The Children of Prosperity

Thirteen Modern American Communes

The Children of Prosperity

Thirteen Modern American Communes

HUGH GARDNER

ST. MARTIN'S PRESS   New York

ACKNOWLEDGMENTS

Excerpts from "Commitment and Social Organization: A Study of Commitment Mech-
anisms in Utopian Communities" by Rosabeth Moss Kanter, *American Sociological
Review* 33:4 (August 1968). Reprinted by permission of the author and the American
Sociological Association.

Excerpts from *Communes U.S.A.: A Personal Tour* by Richard Fairfield (New York:
Penguin Books, 1972). Copyright © Alternatives Foundation, 1971. Reprinted by
permission of Penguin Books.

Excerpts from *Getting Back Together* by Robert Houriet. Reprinted by permission of
Coward, McCann & Geoghegan, Inc. from *Getting Back Together* by Robert Houriet. Copyright © 1971 by Robert Houriet.

Excerpts from *Celery Wine: Story of a Country Commune* by Elaine Sundancer. Reprinted by permission of the author from *Celery Wine: Story of a Country Commune*,
published 1973 by Community Publications Cooperative, Box 243, Yellow Springs,
Ohio 45387. © 1973 Elaine Sundancer.

Excerpts from "Cookbook for a Sacred Life," Book 3 of *Be Here Now* by Baba Ram
Dass et al. (Lama Foundation, 1971). Reprinted by permission of the Lama Foundation.

Excerpts from *Cooperative Communities—How to Start Them, and Why* by Swami
Kriyananda (Ananda Publications, 1971). Reprinted by permission of Swami Kriyananda and Ananda Publications.

PREFACE

Starting in 1965 with a band of college dropouts in a Colorado goat pasture and a handful of like-minded peers on the West Coast, the back-to-the-land commune movement grew to include at least five thousand and possibly ten thousand communal retreats in rural America over the course of the next decade. Still more communal groups of various sorts were formed in our cities and college towns. Altogether, at least a half million young people were involved, at least for a while, in the communal experience. No one knows for sure just how large this massive generational upheaval really was. We can only be sure that it took place on a scale unprecedented in our history, involving more people and more organizations than all previous commune movements in America combined.

The Children of Prosperity is an account of how the commune exodus got started, how it surged into one of the most significant social movements of our time, and how its vitality faded in the recession years of the mid-1970s. More specifically, this book is a study of thirteen representative rural communes over this tumultuous period— how they came to be formed, how they structured themselves as organizations, what life in them was like, what happened to them over time, and why they succeeded or failed.

My interest in the commune movement began in 1967. From the first, I was more curious about the back-to-the-land groups than their urban counterparts. Communal living was radical enough as a lifestyle, but dropping entirely out of the modern urban economy was even more extreme. Informally, I started gathering information about these groups and planning a study of them.

In 1968 I discovered Dr. Rosabeth Kanter's remarkable work on nineteenth-century communes, eventually published in her book *Commitment and Community*. To account for the success or failure of the historical groups she studied, Kanter devised a powerful theory of communal commitment and a research methodology derived from this theory to analyze the structure of communal organizations. Her approach is discussed at length in the pages that follow and need not be portrayed here, but I would like to take this opportunity to record my debt to her for providing the conceptual tools that later proved so useful in my own work.

In response to the cultural and political shocks of the time, by 1969 the commune movement was in full swing. Motivated now by personal sympathy as well as my research interests, I wanted to see and experience for myself what was happening. Accordingly, I adapted Kanter's methods for ethnographic fieldwork and planned a personal tour of the major communal enclaves of the western United States.

During 1970 I visited about thirty communes in Colorado, New Mexico, California, and Oregon. Some were urban groups, but most were rural. I concentrated my formal research efforts on the latter because to me they represented more serious and ambitious attempts to start new societies. At each community I visited, my goals were to reconstruct the group's history, complete a detailed profile of its organizational structure, and record what happened to me as a participant-observer.

I repeated my itinerary in 1973 to see how these groups had fared over the intervening years, both to test Kanter's theory of commitment and to update my historical documentation. The thirteen case studies that ultimately resulted from my two expeditions are presented in chapters 2 through 13 of this book. Taken together, these reports represent a cross-sectional and longitudinal portrait of the early years of the commune movement in the rural West.

To set the scene for these reports, chapter 1 includes a brief history of American communes before 1965, a close look at the rise of the modern movement in the late 1960s, and a discussion of the theory and methods I used in my fieldwork. The group chapters that follow are arranged in the approximate sequence of my travels through the Rockies and the West Coast. Chapter 14 analyzes the thirteen groups in terms of Kanter's theory of commitment and contrasts the successes and failures of the modern movement with Kanter's findings from the nineteenth century. The concluding chapter provides an overview of the commune movement's outcome and its impacts on American society. Two appendices include further information about my research protocol and fieldwork experiences.

Today the surge to rural communes has long since waned and lost its impetus as a social movement. With the end of the Vietnam War and the draft, it lost two of its most important moral imperatives. With the coming of economic recession, it lost the climate of abundance which originally let it flower and grow. As this book shows, however, some of the original communes succeeded nevertheless. They may not have changed the world overnight, but they changed their own part of it, often changing those around them too.

The surge to the country, however, continues unabated. Today it transcends the middle-class generational revolt that started it and includes people of all ages and social backgrounds. The most lasting imprint this revolt left on our society was not communalism per se but the idea of getting back to the land. The modern rural commune movement was the beginning of a population trend out of the cities and suburbs which has grown throughout the 1970s, reversing all previous migratory patterns in American history. The back-to-the-land hippies were the early warning system of a much broader revolt against post-industrial urbanism which is still gathering strength today. The Vietnam War is over, but other issues that motivated the rural commune movement remain the same—pollution in our cities, alienation in our workplaces, powerlessness in our political system, and most of all, perhaps, the loneliness of our urban and suburban communities.

As representatives of my generation, the people I have called "the children of prosperity" included some of the best and some of the most disturbed. What they all had in common, though, was the highest human aspiration: to be free. I trust that history will remember their efforts to usher in the New Age in one great leap.

HUGH GARDNER
Denver, Colorado

ACKNOWLEDGMENTS

The people who were most helpful in bringing this book into being include my parents, Oscar and LaVera Gardner, who helped support me while I wrote it; Dr. Warren O. Hagstrom, my graduate advisor, who always encouraged me to chart my own course; Maya Vickers, who helped cure me of some personal illusions; Laura Audrey, whose friendship kept me going; Diane Minner, my sister, who typed the manuscript and still managed to be wholeheartedly supportive; Dan and Darlene Minner, who offered work space and more free meals than I could accept; Tom Broadbent, my publisher, and Nancy Perry, my editor; songwriter Carol George, who put me in touch with Tom; and Jack Calloway Steele, who was born free.

Above all others, I acknowledge the communards who tolerated my snooping, helped me on my way, and gave me some of the most fascinating experiences of my life. This book is dedicated to them.

ACKNOWLEDGMENTS

CONTENTS

But whereunto shall I liken this generation? It is like unto children sitting in the markets, and calling unto their fellows,

And saying, We have piped unto you, and ye have not danced; we have mourned unto you, and ye have not lamented . . .

I thank thee, Lord of heaven and earth, because thou hast hid these things from the wise and prudent, and hast revealed them unto babes.

ST. MATTHEW

The Children of Prosperity

Thirteen Modern American Communes

1

The Evolution of the Modern
Commune Movement

I

America, with its melting-pot hybrid of peoples and its seemingly endless succession of frontiers, has a long and rich heritage of
utopian social experiments stretching back even before the nation
itself was born. The first known American utopian community was
established by Mennonites in Delaware in 1663, more than a century
before the Declaration of Independence. Altogether there were at
least twenty such communities, mostly Moravian or Seventh-Day
Baptist, established before 1776.

After the Revolution, the impetus shifted to the Shakers, who
dominated utopian history for the next fifty years with over two
dozen new communitarian settlements pushing the frontier as far west
as Ohio. With only one or two exceptions, virtually all of the fifty-odd
utopian societies established before 1825 were Christian and sectarian. America in that period was a haven of religious tolerance by
European standards, a place where pietist and separatist religious
groups stood a fair chance of being left alone, if for no other reason
than the vastness of the landscape. In the words of a Shaker revival
song, it was "the place just right."[1]

In 1825 American utopian history entered a new phase of community experimentation based on the socialist political ideas then
emerging in Europe in response to the squalor and inequities of industrialization, which were beginning to affect America as well. The first
group of its type was New Harmony, an Indiana community comprising nine hundred followers of the English radical Robert Owen. Owen

1

inspired about a dozen related colonies over the next twenty years, most of them short-lived. In the 1840s about two dozen similar groups were founded by followers of the French socialist Charles Fourier and were similarly short-lived. From 1825 until the Civil War, there were over a hundred new communitarian settlements formed, the majority of them based on political rather than religious ideologies. Most of the longest-lived communities over this period, however, were religious. Many of the Shaker colonies continued successfully through this era, and the Mormon church, which was established in the 1830s, likewise went through a communal phase in its early history. Although it was a time of great social and political ferment in America, the spiritualists survived better than the radicals.[2]

For about ten years after the Civil War, most of the new communal settlements founded in America continued to be political, mostly communistic or cooperative in their philosophies. Some were established as far west as Colorado. In the twenty years following the depression of the 1870s, until the mid-1890s, a much bigger surge of new communal societies (numbering about one hundred) appeared, based on philosophies combining religion, ethnic identity, and economic necessity. In the 1870s the Mormons went through another brief communal phase (lasting about three years) in their second migration to Utah, where they set up about thirty new colonies. In 1877 the first colony of Hutterites, a German immigrant sect which later became highly successful as communitarians, was established in South Dakota. In the 1880s some twenty additional settlements were founded as far west as Oregon by immigrant Jews. Most of the Jewish communities, like the Mormon settlements, were communal only temporarily. Despite the prolonged economic depression of the 1870s, very few communal settlements in this era were founded in opposition to industrial capitalism or its injustices.[3]

In the mid-1890s, though, with the railroads and the robber barons approaching the peak of their power, a new wave of socialist, cooperative, and other politically inspired groups began to form. At the same time, there was also a continuing proliferation of religious and ethnic communitarian settlements. In the period from the mid-1890s until World War I, the country became dotted with a crazy-quilt array of Ruskin Socialists, Theosophists, Christian Socialists, Hutterites, Bohemians, Single Taxers, Pacifists, Dutch Cooperators, Sandfordites, Jews, Shakers, Anarchists, and many others—about one hundred more new settlements in all. The communal landscape was just as much a melting pot as America itself was becoming from the flow of immigrants. The communal geography now spread from coast to coast.

During the Roaring Twenties this surge of new communal

settlements died down again, and few new groups were formed. During the Depression of the 1930s the utopian impulse almost vanished—except within the halls of government. As part of its New Deal, the Roosevelt administration subsidized and assisted the formation of about 150 homestead communities and farm cooperatives around the nation, mostly in the South, as a means of helping thousands of impoverished rural families get land and form local cooperative economies. These settlements were only quasi-communitarian in nature and generally did not outlast the Depression. But they clearly deserve their place in utopian history if only because historians so often ignore them.[4]

During World War II the only significant new communitarian movement in America was the Catholic Workers, who formed about a dozen communities. After the war the next two decades of utopian history belonged to the Hutterites. Migrating from war-torn Europe in large numbers, they established over fifty new communities across America's northern plains. Virtually all the Hutterite settlements have lasted until the present day with their communitarian philosophy intact. If the Shakers were America's communal success story over the first century of its history, the Hutterites clearly became the success story of its second, numbering about 25,000 souls in over 170 North American colonies (including those in Canada) by the 1960s.

All told, including the New Deal cooperative farms, America had played host to over six hundred communitarian societies by 1965.[5] Although 70 percent or more did not last longer than five years, the utopian urge itself is timeless. In one wave after another it has reemerged throughout our history in periods of crisis and rapid social change.[6] In general, this wave seems much more likely to emerge in prosperous times than depressions. It also seems to last longer when its basis is religious rather than political.

But everything communal that happened in America in the three hundred years before 1965 was dwarfed by what happened in the five short years that followed. By 1970 there were at least twice as many rural communes in America as there had been throughout all previous history. An even greater number of communes had been established in America's cities. This surge came at a time when America had reached a level of wealth and material abundance greater than any other society had ever enjoyed before. Yet it was the children of that prosperity, those who were ostensibly its prime beneficiaries—the young, white, educated sons and daughters of the middle and upper classes—who established and populated these small backwoods communities that in every way seemed to be the negation of their inheritance. These young communards were one of the leading edges of a generational revolt the likes of which our country, and perhaps the world, had never seen before.

The young people who turned their backs on modern society to form isolated rural communes were almost totally unaware of the communal history that had gone before, and they were not much interested. Nor, for the most part, were they motivated by any particular political or religious ideology, social tradition, or ordered set of intellectual ideas and principles. Instead, their retreat to the country was an intuitive response to the circumstances of their lives and times. For the children of prosperity who abandoned the cities in the late 1960s, America had passed beyond redemption into a complete social, political, cultural, moral, and ecological wasteland. As journalist Robert Houriet said in his description of the flight of a Minneapolis group to the countryside:

> They had no time to assess the historical parallels or to make careful plans for the future. Their flight was desperate. They needed no help from Orwell and Huxley to know that America was marching lockstep toward *1984, Brave New World* and ecocatastrophe. How could they resist the all-pervasive, life-consuming monster which they believed urban America had become? Resistance had proved futile. Neither peaceful demonstration nor sporadic gestures of violence could change the mentality of police who threatened to close down their city commune; could vitalize the towering glass apartment buildings and asphalted shopping centers; could breathe life into decayed churches or humanize inflexible corporations. The only option was to split.
>
> Instinctively, they took the escape route so characteristically American. . . . They went back to the land . . . headed for the wide open country that held the blank promise of a fresh start.[7]

The promise of a fresh start for the rural communards was indeed blank. Young, inexperienced, with no training in rural living and cut off from urban economies by their own choice, they faced the problem of building their new communities from the ground up. There was land to buy (or borrow), rules to make (or reject), work to organize (or ignore), goals to agree on (or dispute), and interpersonal conflict to confront (or avoid). Like latter-day Pilgrims, they started from scratch just as surely—or unsurely—as their ancestors did. This book is a study of how thirteen such groups managed to deal with these problems—or failed to deal with them—over a period beginning in 1965 and ending in 1973. My work is concerned only with rural communes, which I believed then and believe now were far more radical departures from mainstream American society than their urban counterparts.

II

The genesis of the commune movement, of course, was the postbeatnik bohemian youth culture that developed in the early 1960s with the proliferation of psychedelic drugs like marijuana, peyote, and LSD, the latter two then legal. In 1965 the young bohemians were tagged with the name "hippies," a term coined by *San Francisco Chronicle* columnist Herb Caen in his commentaries on the strange people running around the Haight-Ashbury district with long hair, beads, bells, and flowers. The name immediately caught on, and the hippies became a sensation in the national press. At the time, they were a relatively tiny handful of people living scattered double lives or lumped together in colonies in major cities on the East and West coasts (primarily the latter) and a few scattered college towns in between. Until the late 1960s they were almost exclusively an urban phenomenon.

In the meantime, the children of the postwar baby boom had come to college in record numbers in the wake of the Sputnik scare and an urgent new emphasis on the necessity for higher education. Over the course of the decade, college students became steadily more involved in political causes: first, the civil rights movement; later, anti-Vietnam War protests; and, ultimately, opposition to American capitalism and social institutions *in toto*. More than anything else, the conjunction of these two developments—visionary psychedelia and political defiance—led to the great commune surge of the late 1960s. Of the hundreds of communards I met in my travels and interviews, I could count on one hand those who did not have a long list of experiences in both respects.

Over the years many different interpretations have been assigned to the psychedelic experience, but they all agree on at least one point: preexisting social and perceptual programing is altered and undermined, coming to be seen as essentially arbitrary and random in the mind of the user, without any ultimate validity other than social convention. Typically this is accompanied by feelings of ego-loss, godlike cosmic insight into the unity of all life, and the unmasking of society as a transparent system of games. What users, observers, and ex-users seem unable to agree on is whether this experience is good or bad. On the one hand, it can lead to a profound religious awakening, a new and more authentic discovery of self, and a visionary commitment to a better society. On the other hand, it can lead to existential terror or the warped antinomianism of a Charles Manson.

In either case, the overwhelming significance of psychedelic drug use is the erosion of the old social order in the mind of the user: the breakdown of society's conventional value system, the dislocation of users from the life plans and career tracks marked out for them, and the consequent exodus in search of new worlds, new fulfillments, and new selves. "Once experienced," writes psychiatrist Arnold Mandell of the drug-expanded mind, "this other part of the brain colors the rest of life."[8]

In effect the drug experience stirs within the user a euphoric vision of a new humanity that is the very antithesis of the Protestant Ethic psychology of industrialization that helped bring modern society to its present state. Set against the "bourgeois style of life that emphasized calculation, foresight, and efficiency, and made regularity of work an almost religious obligation,"[9] the hippies represented spontaneity, living in the here and now, and an indifference to work or achievement beyond minimal sustenance. Contrasted with the "cool, detached, sensually and sexually dull, manipulating, and manipulative individual"[10] that is industrial bureaucratic man was a warm, involved, sensually and sexually omnivorous postindustrial hippie who valued people as ends in themselves. The critique the hippies put forward, then, was cultural and psychological. From their point of view, there was no longer any need to subordinate what Lawrence Veysey has called "mankind's long-buried capacity for ecstasy and unguarded sharing" to the oppressive regimen of the work ethic.[11]

And there have been many scholarly observers of the hippies who fundamentally agree with them. Analysts like Theodore Roszak, Philip Slater, Charles Reich, and numerous others all viewed the hippies as a revolutionary force. Sociologist Keith Melville wrote:

> The common belief—one that I share—is that the success of industrial civilization has in large part rendered the assumption of scarcity obsolete. As a consequence, both the mental habits and the life-style appropriate to an era of scarcity can be, and in fact should be, replaced. Most of these analysts emphasize, as I have, what the counterculture has to offer at its best: a vision of a different and better society.[12]

As communal scholar Benjamin Zablocki points out, another important contribution of psychedelic drugs to the development of the commune movement was that they fostered the experience of euphoric communion with others and led to the social institution of the "crash pad." For many young people, crash pads were a zesty first taste of communal living and often led directly to the formation of more serious groups in the countryside. Many communes, Zablocki notes, were also born of group LSD trips where the experiences of oneness and communion while high convinced the participants that the group "belongs together" as a "true family, brotherhood, or tribe." In a certain sense, he adds, "drugs can provide a functional equivalent to religious experience, at least in the early stages of the life of a commune."[13] Another important consequence of drugs, of course, was that the users were criminals under American law, thus greatly reinforcing the significance of the age-graded peer-group relationships that they had been raised with all their lives and would later extend to rural communal retreats. According to Zablocki, drugs were the "triggering mechanism," or immediate cause, of the present-day communitarian movement.

The passage of communes from a marginal social phenomenon to a major social movement was also the result of another triggering mechanism of equal or even greater importance: the steady, dialectical escalation of protest and repression resulting from the war in Vietnam, which was singularly responsible for convincing many would-be communards that there was no other way out. The timing of the growth in the number of communes around the country over the course of the decade, which corresponds step by step with the growth of the student protest movement and the responses it engendered, suggests this connection very strongly.[14]

Until 1965 and the beginning of systematic bombing in North Vietnam, the first antiwar teach-ins, and the first antiwar march on Washington, only three rural communes existed in America that could be described as even remotely "hip": Gorda Mountain (Big Sur, California, 1962), the first of the open-land communities; Tolstoy Farm (Washington State, 1963), open land for ideological pacifists; and Drop City (Colorado, 1965), the first truly intentional hippie commune.[15] From 1965 through 1967, the time of the first "Human Be-In" in Golden Gate Park, the peak of the Haight-Ashbury, "Vietnam Summer," and the first draft-card demonstrations, perhaps a dozen more rural communes are known to have been formed.[16] In these early precommunal days of the student movement, little doubt existed in the ranks that the ills of America could be redressed through the political process and that the American system was basically salvageable through protest and dissent. Indeed, this feeling grew throughout the period, although it declined later. In the meantime the drug culture spread even more rapidly but produced no more than about fifteen new rural communes.

The turning point for the student movement and the commune movement alike came in 1968, with the first bombings of ROTC facilities at Stanford and Berkeley; the shooting of three black students by state troopers in Orangeburg, South Carolina; the assassinations of Martin Luther King, Jr., and Robert Kennedy; rebellions and strikes at Columbia, San Francisco State, Wisconsin, and several other universities; and the battle of the Democratic National Convention at

Chicago. Roughly one hundred rural communes are known to have been founded in 1968.[17] During this year the drug culture was continuing to spread among the young, but not nearly so rapidly as political cynicism and despair. As journalist Hunter S. Thompson put it, " 'Consciousness Expansion' went out with L. B. J. . . . and it is worth noting, historically, that downers [depressant drugs] came in with Nixon."[18]

Over 1969 and 1970, the student political movement and the agents of authority squared off against each other for two years of skirmishes, sabotage, and open warfare. In November 1969 over 500,000 people demonstrated against the war in Washington, D.C., while Richard Nixon watched television. The same year also saw the mawkish "Chicago conspiracy trial" get underway, along with more strikes on campus, a series of police murders of Black Panther leaders, and a new wave of bombings at corporation headquarters as well as ROTC buildings. In 1970 the Nixon administration, through Vice-President Spiro Agnew, declared that it was time to settle the hash of "bums, radicals, and other criminal elements," and the governor of California, Ronald Reagan, publicly stated that a "bloodbath" might be necessary to solve the student "problem." Infiltration of legal political activities by *agents provocateurs* and informers from the FBI and other police forces was in full swing. In May 1970 came what more or less marked the end of the student protest movement: the murder of four students at Kent State University during a protest of the American invasion of Cambodia.

According to the Senate Government Operations Permanent Investigations Subcommittee, there were 602 bombings and attempted bombings nationwide in 1969 and 586 bombings in the first six months of 1970. "It is important to realize the full extent of political violence of these years," writes Kirkpatrick Sale in *SDS,* his history of Students for a Democratic Society, "especially so since the media tended to play up only the most spectacular instances, to treat them as isolated and essentially apolitical gestures, and to miss the enormity of what has been happening across the country."[19] But the enormity of what was happening was not lost on the thousands of young people who now looked to country communal living as a last wistful hope for a peaceful and happy life. From 1968 to 1970 the number of rural communes multiplied exponentially.

By 1970, according to Zablocki's estimate, there were at least a thousand rural communes in America.[20] A *New York Times* survey that year, however, turned up a total of two thousand "permanent communal living arrangements of significant size" in thirty-four states, stating that that number was "conservative" and "does not include hundreds of small, urban cooperatives and collectives."[21] According to Judson Jerome, who did an extensive survey of communes in 1972–1973, "the ratio of public to private (that is, undiscovered) communes is between one to three and one to six—let us say one to four as a conservative estimate."[22] If this tip-of-the-iceberg multiplier is accurate, then the *New York Times* estimate should be adjusted to a total of ten thousand rural communes abroad in America in 1970. My own estimate would be roughly three thousand, suggesting a thirty-fold increase in rural communes in the two years since 1968, with perhaps another two or three thousand attempts by 1973.

Regardless of which estimate is most accurate, it is next to inconceivable that drug use spread across America as fast as the number of rural communes multiplied in just two short years. If the hippies had actually not quite died in 1967, when the original residents of the Haight-Ashbury held a mock funeral to declare the "death of hippie" from overexposure, they had certainly lost momentum by 1968. The brief and luminescent revival at the Woodstock Festival in 1969 was shortly followed in 1970 by Charles Manson and public murder at the Rolling Stones concert at Altamont, California, while thousands of hippies stood by passively. But to quote Hunter Thompson again, "The orgy of violence at Altamont merely *dramatized* the problem. The realities were already fixed; the illness was understood to be terminal, and the energies of The Movement were long since aggressively dissipated by the rush to self-preservation."[23] By 1970 the student movement and the hippie movement had become united in a moribund backwash of fear and bile. America the Beautiful became "Amerika the Death Culture," and all that many thousands of people wanted—hundreds of thousands or even millions—was out.[24]

In essence, then, the rural commune phenomenon was born of the convergence of two overlapping youth movements of the middle 1960s: the drug-based hippie culture and the student-based political movement joined in a shared vision of the apocalypse. The year 1968 appears to have been the watershed. Keith Melville, in his perceptive history of the era, writes:

> Things happened so quickly and changed so convulsively from 1964 to 1968 that it is difficult in retrospect to sort it all out. The combined effect of the war, the Johnson administration, the racial crises in the cities, and the failure of the universities to respond to student demands for full citizenship was to kill all the hopefulness of the civil rights era and to transform the protest movement into a radically disaffected insurgency.[25]

In the meantime, "hippies had been radicalized by busts, official harassment, and the Selective Service Commission."[26] By 1968, less than a year after the "death of hippie" ceremony held by the original residents of Haight-Ashbury,

> the migration to rural communes in Sonoma and Mendocino counties north of the city began. Those who were serious about finding a place for the new culture realized that it was much too fragile to survive in the city. If there was any place left where people could get by with a little help from their friends, where they could escape reporters and harassment, it was the country.[27]

In the years immediately following 1968, the rapprochment between the two streams of the youth culture became increasingly evident in the leapfrogging growth of communal retreats outside the cities. "For them," says Melville, "the lesson of the sixties [was] the futility of political reform, and the only viable radical alternative [was] to begin to create a new society in microcosm, to plant the germ cells of a new social organism."[28] The communal experiments of the early hippies were the model, and the flood of dropout *émigrés* from the cities and colleges turned a model into a social movement.

III

But there was much more to the development of rural communes as a social movement than drugs and politics, even if these were the two most distinctive phenomena leading to the surge to the countryside. For a more complete understanding of this evolutionary process, it is helpful to turn to one of the leading scholars of social movements, sociologist Neil J. Smelser, and the scheme he has developed for analyzing them.[29] According to Smelser, there are six basic categories of "determinants" that lie behind the development of any social movement: "structural conduciveness," "structural strain," "the spread of a generalized belief," some kind of "precipitating factor," "mobilization of the participants for action," and "the failure of social control." As a predictive model, Smelser's scheme works much better in hindsight than foresight, but it is very useful in understanding the development of a social movement in retrospect.

Structural Conduciveness   One prerequisite for any social movement is a social base to give it members. As all observers agree, the social composition of the commune movement was overwhelmingly white, under thirty, and from economically, educationally, and socially privileged families. Only a relatively small fraction of young Americans who could be described by these terms, of course, ever became involved in the commune movement; the point, instead, is that the vast majority of those who *did* become involved came from a uniform background of privilege and leisure. It was, in effect, an elite movement originating from the second-generation middle class and the still more prosperous upper classes. The social system in which the children of prosperity grew up was structurally conducive to their revolt by providing them the leisure, education, and security to find fault with it; by providing them a vantage point, so to speak, from which to criticize the prevailing order and explore other options.

The key to this conduciveness was the prosperity of the middle and upper classes in America in the 1960s, especially during the booming war economy of the latter half of the decade. This abundance, combined with the post–World War II baby boom, the post-Sputnik emphasis on education, and the threat of the draft, brought record enrollments to colleges and universities. For the children of prosperity, already protected from adult responsibilities well beyond sexual maturity by the nuclear, child-centered family and age-graded, peer-group institutions, this increase of time and resources devoted to their schooling had the effect of extending the adolescent phase of leisure and exploration well into their early and middle twenties. The children of prosperity, even as legal adults, were subsidized by parents and the state, free of the need to work, and protected from the draft as long as they stayed in school.

For many, these experiences were positive and pleasurable. Understandably, they were loath to give them up for the "real" world, about which they were becoming increasingly sophisticated and critical, and they sought instead to find means to continue having such experiences in peer-group societies like communes. In an economy of abundance, there was little need for anxiety among the privileged young about jobs or careers, and there was plenty of time for experimentation with other possibilities. It was a massive social opportunity to discover, for instance, that poverty and racism existed in America despite our national ideals, that drugs were interesting, or that the war in Vietnam was bad policy if not totally immoral.

At the same time, the protracted leisure and educational opportunities of the children of prosperity brought them into contact with many different cultures and a vast array of alternative models for arranging their lives and identifications. The development of television brought forth an endless variety of information and fantasy for the appraisal of this, the first TV generation. (According to Marshall McLuhan, television by its very nature generates a culture of multi-level simultaneity, a kind of "tribal consciousness" that would naturally foster an interest in face-to-face communal living.[30]) To paraphrase poet Gary Snyder, one of the prophets of the commune movement, this generation was the first in history to have all the world, past and present, from which to choose how to live.

Structural Strain   But the backgrounds of the children of prosperity brought only a certain social potential to the development of the rural commune movement. According to Smelser, the next step in the development of a social movement is "structural strain" in the norms and values of society (the strain, for instance, between the American dream of abundance and equality and the realities of poverty and racism). The concept of structural strain can also be applied in terms of the internal contradictions of capitalism or the negative social consequences of the long-term master trends of the modern era, usually seen to be industrialization, urbanization, bureaucratization, and for some, imperialism.

Industrialization, for example, brings unprecedented material abundance, but it also has by-products like pollution, trivialized work, and dependence on an anonymous market economy to meet all basic material needs. Likewise, urbanization may bring better jobs in more exciting settings, but it also brings higher rates of crime, pollution, congestion, and the decline of neighborly communities. Bureaucratization increases the efficiency of planning and administration in providing society's needs, but it also creates hierarchical and impersonal relationships as the scale of social organization grows steadily larger and farther away from individual and local control. Imperialism spreads the scale of cultural and economic exchange throughout the world, but it is also exploitative and leads to foreign wars and oppression. All these factors, of course, contributed to the urge to form isolated, intimate, decentralized, face-to-face communities, detached from modern society, where the consequences of such trends could be avoided. But only in the late 1960s, and then only because of other factors and events, did this line of reasoning become incorporated into the sweeping countercultural ideology that gave rise to rebellion on a mass scale and gave birth to the commune movement.

Still another view of structural strain, adopted by a great many observers of the modern communal era, stressed the contradiction between the technological abundance of the postindustrial economy of modern America and the "scarcity assumption" on which it was built. Why work, slave, and sacrifice, asked the hippies, when modern technology has the capacity to produce abundance and leisure for everyone and free them of their inherited compulsions not to enjoy themselves? And why, asked the radicals, is there not a more just distribution of this wealth and of the opportunities to get it?

But social movements come to nothing without a perception of such strains at an individual level. For the children of prosperity who later became rural communards, the flowering of these contradictions in the civil rights and early hippie era was mostly expressed in conflicts over political and life-style values with parents and youthful identification with oppressed minorities or bohemian cultural heroes. But in 1966 and 1967, with developments like the outlawing of LSD, the escalation of the Vietnam War, and police assaults on student demonstrators and hippies, these strains began to affect the self-interest and, indeed, the safety of the would-be communards themselves. Taking drugs meant risking criminal punishment and, in most states, a ruined life. Political activism brought repression and incarceration on a steadily more vitriolic level. The threat of being drafted to fight a hated war became increasingly ominous with the escalation in Vietnam and the phaseout of student draft deferments. The very appearance of the young rebels became simultaneously an act of courageous defiance and an invitation to chronic confrontation with authority.

As the late 1960s struggled on, the scope of alienation among the communards-to-be grew steadily more total and negative with the simultaneous growth of the counterculture and the antiwar movement; new concerns like ecology, feminism, consumerism, and antiurbanism; and disillusionment with venerable institutions like science and universities. But the strains were most intense where they were the most personal, for there they hit the children of prosperity where they hurt most: in their freedom and in their futures. If they, *la crème de la crème,* were abused so awfully, what hope was there for America at large? For those who were later to make up the rural commune movement, this process gradually dissolved the optimism of the civil rights and flower child era and evolved through self-interest into a crisis of disbelief in American culture and institutions in general.

Spread of a Generalized Belief   As disillusionment deepened into despair in the late 1960s, so too spread the general belief that the American system *in toto* was morally bankrupt, evil, and unredeemable. This was another link in the development of the surge to rural communes. But sweeping negative criticism was only part of the ideological development of the commune-tending counterculture. Another, more positive general belief was needed: that some sort of viable alternatives either existed or could be created.

As many observers have noted, the counterculture had a way of defining itself in diametric opposition to the prevailing social order; that is, whatever negative results the system produced, the counterculture would idealize the opposite as positive.[31] If industrial technology brought trivial jobs, waste, plastic goods, and materialistic greed, for example (mere abundance being taken for granted), then a good alternative was craftsmanship, doing more with less, and idealizing subsistence living and preindustrial technology. If bureaucratization meant impersonal, phony relationships, calculated uniformity of dress and behavior, smothering overorganization, and oppressive hierarchies, then the alternative was unplanned spontaneity, rigorous equalitarianism, uninhibited expressiveness, and valuing other people as subjects rather than objects. If urbanization meant fouled, congested cities, overstimulation, freeways, anonymous and lonely living, sterile suburbs, and imprisoning ghettos, then the alternative was the rural countryside, clean air, green grass and trees, relaxation, and small, face-to-face communities.

A specific term summing up all these positive ideological components and shared by all in the movement was never developed in the counterculture, beyond a diffuse interest in getting back to the land. One term that did emerge, however, was "voluntary primitivism," originating at the Morning Star Ranch commune in California in 1966.[32] Although the term never achieved very wide currency even within the commune movement itself, in retrospect it seems most appropriate. The essence of voluntary primitivism was a deliberate withdrawal from the institutions and structures of modern life and the voluntary acceptance of a reduced standard of living, both as a way out of a destructive and oppressive social system and as a positive, freedom-enhancing end in itself. As the communards-to-be came under increasing personal stress in the late 1960s, the logic of voluntary primitivism gradually came to make more and more sense as a plausible response to the dilemmas of their lives.

"The crystallization of a generalized belief," writes Smelser, "marks the attempt of persons under strain to assess their situation."[33] If we are to understand how the children of prosperity could ever make such an assessment as to reject their inheritance for voluntary primitivism, we must remember again the vantage point of abundance to which their heritage had brought them. From such a vantage point, the privileged young could *afford* to view the American scene as dull, standardized, and uninspiring. Indeed, they were encouraged by America's celebration of youth and the high expectations of a prosperous, educated upbringing to view the demands of America-as-usual as *beneath* them. As Berkeley activist Mario Savio said in the early days of the student movement:

> American society is a bleak scene, but it is all a lot of us have to look
> forward to. Society provides no challenge. American society in the
> standard conception it has of itself is simply no longer exciting. The
> most exciting things going on in America today are the movements to
> change America. . . . The "futures" and "careers" for which Ameri-
> can students now prepare are for the most part intellectual and moral

wastelands. The chrome-plated consumers' paradise would have us grow up to be well-behaved children.[34]

In a sense, then, many of the children of prosperity anticipated a disappointment of their career and moral expectations and a drop in their self-esteem within the system as then constituted, a psychological condition which very commonly gives rise to strong sentiments for social change. They had been conditioned to expect better. The righteousness of their political causes and the godlike illuminations of their drug experiences only enhanced their frustrations.

It is important to remember, too, that a decision for voluntary primitivism in the countryside was made a great deal more probable by the economic prosperity of the late 1960s. In depressed times, like the early 1970s, this choice became less realistic. But in the 1960s the economy was booming. Jobs were not scarce, especially for the children of prosperity, and one could always be had in a pinch. America's economy in this period was so abundant, in fact, that the communards immediately discovered how easily they could live off its waste and discards. They were scarcely faced with worrying about money at all. In the communes of the 1960s creative scavenging was a point of pride and a way of life. The children of prosperity always had the *option* to return to the system, hit their parents for money, or resume careers. The actual *costs* of a decision to split the cities—while the economy prospered—were indeed quite minimal. In addition, they were young, generally had no family responsibilities and little property, and in short could quite well afford to experiment with communal living. This assessment, in other words, awaited only a sufficient level of alienation to be taken seriously as a plausible alternative.

Precipitating Factors   Another key step in the development of a social movement, suggests Smelser, is a "precipitating factor." This step is some kind of highly emotional event which dramatically points out the strains in the society at large, particularly as they affect potential participants in the movement. In the middle 1960s, when the modern rural commune movement began on a very tiny scale, the single most important precipitating factor was undoubtedly the use of psychedelic drugs. One of the very earliest communes, Drop City, was literally christened on the model of Timothy Leary's injunction to "turn on, tune in, and drop out." In 1967 and early 1968, the most important factor was probably the collapse of the Haight-Ashbury district of San Francisco under the combined assaults of the media, the city administration, and a flood of transient immigrants and tourists, a dispersal which seeded several new rural communes throughout the West.

From 1968 through 1970, though, when the number of communes began to multiply exponentially all over America, the most important factors were events like the Democratic National Convention at Chicago, the university rebellions, and most of all, perhaps, the shootings at Kent State University in 1970. These events not only indicated the strains of society but, more importantly, impacted directly on many thousands of prosperity's children and indirectly on millions more via peer identification. Nixonian America openly declared war on its young, and the search for alternatives took on a desperate as well as an alienated tone.

Mobilization of Participants   In order for a social movement to swing into motion, however, something more than alienation or even desperation is required: there must also be some sort of shared, positive vision of alternative values, role models, and institutions to convince would-be participants in the movement that action is possible, that the time for action is now, and that the goals of the movement can be realized. In this respect, according to Smelser, the functions of leadership and communication are especially important.

But looking for leaders on the commune scene of the 1960s would be a largely futile undertaking. It was, above all, a diffuse, decentralized movement without any form of deliberate, centralized guidance. Scholars who would trace the development of the commune movement to social thinkers like Herbert Marcuse, Murray Bookchin, Norman O. Brown, Marshall McLuhan, Theodore Roszak, B. F. Skinner, or Buckminster Fuller; to the "traditions" of earlier communal or radical movements in American history; or even to the legacy of the beatniks of the 1950s would largely be indulging themselves in exercises of intellectual vanity.

To be sure, the movement did have its elder prophets, exemplars, and wise men, such as Lou Gottlieb of Morning Star Ranch, poet Gary Snyder, Mildred Loomis of Heathcote, Steve Durkee of the Lama Foundation, and Timothy Leary, as well as some of the theorists listed here and others. Traces of influence could be detected for each. But for positive alternatives, the college students and hip dropouts of the 1960s looked mostly to each other, as they had been trained to do all their lives by age-graded cultural and child-rearing institutions which had unwittingly conspired to help create a generational consciousness. They were not taught the history or sociology of communes in America by their professors, nor were they very interested; they certainly knew little about them. Nor were they particularly informed about or interested in the wealth of past and present utopian theory.

Instead they created "free universities" taught by themselves to learn the practical and "relevant" specifics they wanted to know; practiced nonauthoritarian forms of decision making in their political groups; experimented with communal living arrangements in their private lives free from the oversight of parents or authority figures; tested the zest of community for themselves in their demonstrations, music festivals, and crash pads; and looked through their own eyes and the eyes of the media for role models and examples among their peers. For leaders they relied mainly on the most skilled and visionary among their own on a small-scale, affinity-group basis. To some extent the role of leadership was filled by youthful charismatic prophets like Mel Lyman (Massachusetts's Fort Hill Community) or Steve Gaskin (The Farm in Tennessee, transplanted from San Francisco), or later by opportunistic religious organizations like the Children of God, Krishna Consciousness, the Divine Light Mission, and others. But for the most part the commune movement of the 1960s was hatched in Free U discussion groups, crash pads, friendship cliques, festivals, group drug trips, demonstrations, and other assemblies of alienated, like-minded peers.

The role of communication, though, could scarcely be overestimated. Of the major media, television was probably most important negatively, as it gave millions of young people a direct look at the political demonstrations being created by their peers and the increasingly depressing consequences as the 1960s progressed. Television's positive role basically began and ended with the limited coverage it gave to the precommunal hippie movement in San Francisco.

A more important role, both positively and negatively, was that of music and the record and radio industries that hastened to merchandize it to the young. Through the magic of electronics and the purchasing power of middle-class youth, music created by the young for the young carried the message more persuasively and with more feeling than television ever did, especially when the communal living arrangements of many of the rock groups carrying the message, such as the Grateful Dead or the Jefferson Airplane, became commonly known. From the depths of despair, the music carried lines like "Tin soldiers and Nixon coming, we're finally on our own" (Crosby, Stills, and Nash, "Ohio"). From a shared vision of hope came words like "We are stardust, we are golden, and we've got to get ourselves back to the Garden" (Joni Mitchell, "Woodstock"). The most popular and influential youth magazine today, *Rolling Stone,* was founded in the late 1960s precisely on the premise that it was music, not politics, that truly carried the "revolution" forward. *Rolling Stone*'s success over the years proves that even if this premise was not necessarily right, it was certainly not wrong. Today, the wisdom and advice to which millions of uncertain young people pay the most attention comes over the airwaves from strangers they have never met.

To a lesser extent, films were also important to the birth of communes, in particular, Dennis Hopper's *Easy Rider*. One of the most popular cult films of modern times, *Easy Rider* was a generational epic tracing the adventures of two motorcycling nomads who, in their search for America, are finally destroyed by the forces of bigotry and hate. At one point about midway through the film, the protagonists visit a rural commune in Taos, New Mexico (actually filmed at the Taos Indian pueblo there, since the real communes turned Hopper down). Toward the end, Peter Fonda as Captain America pronounces the film's fatal message, "We blew it." The line was almost universally interpreted to mean that communal living with their peers had slipped them by as the correct answer to their search. The release of the film in 1969, combined with this interpretation, was a powerful stimulus to the momentum of the commune movement. *Easy Rider* more than any other single factor was responsible for the hip inundation of Taos that summer on a scale approaching the invasion of Haight-Ashbury two years earlier.

The print media, too, were vitally important in the birth of the new communes, especially newspapers and magazines (books specifically about communes did not begin to appear until 1970). A perusal of the *Reader's Guide to Periodical Literature* shows clearly that the press followed just a step behind the growth of the hippie culture, and later the communes, with a growing volume of stories from 1965 until 1971, when the movement lost momentum and the press abruptly ceased covering it and thereby feeding it. *Life, Look,* newspapers everywhere, *Time, Newsweek, Harper's, Esquire*—altogether the national press was fascinated by the hippie communes. No matter how they were described—and they were often described favorably—they made good copy. There is no question that press attention stimulated to even greater growth a movement already underway for its own reasons.

But the press, simply by overexposure, also stimulated the growth of communes negatively and in the direction of a rural rather than an urban habitat. The attention given the Haight-Ashbury from 1965 through 1967 prompted the residents of that district, in their death of hippie ceremony, to declare that "hippies" were only a creation of the media, that they were actually just trying to be "free men and women," and that the flood of incompetent and spaced-out transients which ruined the community and set the rural migration into motion had been the media's fault. Within many of the rural communes that developed later, reporters (and to a lesser extent sociologists) were considered second only to the police as bearers of the plague.

An equally important media development in the late 1960s was the creation of the "underground" press. Along with music and travel, the underground press was a vital communications link among the young, carrying stories about the new communes as well as the latest in protests, political issues, drug busts, muckraking, psychedelic art, social satire, and splenetic diatribes. Relatively cheap and simple to set up, most links in the underground press network were short-lived local and campus newspapers, which just as readily fell apart. Only the largest survive today, but around 1970 there were hundreds of them.

Even more important to the development of the rural commune movement was the creation of several underground periodicals devoted specifically to the back-to-the-land audience on a national scale. Some—like *The Modern Utopian*, founded in 1966; *Alternate Society*, originating in Canada in 1969; and *The Green Revolution*, an old decentralist tabloid reoriented by young people in the 1960s—were devoted specifically to communal living. Altogether these three publications never reached a combined circulation of more than about twenty thousand, but their impact was significant in the sense that they directly tapped and stimulated the interest of the most enthusiastic potential communards.[35]

Other, more above-ground publications addressed themselves with more polish and sophistication to the back-to-the-land movement in general and became enduring national success stories. *The Whole Earth Catalog*, a compendium of tools, books, and ideas for independent living, including a considerable amount of commune news in its late-1960s "Supplements," leaped from sales of 1,000 at first publication in the fall of 1968 to a circulation of 160,000 just one year later.[36] *The Mother Earth News*, created in the wake of *The Whole Earth Catalog*'s early success, soon became another publishing phenomenon of equal national importance (with a circulation of 400,000 today). In its early years, *The Mother Earth News* not only carried commune news among its folksy hints for successful rural living, but also, as *The Modern Utopian*'s "Communal Matchmaking Service" had done on a smaller scale, printed a great many letters from people seeking communes to join, communes seeking new members, and people seeking people with the object of forming a commune. Though both of these publications phased out their communal coverage as the movement lost its thrust in the early 1970s, for a few years their impact on it was incalculable. Copies of both could be found in any rural commune in America.[37]

Social Control   According to Smelser, the final determinant of a social movement is the failure of the forces of social control to stop its proliferation. Clearly, many social control mechanisms were on the decline in the 1960s, opening the way for novel and atypical life-style experiments like communal living. The failure of the legal process to thwart the spread and deconditioning effects of psychedelic drugs, the support of the courts for the early protest movements, and the collapse of the principle of *in loco parentis* on university campuses are among many possible examples. But as we have seen, the growth of the rural commune movement was equally a product of the *effectiveness* of the agents of social control. In crushing the student political movement of the 1960s, taking away a sense of efficacy in continuing to struggle for social change in that direction, and in deliberately harassing the longhairs of the cities, the powers-that-were had a profound influence on the quest for new social alternatives in the countryside because of their success even more than their failures.

Indeed, the communal flight from the cities was motivated in good part by the desire to escape these forces and move to places where they were weaker. In 1970 most rural communes of America were concentrated in three rather delimited geographical regions: northern California/southern Oregon, southern Colorado/northern New Mexico, and rural New England. In each of these regions the land is hilly, rocky, infertile, arid, or otherwise unsuitable for commercial agriculture and therefore relatively cheap. Each of these regions is also relatively poor, sparsely populated, isolated from urban police departments, more liberal than commercial farming areas, much more liberal than cities with respect to building and health codes, and a good place to hide in a social cataclysm.

With a few notable exceptions, these areas were not bourgeois enough, outraged enough, or organized enough to bring the powers of authority to bear on the new communes to any significant degree. Few rural communes perished because of chronic confrontations with local agents of social control, although they did occasionally, as we shall see later. It was often said in the rural communes of that era that the American legal system was based on the rights of property rather than the rights of people. This feature of the system the communards deliberately sought to turn to their advantage by landholding in isolated regions. The geographical distribution of the new communes, then, reflected an intuitive and often conscious recognition that social control would be weakest in these areas.

Of social control and communes as a social movement, one important question remains to be considered: To what extent were the new communards interested in or capable of exercising social control over themselves? It was on this question that the success or failure of the new communes would ultimately depend, since the external forces of social control largely left them alone as they desired.

Whatever the features of modern American society that repelled the children of prosperity, the fact remains that their heritage placed them at a pinnacle of unprecedented freedom, mobility, and choice. As Benjamin Zablocki put it, "Modern Western man is the product of a half dozen generations that have rebelled against the restrictions of community (family, church, village) in search of freedom."[38] This kind of individualism, underlined by the erosion of kinship networks, the anonymity of the cities, and the dazzling, almost paralyzing variety of alternative realities available in a rapidly changing electronic culture, creates both an urgent need for the experience of community and a rootless, choice-burdened incapacity for it. The fate of the new communes would be determined by the extent to which their members could commit themselves to what they were doing and build new organizations that would reinforce this commitment—or by failing to do so, choose to value their personal freedom over the roots and obligations of life in community. This is the basic problem to which this study is addressed.

IV

The primary goals of this book are threefold: first, to compile an accurate history of the background and formation of a reasonably representative sample of the rural communal groups established over the period 1965–1970; second, to provide a comprehensive descriptive account of their social and organizational structure through the lens of a uniform analytical framework; and third, to follow through at a later period with a report of subsequent events and an assessment of each group's success or failure over time.

My interest in this subject began to develop in 1967 with a personal curiosity about the new communes then beginning to be reported in the media and discussed among some of my friends. My interest became earnest in 1968 with the discovery of some outstanding work on nineteenth-century communes by Rosabeth Moss Kanter, published in condensed form later that year in the *American Sociological Review*,[39] and in revised and expanded form as *Commitment and Community: Communes and Utopias in Sociological Perspective*.[40] In 1968 I began to collect all the information about communes I could locate and to plan research of my own, using Kanter's ground-breaking work on earlier communes as a model for field studies of the groups of our own age. Kanter's central thesis was that the success or failure of communal groups over the years is a function of *commitment,* which can be measured in terms of organizational structures that either promote commitment or weaken it. In general, her study of thirty-one American utopias founded between 1780 and 1860 demonstrated very persuasively that her theory was true. Since her concepts and findings were of central importance to my own efforts, they are presented here in some detail.

"Commitment," writes Kanter, "may be defined as the process through which individual interests become attached to the carrying out of socially organized patterns of behavior which are seen as fulfilling those interests, as expressing the nature and needs of the person." In short, commitment is a process which relates the need of an organization for members to the needs of individuals for membership in the organization. Commitment is especially crucial to voluntary intentional communities like communes, which must meet their practical organizational needs in a way that keeps members positively involved, loyal, and dedicated to the group. As Kanter puts it, "This requires solutions to organizational problems that are simultaneously mechanisms for insuring commitment through their effects on individuals," fostering the "willingness of social actors to give their energy and loyalty" to the group and promoting "the attachment of personality systems" to the group's social relations.[41]

The thrust of Kanter's thinking, then, was to develop a conceptual framework for understanding the "structural arrangements and organizational strategies which promote and sustain commitment."[42] It was not possible, after all, to go back and ask members of nineteenth-century communes how committed they felt to their groups. Instead, Kanter sought to understand how some kinds of group structure inspire personal commitment and how others tend to minimize it.

To do this, Kanter borrowed from Parsons and Shils's "social action theory"[43] to derive three different kinds of commitment that bind people to organized groups. These she calls "continuance," "cohesion," and "control." On the one hand, these three types of commitment reflect an organization's need for members who stick around, who are loyal to the other people in the group, and who agree with the group's rules and principles. On the other hand, they relate to three different dimensions of human psychology: rational thinking, emotional feeling, and social values.

Continuance commitment, Kanter says, is a function of group members' *cognitive orientations* to the *social roles* of maintaining their membership. That is, group members weigh the rewards and costs of their membership in deciding whether to join, stay, or leave. Continuance commitment is basically a question of individual profits and losses, rewards or punishments, in either continuing as a member of the group or leaving it behind for something else. A committed member, in other words, would find "that the cost of leaving the system [in this case, the commune] would be greater than the cost of remaining: 'profit' compels continuing participation."[44] This is rational, economic thinking about things invested and things given up, the bottom line of group continuity.

Cohesion commitment, Kanter's second category, is a function of group members forming positive *cathectic orientations* to the *social relationships* available in the community. This kind of commitment is basically a question of group togetherness and interpersonal loyalties. Committed members form strong emotional ties with each other; less committed members have weaker personal bonds with the group. The bonds of cohesion commitment reflect how close people come to feel about each other. When the bonds are intimate, membership loyalty is increased, because to members emotional happiness is partly or wholly dependent on maintaining these relationships. A cohesively committed membership, in short, "sticks together" with high emotional solidarity and little infighting, backbiting, or jealousy.[45]

Control commitment, the third of Kanter's types, is a function of group members forming positive *evaluative orientations* to the *social norms* of the group. The issue here is a member's moral judgment of the group's rules, values, goals, and institutions. A member who sees the group as righteous will be more agreeable to playing by the rules, to submitting before the group's need for social control. As Kanter says, "Demands made by the system [that is, the group] are evaluated as right, as moral, as just, as expressing one's own values, so that obedience to these demands is a normative necessity, and sanctioning by the system is regarded as appropriate."[46] In a way this resembles the psychological concepts of "internalization" and "superego," for to a committed member the values and demands of the group converge with the core beliefs of the inner self.

As Kanter points out, "The three kinds of commitment can also be seen to form a scale similar to that which may be proposed for the development of morality in children; the child first obeys social system demands because of rewards and punishments, then because of emotional attachment to others, and finally in terms of an internalized moral code."[47] In psychological terms, the three kinds of commitment could be described as compliance, identification, and internalization.

Each of the three types of commitment ties the personality systems of members to the organizational system of the group, each in its own way. And each of the three types, Kanter says, will result in different kinds of consequences:

> Groups in which members have formed cognitive-continuance commitments should manage to hold their members. Groups in which members have formed cathectic-cohesion commitments should be able to withstand threats to their existence, should have more 'stick-together-ness.' Groups in which members have formed evaluative-control commit-

ments should have less defiance, challenge to authority, or ideological controversy. . . . Systems with all three kinds of commitment, with total commitment, should be more successful in their maintenance than those without.[48]

By the same token, Kanter reasoned, differences in the way that social groups organize themselves will be reflected in the degree of member commitment they inspire. "The proposition follows, then, that groups whose existence is dependent on the commitment of their participants should be more successfully maintained if they utilize social arrangements which promote commitment of all three types."[49] Since Kanter could not go back to the nineteenth century and measure how much commitment the communards felt personally, she went to historical records and reconstructed each group's social structure, measuring each for characteristics that either dampen member commitment or enhance it.

To do this, Kanter reasoned that each type of commitment would have both a positive and a negative side. "For each kind of commitment defined earlier," she wrote, "two processes were conceptualized—one a dissociative process, which would operate to free the personality system from other commitments, and one an associative process, operating to attach the personality to the current object of commitment."[50] For each of the three categories of commitment, then, she developed both a positive ("associative") and a negative ("dissociative") list of organizational-structural characteristics which function to promote group commitment. These lists are described in detail below, since they form the basis for the information-gathering procedure used in the study behind this book. In Kanter's study of nineteenth-century communes, these characteristics were measured and compared to the success or failure of the groups she analyzed. To compare communal "successes" and communal "failures," Kanter defined "success" as group survival for twenty-five years or longer, noting that this is the sociological definition of a generation. Except for the differences between historical research and personal fieldwork (like a much shorter "group survival" period today), the procedures used in my study follow hers very closely.

Continuance Commitment   In the first of the three categories, Kanter argued that for each member of a communal organization there is a "profit" associated with continued participation and a "cost" associated with leaving:

Thus *sacrifice* (negative) and *investment* (positive) are among the components of cognitive-continuance commitments. Sacrifice involves the giving up of something considered valuable or pleasurable in order to belong to the organization; this stresses the importance of the role of member to the individual. Sacrifice means that membership becomes more costly and is therefore not lightly regarded or likely to be given up easily.[51]

As indicators of "sacrifice," Kanter suggested that various forms of oral, sexual, or other abstinence, plus austerity in the physical conditions of group life, should lead to greater commitment and group survival. In the case of "abstinence" particularly, this proved true in Kanter's study. A harsh setting and harsh rules, at least in the nineteenth century, promoted group survival.

As indicators of "investment," which would give the individual member "a stake in the fate of the organization," Kanter suggested such communal mechanisms as the requirement for physical participation of all members, financial contributions and/or signing over of property at admission or while a member, and the irreversibility of member contributions of money, property, or labor (that is, investments would not be returned or reimbursed, thus committing the donor indefinitely). Here again investment mechanisms were generally much more prevalent in successful nineteenth-century communities than in unsuccessful ones.

Cohesion Commitment   What Kanter calls "cohesion commitment" involves the development of emotional ties among the group which bind members to each other and strengthen them collectively against outside threats to their existence:

> This kind of commitment requires, first, that members relinquish any attachments which might compete with their emotional involvement with the entire group. Second, it requires that members be brought into meaningful contact with a collective whole, that they experience the fact of oneness with the group. Two general processes work toward these ends: *renunciation* (of other ties) and *communion* (with the group as a whole). The use of mechanisms supporting renunciation and communion should thus distinguish successful and unsuccessful utopian communities.[52]

As indicators of the negative side of cohesion, "renunciation," Kanter proposed such factors as geographical isolation and other forms of group insularity like a lack of contact with outside media, strict "cross-boundary controls" regulating the passage of members to the outside and visitors to the inside of the group, and renunciation of the conventional family-child unit in favor of loyalty to the group "family" as a whole. Except for physical isolation—an important exception—all of these factors divided successful from unsuccessful groups fairly clearly.

In deriving positive indicators of "communion" mechanisms, Kanter's emphasis was on things like intense group participation, which makes group members feel equal parts of a whole rather than differentiated individuals acting alone:

> The need for member equality, fellowship, group consciousness, and group dependence may be supported by various kinds of structural arrangements. These arrangements include homogeneity of religious, class, and ethnic background, as well as prior acquaintance; communistic sharing, in which the individual relinquishes both control over his own goods and private symbols of identity, in favor of group control and ownership; communistic labor, which emphasizes joint effort, with all members performing all tasks for equal reward, including communal work efforts like "bees"; and regularized group contact, via communal dwellings and dining halls, limited opportunity for privacy, and frequent group meetings, which insure participation and involvement. Group ritual, which involves collective participation in ceremonies or recurring events of symbolic importance, also enhances communion. . . . Finally, an experience of persecution welds the group together in the face of a common threat and "heightens the symbolic intensity of a group's values."[53]

Except for communal dwellings and communal dining halls, which had effects opposite to those predicted, each of these communion factors distinguished successful from unsuccessful utopian communities. For Americans, who were known to be individualistic even in the nineteenth century, communal sleeping and eating shortened a utopia's life span.

Control Commitment The third kind of commitment Kanter studied was "evaluative" commitment to the norms and rules affecting social control within a group. Optimally, the demands of the group are considered "right" in terms of a member's self-identity, and obedience to group authority becomes a moral necessity:

> An individual whose personality system is attached to the norms of a social system should see himself as carrying out the dictates of a higher-order system, a system which orders and gives meaning to his life. This kind of commitment requires that the individual see himself as humble and hapless without the group, that he reformulate his identity in terms of meeting the ideal conditions set by the system. And, at the same time, he must experience the great power represented by the organization, so that he will attach the meaning of his life to the carrying out of

the demands of this power. Thus, *mortification* (a negative process) and *transcendence* (a positive process) are among the components of evaluative-control commitments.[54]

In noncoercive groups like communes, "mortification can be a sign of trust in the group, a willingness to share weaknesses, failings, doubts, problems, and one's innermost secrets with others. At the same time," Kanter continues, "its use is also a sign that the group cares about the individual, about his thoughts and feelings, about the content of his inner world." Mortification "thus facilitates commitment . . . and generates loyalty . . . through the system's invasion of phenomenological privacy.[55] In effect the function of mortification mechanisms is to "erase the sin of pride" from interfering with the group's moral and normative integrity.

Kanter proposes several possible group "mortification strategies" which reinforce commitment to group social control as indicators of this negative control process. "Confession and mutual criticism" sessions and "surveillance of the behavior of members," for example, were one variety of mortification procedures that generally distinguished successful from unsuccessful nineteenth-century groups. The "spiritual differentiation" of some members from others was another cluster of factors generally separating failures and successes. Nineteenth-century communes were more successful if they permitted the distinction of some members over others on moral or spiritual grounds, formal deference to those of higher moral status, the segregation of new members from old, formal probationary periods with limited privileges, and instruction in community doctrines and rules. Yet another set of devices used more frequently by successful nineteenth-century groups were "mortifying sanctions" such as public denouncement of deviants, expulsion, denial of privileges, and other forms of punishment. Finally, successful groups were much more likely than unsuccessful groups to use "de-individuating mechanisms" like requiring members to wear standardized uniforms.

The more positive side of "control commitment," according to Kanter, is reinforced by what she calls "surrender mechanisms" (later renamed "transcendence mechanisms" in her book *Commitment and Community,* a usage which will be followed here). "Transcendence involves the attaching of a person's decision-making prerogative to a greater power, total involvement with a larger system of authority which gives both meaning and direction to an individual's life. . . . For transcendence to occur, the individual must first experience great power and meaning residing in the organization." Often this experience is transmitted by charismatic leaders, but Kanter argues that for long-term commitment to persist independent of one person, "charisma diffused throughout the corporate group is required. I call charisma in this form 'institutionalized awe,' a characteristic of an on-going, formalized social system which imbues the system with power and meaning."[56]

She then divided "institutionalized awe" into two subcategories: "ideology" and "power and authority." As indicators of the ideological dimension of institutionalized awe, Kanter looked for the presence or absence of elaborate philosophical systems explaining the essential nature of human beings, an ideology relating the community to historically important leaders or teachers, the imputation of special magical powers to some or all group members, and higher-order principles which justify decisions and legitimate group demands on individuals. As indicators of institutionalized awe in the form of power and authority, she looked for the presence or absence of authority hierarchies and various forms of privileges and immunities for leaders; she questioned whether leaders were founders or their groomed successors and whether the membership had impeachment and recall powers over them. Successful nineteenth-century communes generally had more of these positive control mechanisms than unsuccessful groups, and hence more transcendence-inspiring "distance and mystery" pervading their organizations and leadership arrangements, than unsuccessful communes. In addition, Kanter also found that "transcendence" and group success were promoted by fixed daily routines and other instances of behavioral programing; by conversion techniques like vows and tests of faith; and by traditions derived from prior, precommunal forms of group organization where such existed.

Altogether, Kanter found that all three kinds of commitment, in both their positive and negative forms, were related to communal survival in years. The effects were strongest for "transcendence" and "communion" ($p < .05$), somewhat less strong for "sacrifice" and "renunciation" ($p < .10$), and least strong for "investment" and "mortification" ($p < .15$). But all had a bearing on communal longevity. Since all the "successful" groups in her sample were strict, hierarchically organized religious societies, in a way her results merely confirm the well-understood principle that religious communes tend to survive longer than nonreligious ones because they are stricter and more structured. On the other hand, the theoretical scheme she created is very thorough and detailed. It is an excellent means by which to describe and analyze the structure of communal groups whether they are religious or not; nonreligious groups, after all, can share many of the structural aspects of religious groups or functional equivalents of them.

Another great virtue of Kanter's methodology is that it permits us to bypass the very irksome and most likely insoluble problem of defining exactly what a "commune" is. Even the "one central characteristic" that Kanter uses to define communal systems, "their mutually expressive goals," is not theoretically crucial.[57] Instead, one can simply speak in terms of "intentional communities" (as opposed to unplanned or commercially evolved towns and villages) and leave the degree of "communalism" open to the variation it naturally assumes from group to group. In a definitional sense, it does not matter whether the membership of a given group prefers to call itself a "commune," a "tribe," a "family," an "anarchy," an "ashram," an "order," an "association," a "society," or a "community." Nor does it matter for the purposes of definition how communistic it is, how religious or structured it is, how separated from the larger society, and so on. Common to all is a choice of structural variables that either may or may not be used to organize itself. As Kanter says, and I think quite correctly, "all of these are empirical questions for communal systems rather than theoretically defining values."[58] Indeed, her scheme could be used to analyze commitment in any social collectivity.

Kanter's work, then, formed the basis of the data protocol used in my own. This protocol, slightly modified from the original to fit the conditions I expected to face in latter-day communes, is reproduced in Appendix B. The protocol is organized in terms of the six categories of commitment mechanisms—sacrifice, investment, renunciation, communion, mortification, and transcendence. Each contains a number of specific structural indicators which together produce an additive scale for each category of commitment. These subtotals, in turn, may be added together to produce an overall index of the strength of a communal organization's commitment-producing features.

In measuring "regularized group contact," for instance, a score of 0 was assigned to a group that had no communal dwellings, a score of 1 to a group that had some communal dwellings, and a score of 2 to a group where all dwellings were communal. Similar values were assigned to other indicators of "regularized group contact" like the frequency of communal dining (weekly or less, 0; once daily, 1; twice daily, 2), the frequency of group meetings (once a month or less, 0; biweekly, 1; weekly, 2; daily, 3), and so on. These scores added up to a "regularized group contact" subtotal, which could then be added to other "communion" subtotals like "social homogeneity," "communistic sharing," "communistic labor," "ritual," and "persecution experiences" to produce a total score for "communion commitment." This score, in turn, was one of six such scores comprising overall commitment. Using Kanter's methods permitted not only a test of the relationship between commitment and group survival, but also a conceptual method for gathering the comprehensive descriptive accounts of modern American communes that I spoke of earlier as one of the goals of this project.

V

This book is based on thirteen rural communitarian groups in four western states (Colorado, New Mexico, California, and Oregon) which I visited on two extended trips, in 1970 and in 1973. As a representative sample it is small. Qualitatively, it probably overrepresents open-land groups like Morning Star East and Wheeler's Ranch, since these were more common in the West than in the East, where I did not travel. It probably underrepresents secretive and unpublicized groups like Crook's Creek and LILA, which like most communes in 1970 were not well known outside their immediate area. Further consideration of the sample, the circumstances of my research, and some of the problems I encountered can be found in Appendix A. Apart from limitations imposed by setting and circumstance, the thirteen groups taken together form an accurate profile of the American commune scene circa 1970.

The chapters which follow, one for each of the thirteen groups (except one instance in which two groups are discussed together), are presented in three sections each. The first section of each chapter sets out the group's history up until my first visit in 1970, in some cases going back five years but most often about two. In compiling these histories, I have drawn on my own interviews with participants and ex-participants, books and other documents produced by the communards themselves, reports in the underground press, and the descriptions and accounts written by various reporters who either preceded or followed me with visits of their own to groups in the study. Of these I owe a special debt to journalist-farmer Robert Houriet, whose *Getting Back Together* is the most scrupulously accurate and reliable commune-tour book of all those published in recent years,[59] and to Richard Fairfield, former editor of *The Modern Utopian,* whose *Communes U.S.A.* contains several invaluable interview transcripts with figures of note in the commune movement of our time.[60]

In general, however, I have relied on the direct quotes recorded by these and other reporters rather than the interpretations they assigned to their experiences or the communal myths they sometimes passed along. A major problem in assembling an accurate history of the communal groups born in the 1960s is that direct, firsthand observations are surprisingly sparse, given all the print that modern communes have inspired. Many communes were given pseudonymous identities in order to protect them from transients and harassment.

With the passage of time and the social climate of fear that then motivated these precautions, I feel that explicit historical accuracy is of higher value and that the cloak of anonymity can now be dropped in favor of honest assessments. (Regrettably, it became necessary to make one exception to this principle, which is explained in Chapter 13.) I have often avoided using personal surnames, however, where there seemed any chance that the revelation of personal identities might bring reprisals to individuals involved.

The second section of each chapter is a structured description of each group as it was organized at the time of my initial visit in 1970. The basic framework, lens, or instrument used in these observations is Kanter's scheme of commitment mechanisms and their detailed components. Each group is systematically described in terms of its organizational structure, following Kanter's six types of commitment. Much of the information recorded in the second and other sections of each chapter is drawn from a daily journal I kept in addition to the interview protocol. Once again the observations of other reporters were often helpful as supplementary material.

The third section of each chapter records what happened to each group over the three-year period between my first and second visits. Seven of the thirteen groups failed and no longer existed as collectivities at the end of this time. In these cases I relied on the accounts of ex-members still in the area, neighbors, previous benefactors of the group, and, in a few cases, local officials. Five of the thirteen had "succeeded" or at least survived this three-year period as corporate entities, and one other lingered on as a nuclear family still trying to be a commune but by no ordinary standards actually being one.

To test whether they thrived or merely lingered, a shorthand index of group "prosperity" was constructed for these groups, using indicators like new population growth, new structures erected, and new utilities installed. This index attempted to distinguish those groups which merely marked time from those which made tangible improvements to their property and the physical conditions of their lives. It is included in Appendix B.

In general I found that the organizational structures which had been adopted in 1970 were still essentially the same three years later, if the group had survived. "Success" as survival over three years is only an arbitrary definition, of course, and the final tallies are by no means in. But in an age of chronic change, three years proved quite enough time for over half of these groups to fail, thus distinguishing them from those which carry on today. Those groups which "succeeded" in 1973 were still succeeding as of this writing.

Finally, two concluding chapters chronicle some of the changes in the commune movement from 1970 to 1973, analyze the differences between those groups which survived and those which did not, and assess the social and historical significance of the commune movement in the 1970s and beyond. The children of prosperity were, of course, only a vocal minority among the youth of their time. Nevertheless, I am one of those who suspects that the impact of their experiments and innovations in politics, education, culture, and social relations will be with us for a long time, even if many of their early attempts at new societies failed. In justifying their study, I second the words of Theodore Roszak:

> The counter culture, far more than merely "meriting" attention, desperately requires it, since I am at a loss to know where, besides among these dissenting young people and their heirs of the next few generations, the radical discontent and innovation can be found that might transform this disoriented civilization of ours into something a human being can identify as home. . . . It looks to me like all we have to hold against the final consolidation of a technocratic totalitarianism in which we shall find ourselves ingeniously adapted to an existence wholly estranged from everything that has ever made the life of man an interesting adventure.[61]

Notes

1. Elinor Lander Horwitz, *Communes in America: The Place Just Right* (Philadelphia: J. B. Lippincott, 1972), p. 11. This phrase is from a stanza of the song "Simple Gifts."

2. This brief history of premodern American communes was greatly aided by the work of Foster G. Stockwell, a Chicago editor and historian who has compiled the most thorough demographic listing of pre-1965 communes available and kindly gave me access to his information.

3. Two of the best utopian histories to 1880 or so are Charles Nordhoff, *The Communistic Societies of the United States* (1875; reprint ed., New York: Schocken, 1965); and Mark Holloway, *Heavens on Earth: Utopian Communities in America, 1680–1880* (1951; reprint ed., New York: Dover, 1966).

4. Stockwell, private correspondence.

5. Ibid.

6. Based on Stockwell, private correspondence. A 1939 study of 236 historical American communes found that 45 percent broke up within five years. See Lawrence Veysey, *The Communal Experience: Anarchist and Mystical Counter-Cultures in America* (New York: Harper & Row, 1973), p. 457n. On the basis of more complete information, Stockwell concluded that the five-year break-up rate was 70 percent or more.

7. Robert Houriet, *Getting Back Together* (New York: Avon Books, 1972), p. 8.

8. Arnold J. Mandell, "Don Juan in the Mind," *Human Behavior*, 4 (January 1975), 66.

9. Lewis Coser and Irving Howe, "Images of Socialism," in *The Radical Papers*, ed. Irving Howe (Garden City, N.Y.: Doubleday, 1966), p. 14.

10. Benjamin Zablocki, *The Joyful Community* (Baltimore: Penguin Books, 1971), p. 299.

11. Veysey, *The Communal Experience*, p. 379.

12. Keith Melville, *Communes in the Counter Culture: Origins, Theories, Styles of Life* (New York: Morrow, 1972), p. 231.

13. Zablocki, *The Joyful Community*, pp. 300–302.

14. This chronology of the student movement during the late 1960s is indebted to Mitchell Goodman, ed., *The Movement Toward a New America: The Beginnings of a Long Revolution* (Philadelphia: Pilgrim Press, 1970), pp. x–xi.

15. Richard Fairfield, *Communes U.S.A.: A Personal Tour* (Baltimore: Penguin Books, 1972). Fairfield writes of Gorda Mountain on p. 241, of Tolstoy Farm on pp. 284–290, and of Drop City (also covered here) on pp. 202–208.

16. These were founded almost entirely in California and New Mexico, though by 1967 a few were getting started on the East Coast, too. Most are recorded in Fairfield, *Communes U.S.A.*, or in back issues of the magazine he edited from 1966 called *The Modern Utopian*.

17. Estimate based on lists compiled by *The Modern Utopian*, Carleton College Collective Clearinghouse (Minnesota), *The Green Revolution* (Heathcote Center, Md.), and other sources.

18. Hunter S. Thompson, *Fear and Loathing in Las Vegas* (New York: Popular Library, 1971), p. 202.

19. Kirkpatrick Sale, *SDS* (New York: Random House, 1973), p. 634.

20. Zablocki, *The Joyful Community*, p. 300.

21. Bill Kovach, "Communes Spread as the Young Reject Old Values," *New York Times*, December 17, 1970.

22. Judson Jerome, *Families of Eden: Communes and the New Anarchism* (New York: Seabury Press, 1974), p. 18.

23. Thompson, *Fear and Loathing in Las Vegas*, pp. 179–180.

24. The crossover from radical to communard was perhaps typified by Raymond Mungo, founding member of the Liberation News Service who moved to a rural Vermont commune in 1970 and wrote *Total Loss Farm* (New York: E. P. Dutton, 1971). The celebrated tension between radical activists and hip communards was probably always exaggerated, especially by radical ideologues who perceived dropouts as "politically irresponsible" and a threat to the movement. Under duress, as the commune movement demonstrated, the similarities (already encompassing drugs, long hair, and other life-style commonality) became much greater than the differences for the rank and file.

25. Melville, *Communes in the Counter Culture*, p. 60.

26. Ibid., p. 73.

27. Ibid., p. 67.

28. Ibid., p. 80.

29. Neil J. Smelser, *Theory of Collective Behavior* (New York: Free Press, 1963). See chapter 10, "The Value-Oriented Social Movement," pp. 313–381.

30. Marshall McLuhan, *Understanding Media: The Extensions of Man* (New York: McGraw-Hill, 1964).

31. See Theodore Roszak, *The Making of a Counter Culture: Reflections on the Technocratic Society and Its Youthful Opposition* (New York: Anchor Books, 1969).

32. See chapter 9, "The War of Sonoma County," for a discussion of the origins of voluntary primitivism in more detail.

33. Smelser, *Theory of Collective Behavior*, p. 384.

34. Goodman, *The Movement Toward a New America*, p. 70.

35. In *Communes U.S.A.*, editor Fairfield noted that the circulation of his *Modern Utopian* never exceeded 5,000. *Alternate Society* and *The Green Revolution* apparently had even lower circulations.

36. John R. Howard, *The Cutting Edge: Social Movements and Social Change in America* (Philadelphia: J. B. Lippincott, 1974), pp. 199–200.

37. In 1972 *The Mother Earth News* shifted its commune coverage to a new publication called *Lifestyle!*, which proved considerably less successful than *Mother*.

38. Zablocki, *The Joyful Community*, p. 286.

39. Rosabeth Moss Kanter, "Commitment and Social Organization: A Study of Commitment Mechanisms in Utopian Communities," *American Sociological Review*, 33 (August 1968), 499–517.

40. Rosabeth Moss Kanter, *Commitment and Community: Communes and Utopias in Sociological Perspective* (Cambridge, Mass.: Harvard University Press, 1972).

41. Kanter, "Commitment and Social Organization," p. 500.

42. Ibid., p. 499.

43. Talcott Parsons and Edward Shils, eds., *Toward a General Theory of Action* (New York: Harper & Row, 1962).

44. Kanter, "Commitment and Social Organization," p. 500.

45. Ibid., pp. 499–500.

46. Ibid., p. 501.

47. Ibid.

48. Ibid., pp. 501–502.

49. Ibid.

50. Ibid., p. 504.

51. Ibid.

52. Ibid., p. 507.

53. Ibid., p. 510.

54. Ibid.

55. Ibid., p. 512.

56. Ibid., pp. 513–514.

57. See Kanter, *Commitment and Community*, p. 242.

58. Ibid.

59. Houriet, *Getting Back Together*.

60. Fairfield, *Communes U.S.A.*

61. Roszak, *The Making of a Counter Culture*, pp. xii–xiii.

2

Rule by the Woodchucks:
Drop City

I

Drop City was founded in May 1965, a date that more or less begins the "hippie" era of modern communes. The founders were young artists and dropouts from the East Coast, Texas, and the Universities of Colorado and Kansas. The setting they chose, with only $500 to spend, was six acres of goat pasture about four miles from the sleepy southern Colorado town of Trinidad and the somewhat busier I-25 interstate highway. The highway led north to Denver and Boulder, reservoirs of friends, jobs, and materials. Going south it pointed toward Taos and Santa Fe and similar connections. The Droppers took their name from Timothy Leary's injunction to "Turn on, tune in, and drop out," which was exactly what they proposed to do—but not too far from the freeway.

In more ways than one, Drop City was an integral part of the birth of the counterculture. Architecturally, it was the first commune to build and live in geodesic domes, thereby establishing a fashion in building that would later spread throughout the underground. Artistically, their paintings and psychedelic "Droppings" were then among the most original. Politically, the Droppers followed closely behind Ken Kesey's Merry Pranksters in techniques of transforming American culture through visceral entertainment experiences. They traveled far and wide with their message and their show. Even their name carried the message in code: drop out, drop *all* the way out, go out and make a new way of life.

> Droppers absolutely put down power; Droppers absolutely put down money, hoarded energy; we absolutely put down ownership—everything we have is yours, everything you have is ours. GET RID OF YOUR HANGUPS, HELP US GET RID OF OUR HANGUPS.[1]

What they had to offer as an alternative to straight society was an enticing vision of joyful community combining Eastern mysticism, avant-garde art, and an American Indian's sense of tribal place and unity (interpolated via Texas peyote):

> Drop City is Home. We dance the joydance, we listen to the eternal rhythm, our feet move to unity, a balanced step of beauty and strength. Drop City pivots on a sublime paradox; opposing forces exist side by side in joyous harmony, mystery and metaphor are the roots of the joy-force, creation is joy, joy is love, life-love-joy-energy are one. We are all one.[2]

These passages were written by "Peter Rabbit," one of Drop City's founders and author of a book about its early history. The first is an appeal to personal liberation, while the second is a paean to perfect communal harmony. Where in practice these goals might be assumed to conflict, in Drop City's vision they were almost the same thing: both could be achieved by spontaneity, ego-detachment, antimaterialism, and equalitarian social cooperation. Self-fulfillment would emerge in paradoxical symmetry with self-loss. But despite the religious overtones, the Droppers were by no means pious and retiring. In their first two years, they were activists dedicated to changing society as well as themselves:

> Droppers travel around doing Droppings—total media environment intermix. Every Dropper does his thing, helps the other Droppers do their thing, all an energy center pulsing out, sucking everyone in. Soon they're over their heads—blown minds—joydancing—lovechanting. A Dropping is a fine thing.[3]

From 1965 to 1967, an era when they made many forays to college campuses, the Droppers felt something powerful coming out of the underground and viewed themselves as its carriers, agents, and spokesmen. Their method was to stimulate and service a growing curiosity about light shows, psychedelic music, independent film making, and architectural novelties like their domes, made out of junk car tops for next to no cost. In every respect Drop City summed up the optimism, creativity, and sense of self-importance with which the commune movement began. They even produced a movie about themselves called *The Drop City Document*. They were especially proud of their domes, which won "The First Buckminster Fuller Dymaxion Award" for "poetically economical structural achievement." Their missionary zeal and sense of historical destiny sometimes approached pure hubris:

> Soon domed cities will spread across the world, anywhere land is cheap—on the deserts, in the swamps, on mountains, tundras, ice caps. The tribes are moving, building completely free and open way stations, each a warm and beautiful conscious environment. We are winning.[4]

The strange doings at Drop City were first brought to national attention in 1966, when the *Denver Post* sent a reporter to Trinidad to check out the rumors. The reporter got an impish reception and went away to write a bizarre fairy tale (spoon-fed by the Droppers) about dwarfs and elves contacting Drop City because they were concerned about a nuclear disaster. The wire services picked up the story, and Drop City soon made the "Talk of the Town" column in *The New Yorker*. One Dropper was even commissioned by the tattle tabloid *National Insider* to write their story, which was printed as "The Heretics: Work Kills the Human Spirit—Why Not Quit Today?"

In practice, the Droppers' vision of quitting included permission to "liberate" the system's resources for themselves and their message of change. For the most part they were creative scavengers, but on occasion they were also thieves. Above all, though, the Droppers were artists in search of an audience. They actively promoted themselves through mimeographed newsletters and flyers which they sent throughout the nation. These reached, among other places, the headquarters of a new magazine devoted to communes called *The Modern Utopian*. Its editor, Richard Fairfield, later wrote that the Droppers "advertised themselves as a community of artists who were innovating not only in the area of buildings and life-style, but also in a multi-media approach to art."[5] In short, they were after self-serving public exposure as part and parcel of their communal proselytizing. With their Droppings, lecture appearances, metropolitan art shows, flyers, articles, and other efforts to spread the word, they soon got the notice they were after.

And their fame soon backfired. In 1967, the Summer of Love in Haight-Ashbury, they were inundated by "hoards of teen-age runaways, thrill seekers, sightseers, and miscellaneous dropouts—mostly of the irresponsible variety."[6] In good part, of course, they brought the problem on themselves. In June 1967, they invited anybody and everybody to come to the "Drop City Joy Festival." According to Peter Rabbit's book, it was a fabulous party, visited by hundreds of people and no less a personage than Guru Tim himself. (Completely in character, the Droppers immediately hit Leary for money.) But for Drop City in 1967, the party was soon over:

> And then came the hordes. Drop City was continually overcrowded. The level of consciousness decreased—too many people—the energies were hopelessly dispersed. The kitchen was filthy, the food tasted shitty, disease continuously ran through the commune. People were crashing all over the Complex. Nobody knew anybody else. People would stay a month or so, get themselves a little straight and travel on. The Droppers were going on the same trip over and over again: coolin' out runaways, speed freaks, and smack heads, cleaning up after them, scroungin' food for them, playing shrink and priest confessor—round and round and round.[7]

Drop City's experiences that year almost exactly paralleled those of the Haight-Ashbury district. The invitation to love and joy soon turned into a snake pit. In San Francisco, the countercultural vanguard proclaimed "the death of hippie" that fall and then moved out. The Droppers moved out, too, though in their case (if not the Haight's as well), self-advertisement shared much of the blame. In May 1968 most of the original Droppers left to set up another community—this time more secluded and less open to visitors. By the fall of 1969 all the original Droppers had abandoned their domes, victims of their own success, thereafter to become more jealous of their energies and less embarrassed about their own self-interest.

> In a way the time of dissolution was good; a period of service. But instead of going higher, we were on the merry-go-round. . . . Instead of a community of people dedicated to getting it together on the highest possible level, Drop City became a decompression chamber for city freaks.[8]

The elegy for hippie and the collapse of Haight-Ashbury could not have been put more succinctly: a period of service that got out of hand. Drop City's first generation then moved on to form a more isolated, serious, and permanent community of the sort that would largely replace the open-gate, anarchistic communes by 1970. As a social movement, something died in 1967 in vanguard zones like the Haight and Drop City, even though communes in general began mushrooming. It took four more years for the larger wave to crest, for joy to become sober retreat and finally despair.

In any case, Drop City established a pattern for many communes to come later: a "founding" period of intense energy and optimism, followed by a "period of service" which ultimately becomes debilitating, and ending with a period of becoming more closed to outsiders or moving out. The founders of Drop City more or less abandoned their domes to whoever wanted to come live in them.

II

With the coming of spring in 1970, an entirely new generation of Droppers began filtering in. By the time I arrived in July, the population had grown to a total of twenty-two men, seventeen women, and four children. Of the thirty-nine adults, only four had been in Drop City six months earlier, during the winter. Indeed, twelve of them were temporarily in jail on charges of trespassing during a picnic expedition to a nearby mountaintop. But for most of them, being in jail was like a lark. A friendly jailer even helped them smuggle in wine.

The treatment the arrested Droppers got in jail testified to the fact that, after five years of experience, most of the residents of Trinidad had come to view them with amusement and tolerance. In a sense, Drop City was the biggest show that Trinidad—poor, Chicano, easygoing—had to offer. Over the years the sheriff had tried hard to leave the Droppers alone, showing up only occasionally to let them know if there was a complaint from the neighbors about nudity. To my knowledge no one was ever arrested on Drop City's premises in the eight years of its history.

Except for the complaints about nudity (which were never really pursued), Drop City was thus a kind of "safe zone" just off a major route of hitchhikers and other dropout traffic. As a community, it had the lowest level of commitment of any group in this study. Nothing was required of members, people could stay as long as they liked, and new people came and went on a daily basis. Only 3 percent of the members had been there twelve months. Those who had been there longest occupied the domes of their choice, as couples or friendship cliques. The other buildings, particularly the large Kitchen Complex, were given over to transients and crashers. All of Drop City's domes were within a stone's throw of each other on a small six-acre plot fronting a paved county road. There were no trees, and the nearest neighbor was less than fifty yards away. Tourists drove by daily to gawk, and young kids from Trinidad came out almost nightly. As one Dropper put it, it was like living in a fishbowl. According to the psychedelic sign on the fence, Drop City was a "Butterfly Sanctuary." And truly it was.

By 1970 Drop City was populated by the very sort of people that the original Droppers had moved out to avoid. "They show up here like that," reported *Time*'s William Hedgepeth, "the newly dropped out; the fresh in flight; the fitful, infinitely fragile youths embroiled in bottomless discontent and disillusionment with rigidly citified society whose social symbols suddenly—perhaps as prompted by the catalytic action of some hallucinogen—no longer signify anything."[9] Drop City's average age was less than twenty-one, and a Dropper's education had typically ended with a high school diploma. Of all the communards I visited in 1970, these were the youngest and least experienced. But there were also a number of older Droppers who had lived in communes before and were often quite frank about using Drop City as a free ride or a rest stop. The older residents took little interest in Drop City's affairs, which were largely left to the more spirited and idealistic younger members. Drop City's resident philosopher, Jack, who himself declined to participate but enjoyed observing, described it as "rule by the woodchucks."[10]

The entire commune of forty (give or take a few) people and its constant stream of visitors somehow got by on food stamps and a sporadic income that seldom exceeded $100 a month. If one was simply marking time and interested in having fun, Drop City in 1970 was a very economical way to do it. But fun came at a certain price. The kitchen was filthy, and there was no soap because money was short. Hepatitis had recently swept through the commune, and still no one was motivated enough to see that soap was made available. Sleeping quarters were seriously overcrowded. The outhouse was filled to overflowing, and there was no lime to sterilize it. In 1970 Drop City had become, if it was not from the first, a laboratory dedicated to a totally minimal existence.

Still, Drop City considered its only real money problems to be utility bills (electricity and propane) and property tax, a combined total of perhaps $50 a month. Food stamps helped but always ran out halfway through the month, leading to scavenging runs to the Trinidad Safeway and its outdoor trash cans. The Droppers, like so many communards, liked to make a mystique of where their money came from. "It comes when it's needed," they said, "it just happens." Indeed, they were so obviously impoverished that many outsiders felt impelled to go out of their way to help. When it fell to me, as a visitor-participant, either to go out and buy soap on my own or to accept its absence, I went out and bought soap. Such were the ways the mystique actually worked. "It comes," we might say, "through the gates." The flow of new people and visitors was in fact the life blood of Drop City's economy. When it was inadequate, the Droppers were quite adept at presenting themselves in Trinidad as a merry band of helpless orphans who needed mothering. Even Safeway could not resist them. In a sense, then, Drop City was still in the entertainment business. By 1970, though, the political content was gone, and the question was raw survival.

Even so, the Droppers did not view overdue bills as a communal responsibility but rather as an abstract nuisance, for which a solution would somehow emerge. As individuals, few members assumed any personal responsibility for the group's fate. Nine out of fourteen Droppers I questioned described their stay in Drop City as "temporary" or "not very permanent." This negligible level of commitment was perhaps summed up best by one young member who was asked if he felt a permanent sense of responsibility for the others in the group. "Yes," he replied, "all of them that I *know*."

Sacrifice   Aside from the sanitation and minor money problems, though, there was little by way of personal sacrifice required to live in Drop City and therefore little to inspire this sort of commitment. There were no abstinence rules whatever, and no attempt was made to regulate drugs, alcohol, diet, or sexual behavior. Like so many communes, Drop City paid for this liberty in the coin of physical austerity. Winters can be harsh on Colorado's eastern plains, and most buildings at Drop City were poorly heated. Still, life was harsher at several other communes in this study. Drop City at least had gas for its kitchen dome, year-round water, electricity, and food stamps. Altogether, Drop City had the second lowest level of commitment through sacrifice of all groups studied.

Investment   Drop City was also below average in the level of commitment it inspired through investment. No physical participation in the group was required of anybody, nor was any form of financial participation. There were no fees or property turnovers expected of members, and only the gentlest moral persuasion was used to get members to share their private resources. An average of fifteen to twenty transients poured through the community each week, often many more during the summer, and frequently no one even learned their names. It was quite possible to walk in and pitch a tent at Drop City for days without being expected to help or even challenged for an explanation. Yet for the duration these transients were more or less accepted as "members" if they chose to be. About the only commitment-building investment requirement at Drop City was that any contributions which *were* made were very unlikely to be returned and were usually irreversible.

Renunciation   Drop City again had the lowest score in this study on the commitment-building factors associated with the concept of renunciation. Drop City was not nearly as isolated as most other rural communes which followed it. At a distance of four miles from Trinidad and in clear view of nearby neighbors, Drop City was practically a suburb or a dropout way station on Interstate 25. With several modern media in the community and almost daily trips into town, Drop City was scarcely very insulated from the ordinary world. Nor were there any rules concerning visitation restrictions or any of the many possible ways that new members might be screened. In sociological parlance, Drop City had no "cross-boundary control" over its members or visitors. There was no particularly meaningful distinction between "them" and "us" or "inside the community" and "outside." Drop City drew no strength from the kind of commitment that evolves when a community cuts itself off.

Communion   Working together, sharing together, being a lot like each other, and reinforcing a sense of community feeling with shared rituals and ceremonies—these are the sort of communion experiences that create commitment. In these respects Drop City was more like other modern communes and more or less typical of the "open-land" variation. Most members had known each other only a short time, there were often significant age differences between them, and there was little by way of organized group labor or formal ceremonies. Most communes were more homogeneous and organized. On the other hand, the Droppers were higher than average in sharing with each other what meager wealth they had. They were also above average in the intensity of their daily contact with each other, due to their communal eating arrangements, the low level of privacy, and other factors related to the small size of the commune and the physical density of its life. There were no fixed routines, group meetings, or designated leaders to give the group direction. Politically, Drop City had changed little from the tradition established years earlier by Peter Rabbit and the first generation:

> There is no political structure in Drop City. Things work out; the cosmic forces mesh with people in a strange complex intuitive interaction. Sometimes it's slow, but when it comes out it's good and nobody's head is bent. Only three things have ever come to a vote: in all three cases Droppers went around with their heads bent for days. When things are done the slow intuitive way the tribe makes sense.[11]

The "slow, intuitive way" made especially good sense given the undercurrents of transience and unarticulated personal goals. In good measure, this antipolitical ideology was a romantic patina over the latent conflict under the community's surface, which would probably have emerged in the open if the group had been serious about long-term commitment. It also had a dampening effect on the development of such conflict by making it illegitimate. "Here," reported Hedge-peth and Stock in 1970, "you mention 'purpose' and people say, 'Oh, let's not talk about *that* again.' "[12] And Drop City, in 1970 anyway, never experienced the kind of harassment from outsiders that might *make* them talk about it.

Mortification   There were other aspects of this chaotic community structure that the Droppers pointed to with pride. Nineteenth-century communes, for example, often made extensive use of mortification mechanisms like mutual criticism sessions or making moral distinctions between members. By humbling individual pride, these communes thereby increased group commitment in a rather distasteful but effective way. Few modern communes made very extensive use of these devices in the early days before the commune movement took on a more spiritual character in the 1970s. Drop City used them even less. Mutual criticism was uncommon and entirely informal, and status distinctions on moral or spiritual grounds were considered illegitimate. Nor did Drop City employ devices like probation periods, limited privileges, or formal instruction for new members.

Transcendence   Nor did Drop City employ the sort of structures that build commitment through transcendent experiences of personal surrender before the awesome authority of the group's institutions. Most modern rural communes likewise made little use of these devices, but once again Drop City used them least of all. It had no coherent ideology, and no particular magical qualities were imputed to the group or its members, aside from the vaguely miraculous fact that it survived year after year. Structures of power and authority were out of the question. Neither was there any attempt by the group to program individual behavior, require commitment to certain beliefs, make new members take vows, or otherwise require any form of "conversion." For mechanisms encouraging commitment through transcendence, Drop City had only the tradition established by earlier Droppers, who completely disavowed such practices. The highest virtue was freedom, and when all is said and done, that is what Drop City was designed to permit.

At times this dedication to anarchy could even be fiercely defiant, in certain interesting and nonviolent ways. On the day I first arrived in Drop City, a former member of the Hell's Angels, named Butcher, was just leaving. He had spent two weeks in Drop City "trying to get things organized," but nothing had worked. On one occasion he had gone out and bought a bag of free groceries for the group, including a large bag of white sugar. When he brought it back, one of the young Droppers dumped the sugar all over the ground.

Publicly the sugar-dumping Dropper said he did so because the white sugar was "pseudofood." But privately he was acting "because Butcher was trying to run everything." This line of resistance to patronizing authority left Butcher completely exasperated. To the group he said he had to go to Denver to get his teeth fixed and would be back, but in fact he was disgusted and had no plans to return. "These people are *animals,* man," the plaintive Angel told me. "*Nothin's* ever gonna happen here."

But Butcher was wrong. What was happening was a community offering few material amenities but many social ones in an atmosphere of unrestricted individuality. And for what it offered, little though that might have been, it demanded nothing. For many young American wanderers in 1970, this was a pretty fair definition of utopia.

Daily life at Drop City began anywhere from eight to eleven in the morning, depending on the extent of the partying the night before. The first to wake up went into the Complex to make breakfast for themselves. The proceedings seemed to begin officially when the first record was placed on Drop City's communal stereo, which was in continual operation all day and often long into the night. If the sun was out, the Droppers would loaf around waiting to see what came through the gate or perhaps go to town for food and adventure. If it was a less pleasant day, some Droppers might work on making antler hash pipes or spoon rings for sale in town. Drop City's tiny communal garden was bone-dry and neglected, growing nothing edible but wild pigweed and amaranth. If Bill was around, the goats got milked; if not, they might well suffer until the next day with distended mammaries. All chores were completely voluntary and often went undone. Except for Bill and the goats, there were not even any mutually understood areas of responsibility.

The highlight of an average day was usually the evening meal, which was put together when somebody—usually one of four or five resident women with random voluntary help from both sexes—took the initiative to prepare it. Dinner was the one sure time when Drop City's full population, including nomads and hangers-on, would assemble in one place. No prayers were said, but the bowls were passed around with reverent fairness, as each waited for all to be served before eating. The atmosphere was always jolly, and as often as not somebody was having a birthday, making things even more festive. Old whisky bottles were used as communal drinking glasses because they added to the communal magic (and meant less dish washing). A goat might come in and walk over the table unmolested, a young dog might defecate on the floor, but nothing really mattered, because earthy living was both the object and the requirement of a Dropper's participation.

Drop City was structured, then, with complete individuality and mobility as its most central features. This was reflected in its level of "political equality," which was the third highest in the sample. Why it was not the very highest, as we might expect, is interesting, since the reasons reveal some of the core problems of communal anarchies. First, Drop City had no system to assign areas of responsibility or share tasks fairly among all participants—or if there was such a system, it would have to be described as total laissez-faire. Among the results of this nonsystem was the creation of a two-class social structure, consisting of a freeloading majority and an overworked minority of more permanent or committed members. An additional result, especially when coupled with the lack of incentives to invest anything in Drop City, was the commune's presubsistence economy, in short, its poverty. Still another result was the fact that women, while otherwise sharing equally in Drop City's vague kind of politics, were almost invariably left with the responsibility for feeding the community (though in doing so they enjoyed more sense of purpose than did many of the others).

Drop City's political equality was also lowered by the fact that outside benefactors had control over their destiny. In 1970 the deed holders, the original founders, were acting in good faith with a provision in their nonprofit corporate charter that the land was to remain "free" forever. But if this policy were to be changed, Drop City could be out on its ear—which, in fact, is what ultimately happened.

Finally, Drop City's style of equalitarian politics was weakened by its vulnerability to illegitimate usurpation of authority, particularly by older, more experienced males like the Hell's Angel Butcher. But while I was visiting, at least, those who might have been likely candidates for community elders chose to remain on the margins. Mostly they were like Jack, a twenty-five-year-old asthmatic poet who occupied a small dome alone. Although given to nudity, Jack was otherwise monkish in his habits and sometimes stayed in his dome for days at a time. He might have been the local Zen master, but nobody took him very seriously. He was called Crazy Jack by some of the younger Droppers.

Another typical Drop City elder was Richard, who was in his early thirties and living in a big yellow school bus with his wife. Drop City for him was a supportive parking lot while he worked on the bus and his plans to take an occult version of the Aquarian gospel to the farmers of Nebraska. Richard was a rough-hewn, soft-spoken cosmonaut with two feet of wild, carrot-colored hair. He told me one evening that he had been to Mars twice and to Venus once, as the guest of flying saucers. Richard was very lucid and personable and talked very matter-of-factly about his space travels. "Don't do Venus, man," he advised me, "there's nothing happening *there*." At the time, Richard was in trouble of some kind with the draft. If it came to splitting, he was undecided whether to go to Canada, Europe, or Mars. He and his wife possessed Drop City's only working television set.

As community patriarchs, Jack and Richard were unlikely prospects, though less because of their eccentricities than because of their indifference to leadership. Like the holy fools of primitive tribes, they were left alone, vaguely respected, and asked to do nothing except be themselves. The oldest woman in the community was a working-class mother about thirty-five years old. For being the most experienced cook, she was generally forgiven for her children, who were habitual petty thieves. In July 1970 the most widely respected person in Drop City, the person who displayed more legitimate initiative than any other, was a boy nineteen years old.

III

Over the years Drop City continued to change its population annually, though toward the end there was an attempt to close the commune off from outsiders. During the winter of 1971–1972, I interviewed two women who were then members. They had not been there in 1970 and said that only two or three were left from that generation. But they were optimistic. "We're really getting it together," they told me. "We're not really open to crashers anymore. We think of it as our home."

Ironically, not long after Drop City ended its open-gate tradition, the founders of the community decided to close the gate for good. The founders were by then tired of their responsibilities as Drop City's trustees, and they had other uses for the resources the property represented. They hired a lawyer to remove the embarrassing clause that Drop City was to remain free forever. In March 1973 the property was sold and the tenants evicted. Within a month, Drop City's colorful cartop domes, a kind of hip national monument, had been stripped inside by scavengers and damaged by vandalistic fires. The charming "Butterfly Sanctuary" sign was gone, replaced on Drop City's barbed-wire fence with an ominous red sign saying "Posted."

But even in its demise Drop City was a kind of first. As a stable, sustaining, serious community it was a total flop. Yet it lasted for eight years, a life span that still had not been reached by any other commune in this study by 1975. The population turned over continually, but the group entity and the spirit survived. Had the land not been paid for right at the beginning and had taxes not been so low, Drop City might have perished many times over from its total lack of rational organization. Yet had it not been for the existential fatigue of the founders and trustees, Drop City might still be thriving today.

Drop City's philosopher, Crazy Jack, once explained to me that money is not a need, but a desire, and that the very existence of Drop City proved it. The logic of Drop City's lack of rules, as he saw it, was that otherwise competitive factions would develop. He described Drop City as a uniquely important kind of place where only change is permanent: "a feast of change." Where nothing is permanent, he explained, a new person is born: yourself. "That's what Drop City's all about," he said, returning to work on a novel to be called *Animal Crackers*.

Notes

1. Peter Rabbit [pseud.], *Drop City* (New York: Olympia Press, 1971), p. 29. By far the most detailed and entertaining account of Drop City's first five years.
    2. Ibid., p. 31.
    3. Ibid.
    4. Ibid., p. 29.
    5. Richard Fairfield, *Communes U.S.A.: A Personal Tour* (Baltimore: Penguin Books, 1972), p. 203. An important date in the modern commune movement was September 1966, when Fairfield, then a theology student, founded *The Modern Utopian* in Boston. After moving to California and finishing school, Fairfield spent several months as a Unitarian minister, but "found little challenge or inspiration" in that calling. He then expanded his publishing enterprises into "The Alternatives! Foundation," which offered a wide variety of "alternative life-style" publications and services by 1970, including directories of communes, free schools, and nudist camps, and a communal match program. Though *The Modern Utopian* itself never achieved a circulation greater than 5,000 ("mostly among college students and professors, semidropouts and dissatisfied middle-class professionals," to quote Fairfield), it was for some time (almost three years) the most important magazine of its kind and the only one dealing with communal reports from around the country on a regular basis. *The Modern Utopian* was the major printed commune information switchboard and contact point in America until 1970, when it was supplanted by more sophisticated and successful publications like *The Whole Earth Catalog* and *The Mother Earth News*. Some back issues of *TMU* are still available; for details see the appendix of Fairfield's book. *Communes U.S.A.* also includes a firsthand account of Fairfield's visit to Drop City in 1970, as well as his travels to other groups.
    6. Fairfield, *Communes U.S.A.*, p. 204.
    7. Peter Rabbit, *Drop City*, p. 148.
    8. Ibid., p. 149.
    9. William Hedgepeth and Dennis Stock, *The Alternative* (New York: Collier Books, 1970), pp. 155–156. *The Alternative* includes an excellent on-the-spot account of Drop City in the final transition phase (the winter of 1969–1970) between the first generation and the second. Printed with many outstanding photos in an oversize magazine-style format, this was the first book specifically about the new communes, and it remains one of the most insightful.
    10. Jack was often, however, the Dropper who answered the mail. A reference to "rule by the woodchucks" is also found in sociologist Ron Roberts's book *The New*

Communes. Unfortunately, Roberts overinterpreted Jack's cryptic letter as showing "a desire for quiescence that is common to many hip communes," thereby demonstrating the frailties of studying modern communes through the U.S. mail. More often than not such replies were put-ons. See Ron E. Roberts, *The New Communes; Coming Together in America* (Englewood Cliffs, N.J.: Prentice-Hall, 1971), p. 55.

11. Peter Rabbit, *Drop City*, p. 29.
12. Hedgepeth and Stock, *The Alternative*, p. 157.

3

Living in the Future: Libre

I

The community of Libre was founded in May 1968 by six emigrants from the confusion and turmoil that self-advertisement had brought on Drop City. Earlier that spring, one of these expatriates-to-be had expressed strong disillusionment with the Drop City ideal to an underground newspaper reporter, who noted that a sign had been placed on Drop City's fence saying "NO PHOTOGRAPHS, VISITING HOURS WEEKENDS ONLY, 8 A.M. to 8 P.M."

> "We'll let anyone come for awhile, but only those who contribute can stay," stated a resident. "It has to be that way. We've learned the hard way, by letting too many come who could only take away."
>
> "We're thinking of burning Drop City down," he continued. "We're going to move; start out new in Canada or Virginia or on a farm near here, but this time we'll keep it a secret."[1]

But the public-relations skills learned at Drop City were again in evidence: hundreds of form letters were mailed out asking for contributions to establish a "free community." Thanks primarily to the same benefactor who had made the New Buffalo commune possible north of Taos, Libre's founders were able to buy four hundred acres of timbered mountainside above an isolated valley in southern Colorado. There the land was cheap, starkly beautiful, and deep within a box-canyonlike funnel where very few had reason to travel. There was no commercial development or industry and little potential for it. If the terrain was rugged and the land poor, so much the better for Libre's seclusion, so much the better for setting up secure boundaries around a new home distilling all that its founders had learned in Drop City.

Below Libre's nine-thousand-foot setting flows the Huerfano River, which gives the region its Spanish name, the Valley of the Orphans. "Libre" itself is Spanish for "free." Within five years, as if in keeping with some forgotten prophecy, the valley was populated by over two hundred hip orphans and three more communes.[2]

With the gift of the land, Libre was registered as a nonprofit artistic and educational organization. The land title was transferred to the control of the corporate trustees and officers, who were to be members only. By June 1968 five dwellings were begun. The population doubled by the next summer and doubled again by 1970, but the process of acquiring new members was nevertheless slow and deliberate. Each of the founding members had to approve each new member, and each new member after that had to win the unanimous approval of the entire membership. When the population reached two dozen in 1970, the general feeling of the community was that this was about the suitable number for the land and that no new members would be admitted for a year.

The other rules that guided the community were equally deliberate. Couples were preferred to singles for community stability, although exceptions were made for good friends. Each new couple (or single) had to build their own house. Help would be available from other Libreans, but there would be no shared responsibilities for shelter. In addition, each house had to be built out of the sight of every other, except by explicit permission of those already there. The hilly terrain limited the number of suitable building sites, so another Libre rule was to limit its population in balance with the ecology of the site. "Straight" visitors would be limited to Sundays only. Key decisions would be approved only by unanimous Council. Councils would not be regular, but they would be both serious and obligatory when called. No new members would be admitted unless they satisfied the Council that they had a clear sense of purpose in wanting to live at Libre and showed sufficient competence and self-reliance to support themselves.[3]

Such was the social legacy of Drop City. But the legacy of innovative art and architecture was continued with relish. The ex-Droppers built domes and zomes for the most part, though others chose to build from wood or adobe. The homes of the early members were scattered around the small meadows of Libre's lowlands, connected by paths adorned with modern sculpture and other art objects. When the second half of Libre's membership began building in 1970, they constituted a kind of colony within a colony up on the ridge. The newcomers built equally novel structures, mostly of wood, to suit the sites where they were located. One grew like a multisided crystal around a natural granite boulder, another mounted the crest on the ridge like a spaceship, while another was built on the highest slopes in three levels. Though most of the buildings at Libre were constructed of salvage and lumber seconds, their artistic quality led *Architectural Design* magazine to publish a feature on them in 1971.[4]

But architecture was only one dimension to Libre's evolving definition of art as the everyday experience of a self-constructed life (with Libre of course at the vanguard):

> The other artists here and I are trying to reintegrate our art with life and nature. In a few years, art won't be something restricted to museums and divorced from life. It will be an inseparable part of the process of living.[5]

The members of Libre were also innovators in breaking away from the romantic disdain in the counterculture for modern technology, electronics, and machines. The membership was determined to make a serious community of permanent homes, and every tool helped. In sentiment they echoed the words of Steve Baer, a young new-technology zome pioneer who was instrumental in the early dome building of several communes in the southwest: "All this talk about a self-contained counterculture . . . can you imagine us freaks trying to manufacture plastic, pipe, and glass?"[6]

The members of Libre, then, took what advantage they could of modern tools without embarrassment: electricity, chain saws, polyvinyl chloride (PVC) pipe, fiberglass, and FM tuners. They joked about their reputation as the "Scarsdale of the Underground." There was even talk of getting a computer. For the second generation of Libreans who built on the ridge in 1970, the tone was more back to basics. There was no electricity or water on the ridge, although that seemed to suit the new members well enough and permitted them the amusement of distinguishing themselves spiritually from the "flatlanders."

In 1969 Libre began to attract the attention of the underground press as a "very heavy" commune of "far-out artists." In the meantime, the old Dropper activism had been revived at Libre, though this time with more refinement. When they went on a concert and lecture tour of the East Coast that year, for instance, they did so on a foundation grant. While in New York, their reputation for claiming unusual psychic experiences was put to the test at the Maimonides Dream Laboratory by its director, Dr. Stanley Krippner, who reported that the six Libreans tested demonstrated unusual telepathic ability as individuals and especially as a group.[7] In 1970 this news was reported in both the underground and aboveground press. The tension between the old Dropper desire for notoriety and Libre's founding desire for secrecy was resolved as an intimidating mystique, which seemed to satisfy both sides of the ambivalence at once: here was a famous community of unapproachable artists and spiritual heavyweights that had to be respected but left alone.

Libre also acquired a reputation locally for its gadfly resistance to various branches of the Huerfano County government. Thus they gained the respect of the impoverished Chicanos in the valley, especially for their attempt to set up a school for valley children, which was finally quashed by the county on building code violations. Peter Rabbit, an ex-Dropper and Libre founder, received his nickname from the local people for his ability to hop around and outwit the big shots. It was said that Peter talked to deer before he shot them and ate their warm livers afterwards. Peter and the other Libreans did nothing to discourage these stories (which were true enough anyway), for in the country-and-western ambience of Huerfano County they gave credence to Libre's announced intent to defend its right to exist by any means necessary.

The first three years at Libre were all years of intense building, especially the first and third, reflecting the two major waves of settlement. One member, who built his house for under $100 with salvaged materials, spoke for most Libreans when he told journalist Robert Houriet that "the greatest creative experience of my life was building this house."[8] Apart from occasional changeovers in mates, life inside Libre in the early years was preoccupied with constructing a new village. By 1970 several other communes were building nearby, and the sense of collective purpose had spread throughout the valley. Libre had led the way to the revitalization of half a county and its transformation from a forgotten backwater to a politically important outpost of the counterculture.

II

In July 1970 Libre was in the second of its intense building periods. The thirteen new members who had joined since the winter were all in the middle of building their new homes on the ridge. Libre's energies were necessarily focused inward again, and there was considerable concern about being invaded by an influx of visitors as their communal colleagues in Taos had been in the summer of 1969. As one member told Richard Fairfield:

> We thought we could get away by coming up here, but people just kept following us. We've had at least half a dozen visitors this afternoon and

it's only early spring and a weekday at that. What will it be like when
summer arrives? . . . It's funny. We were here all winter and snowed in
part of the time. Then, we wouldn't have minded visitors. . . . Tell
people not to come here. We're interested in maybe a few more people
joining us but we're in no hurry.[9]

Over the summer there was a steady flow of visitors, but no
great influx as feared. That there were visitors at all was testimony to
Libre's mystique, since the community is truly isolated and hard to
penetrate. First, it is separated from the nearest pavement by fifteen
miles of forking, unmarked dirt roads. The fork that ultimately leads
to Libre deadends when it gets there. Just beyond the gate is a deep
swale, which Libre leaves unfilled as a moat against long, heavy,
late-model American cars, which never seem to bring the right kind of
guests.

Another deterrent was the dispersal of the community over so
many forested, hilly acres. This absence of any "center" to Libre's
diffusion of private homes caused many visitors great feelings of awk-
wardness and gave Libreans a rationale to turn away all but the most
helpless overnight crashers. Other strangers were welcomed, though,
if they made a friend among the membership, showed an interest in
helping out with construction, or otherwise had something to contribute (such as a case of cold beer).

In the summer of 1970 there were twenty-three adults at Libre
and six children. Apart from two single men and one single woman,
the community was paired off in couples. Several couples had been
rearranged in the first three years among the older members. Newer
members were younger and (so far at least) married. The average age
was over thirty for the founding members and about twenty-five for
the newer ones. Almost all had college degrees. Several members
were artists with a notable measure of commercial success; others
were writers, craftsmen, and builders likewise able to market their
skills outside when necessary. Some members were highly skilled in
dealing with the media, government agencies, and philanthropic foun-
dations. In age, education, and experience, the members of Libre
were the oldest and probably most competent group in this study.

After the first two years, four of the six founders—minus two
women—were still present at Libre, and community life was becoming stabilized. Only 43 percent of the total population had been there
twelve months earlier, though this was due not to transience but to
the rapid doubling of Libre's population in the spring of 1970. They
had lost only one member in the previous year, a mere 4 percent of
their population. Libre's acreage, especially per capita, was well
above the average for other groups, and as a whole the community

had ample room to absorb a limited number of guests without any threat to its integrity. But at Libre, unlike Drop City, the flow was carefully measured. Other dimensions of Libre's community structure can be described in terms of their implications for group commitment.

Sacrifice Despite Libre's reputation as the underground Scarsdale, it had one of the higher austerity scores in the sample. The winters were harsh, and the water supply was seasonal, involving tedious trips to a single tap or even outside the community. Sewage treatment was largely Mother Earth's job. The austerity factor was also increased by the fact that there was no preexisting housing. On the other hand, Libre used electricity, propane, and food stamps and gave up no individual oral, sexual, or material pleasures for the sake of group solidarity. Libre's level of commitment through sacrifice was, therefore, about average for the sample, consisting of moderately high austerity and little or no abstinence.

Investment Libre's investment requirements were about average compared to the other groups, the two key features being that all members had to build their own shelter and that nonresident members were prohibited. There were no financial requirements to join or to be sustained as a member, since the land was paid for, and otherwise each member was on his own. With nonprofit incorporation, tax problems were negligible, and little cash income was needed to survive.

Renunciation Libre's degree of renunciation of the outside was the third highest in the sample, reflecting high levels of insulation on every measure. Libre was unusually distant from neighbors and towns, media input was limited apart from radios and a few magazines, and there was no television or telephone. The visitation and new membership rules were among the strictest of all groups studied. In 1970 a new member was expected to rent a house and live in the valley for several months, getting to know the members of Libre slowly and thoroughly. When new members felt ready, they petitioned for membership by calling a Council, where they would submit their motives and plans to the scrutiny of the membership as a whole. Membership would only be extended if approval was unanimous. This process was complicated and intimidating enough to weed out casual applicants almost immediately. If a more serious candidate was going to be blackballed, he was invariably told in advance by someone in the membership to spare him embarrassment. Consequently the blackball mechanism had never been formally used. The informal screening process, based on explicit community goals, was amply effective in regulating the addition of newcomers. Libre deliberately

selected new members who were couples, who had the motivation
and skills to build their own houses, who were old friends or proven
new friends, and so on. Final acceptance required a formal oath to
abide by community principles.

Communion   Libre's most exceptional departure from the other
groups is reflected by its score on this dimension, which is the lowest
in the sample. Libre was not in love with togetherness, which from
their experience was illusory if not founded on individual self-
sufficiency. The members also thought being continually snarled up in
the affairs of others to be a drain on freedom. Libreans were strictly
voluntarists. While they cooperated and shared about as much as any
other commune, the rules of their community were deliberately anticommunal in structure. One member compared them to the self-reli-
ant values of the frontier:

> It's a very American tradition. . . . It's like what the history books told
> us about Daniel Boone, who kept moving west every time he saw the
> smoke from his neighbor's fire.[10]

There was considerable sharing at Libre, though. The community as a whole owned the land, including the dwellings (though the
builders had "priority," they could not sell to outsiders). Tools and
autos were used (but not generally owned) communally, and there
was a large and successful communal garden. But no turnover of
property or income to the community was required. Communal labor,
too, was entirely voluntary, and there were few communal (as distinguished from cooperative) work efforts.

On measures of "regularized group contact," Libre stands out
by scoring the lowest total in the study. There were no communal
dwellings and no regular communal meals. Each member's private
home was considered his inviolable "place," and on the average a
typical member would spend less than 50 percent of his day relating
to others. There were no fixed routines or meetings. When a Council
was called, which was less than once a month, it could take place
anywhere on the land. There was no distinct community meeting
place, nor was there any regular pattern to Libre's daily life, apart
from ordinary neighborly socializing and helping each other when
asked.

The only other major contributor to Libre's communion score
besides a certain measure of sharing was its history of shared harassment and persecution experiences. Questions of water rights
(and culture clash) brought trouble from two neighboring ranchers in
the form of water diversions, potshots, and legal action, in addition

to the trouble experienced with county building inspectors and other officials. Irregular and loose though it was, Libre's community structure was always adequate to the threat. When it came to outside hassles, Libre had a vigorous sense of unity which it seldom otherwise displayed.

Mortification   Like most modern rural communes, Libre made little use of mortification mechanisms. Meetings were few and mutual criticism was low, though informal encounter and bitching sessions occurred sporadically on specific issues. In point of fact there was little to argue about and little by way of grappling for community purpose or authority. Being a corporate officer was a job nobody really wanted. Members were only vaguely distinguished on moral or spiritual grounds, and no member was of such high moral status as to be granted any formal deference from the others. On the other hand, there was some measure of mortification in the probation period required of new members.

Transcendence   In transcendence mechanisms, Libre was again typical of the anarchical bent of most modern communes. There were no authority hierarchies, no structured routine, and only a mild ideology to which a member need submit. The transcendence factors of primary importance were the obstacles of the recruitment process and the intimidating mystique imputed to Libre both by the media and by themselves, with a long tradition of magic and eccentricity going back to Drop City. Beyond that, there was no further programing of behavior that was not self-prescribed. Leadership initiative came primarily from a small group of male founders. Peter Rabbit in particular was considered Libre's "guiding light." But major decisions were never implemented without community consent, and those who led were not rewarded with any special privileges or immunities.

The grand total of commitment mechanisms operating at Libre in 1970 was slightly below average for the study as a whole. Libre's most significant departure from the norm was its uniquely low level of communal activity and regularized group contact. On the other hand, it had an above-average level of insulation from the outside world and stricter cross-boundary controls on visitors and new members. This could be viewed as a functional trade-off. Stricter communal distinctions from the outside averaged out with the pursuit of more individualistic concerns inside.

In terms of political equality, Libre was again more or less average. Decisions had to be unanimous but were routinely managed by a legitimate minority and seldom put to a vote, even when meetings were necessary, which was not often. The tenure of community functionaries at Libre was informal and voluntary, where in more equality-conscious groups these jobs were given terms and formally rotated. Finally, Libre women generally assumed traditional household tasks without rotation but were outspoken participants in Councils and other community affairs when issues fell within their range of interests. This rather traditional division of labor perhaps makes more sense in a rural household community than it seems to in urban communes. In any case, women often worked beside their men in construction, and the men, in turn, could often be found at the stove. Had Libre been organized communally instead of by couples, perhaps women's issues would have come more to the fore. Moreover, the women at Libre could never be described as shrinking violets.

III

I had occasion to visit Libre again in 1972, and by then Libre's houses were more or less complete, though some were still being improved. Only one couple had left the community for good since 1970—the youngest couple in the community, whose house-building efforts had turned out to be inadequate to Libre's winters (a cavelike structure among several large boulders with a poor roof and little light). There was still conflict with the two neighboring ranchers over water rights and more subtle issues of life style, but otherwise Libre was settled and stable. When I returned more formally in 1973, 91 percent of the 1970 population was still there; they in turn totaled 84 percent of the 1973 population. By either measure of turnover, Libre was by far and away the most stable group in the sample.

Libre had also made progress on its water hassles by erecting a large storage tank. Now, even when the stream ran dry in summer or was diverted by the ranchers, they would have a reliable water supply. The purchase of the tank and other water system improvements had been made possible by a donation of $5,000 from one of the female members (from an inheritance). Libre also showed progress in building, in food animals, and in a modest population growth (from twenty-three to twenty-five). The only factor suggesting any community decline was Libre's garden, which was far smaller and poorer in July 1973 than July 1970, a casualty of the prior problem of water supply and the attention required to solve it. In such an arid setting the improvements in the water supply had emerged as a major step in consolidating the community. The water system had replaced housing as Libre's main preoccupation and in the summer of 1973 inspired regular weekly "water meetings."

Overall, Libre was one of only three groups in the sample to show several tangible advances in communal prosperity in 1973. The other two were strictly organized religious groups (Lama and Ananda), both at the other end of the spectrum in terms of formal organization and commitment mechanisms. Libre was the most truly anarchical community of them all, yet compared to the religious groups, it was equally successful. But like Lama and Ananda, there was a religious side to life at Libre that made a difference. From the beginning, some of the members had been interested in the shaman-istic peyote rituals of the Native American Church. In the Southwest it is called the Peyote Road, which is both a figurative religious term and an underground network of practitioners linking Mexico, Texas, Taos, Colorado, and points west and north to the Indians of Ari-zona, the northern plains, and Canada. By 1973 many members of Libre had become "hay-nahs," or travelers on this road to a sepa-rate reality, and ceremonial meetings had become regular, though unofficial, community affairs. The religion is a mystical version of Christianity, well suited to the rugged environment of Libre's life and to the inward-looking concerns of its members.[11]

Since Libre descended directly from Drop City, there are many inviting comparisons that can be made between the two groups, which illustrate the essence and direction of the counterculture in the decade spanning 1970. Drop City was a laboratory, and Libre was the result, a serious new community tempered by experience, adopting the changes needed to keep a more adult version of Drop City's spirit alive and well and out of the mainstream system.

A comparison of anarchism in the two communities, for in-stance, shows that Libre became even more anarchical than Drop City by its great reduction in the amount of regularized, structured contact among the members. Yet at the same time, Libre employed many more commitment mechanisms than Drop City, especially those to control visitors and new members. The spirit of Drop City was thus extended and changed at the same time. Libre was a corporate um-brella under which individualism could flourish better than ever, but this time the umbrella was watertight against the outside, even at the cost of some old ideals.

"We live in the future," Libre's Peter Rabbit once told reporter Robert Houriet. In assessing this claim, we have to bear in mind that Libre was founded on a gift which left it free of mortgage debt from the beginning. It is also important to remember that Libre's residents were older, well-educated, self-motivating people with many flexible skills for meeting their needs. They were well adapted to the life of greater leisure and serial monogamy that the future is supposed to bring us.

If Libre lives in the future, then this is what the future will look like: small, post-middle-class affinity groups of nuclear families set off in small, face-to-face communities of friendly neighbors who are "downwardly mobile" by choice, innovative in the use of cooperative legal and economic structures to shield themselves and cut expenses, tolerant of mate changes as a way of life, and living lives primarily devoted to the pursuit of creative leisure and self-fulfilling work, borrowing freely from both old traditions and new technologies. Demographically, such communities will have moved far beyond the suburbs into the rural countryside. Yet, like suburbs, they will have no significant economic relationship to the land as did the rural settlements of the past. Instead their economic links will be mainly with urban areas, through temporary migrations for jobs and materials and extensive urban ties to friends, business associates, government services, markets, and kin. In this respect, Libre shares something in common with the resort and second-home developments of the wealthy. Both are exurbs, or deliberate new rural settlements made possible by the prosperity and urbane skills of the educated middle and upper classes rather than a local economy. The problem the future will face in catching up with Libre is gathering the resources to make the leap that Libre made through subsidy.

Notes

1. Quoted in Richard Fairfield, *Communes U.S.A.: A Personal Tour* (Baltimore: Penguin Books, 1972), p. 208. Fairfield writes of Libre as "Liberty."

2. The other three communes were known as Ortoviz Ranch, the Red Rockers, and the Anonymous Artists of America. Ortoviz Ranch is discussed (under the pseudonym of "Antelope Ranch") in Hugh Gardner, "Crises and Politics in Rural Communes," in *Communes: Creating and Managing the Collective Life*, ed. Rosabeth M. Kanter (New York: Harper & Row, 1973), pp. 150–167. The Red Rockers were Hollywood hippies originally interested in joining Libre who later gathered the resources and members to found a group of their own nearby. Their first year out (1969) they built and occupied a large communal dome. The following year they began building peripheral, single-family dwellings more on the Libre model, having found communal dome life more intense than they wished. The AAA ("Triple A") commune had once been a successful band called "The Acid Test" in the early Grateful Dead–Jefferson Airplane days of San Francisco rock, when communal living and psychedelic music were almost synonymous. The Triple A lived on a farm in the valley but supported themselves primarily by bar gigs in Denver and nearby towns like Walsenburg and Pueblo. The majority of the valley's freak population lived as renters on savings, local odd jobs, and welfare.

3. Other accounts of Libre and its social system can be found in Fairfield, *Communes U.S.A.*; William Hedgepeth and Dennis Stock, *The Alternative* (New York: Collier Books, 1970); and Robert Houriet, *Getting Back Together* (New York: Avon Books, 1972).

4. *Architectural Design*, December 1971.

5. Quoted in Houriet, *Getting Back Together*, p. 240.

6. Ibid., p. 228. The phenomenal success of *The Whole Earth Catalog* after 1970, which listed the whole array of modern technology side by side with Corona grain mills and tepee kits, showed that a tool's greatest relevance to the counterculture was not its origin but its implications for independent living.

7. Stanley Krippner and Don Fersh, "The Mystical Experience and the Mystical Commune," *The Modern Utopian*, 4 (Spring 1970). See also Hugh Gardner, "Your Global Alternative," *Esquire*, 74 (September 1970).

8. Quoted in Houriet, *Getting Back Together*, p. 235.

9. Quoted in Fairfield, *Communes U.S.A.*, p. 210.

10. Quoted in Houriet, *Getting Back Together*, p. 234.

11. See Weston LaBarre, *The Peyote Cult* (New York: Schocken Books, 1969), the standard reference on peyote use by American Indians. For a participant-observer's account of a peyote ceremony at the New Buffalo commune, see Houriet, *Getting Back Together*, pp. 201–207.

4

The Triumph of Monogamy:
The Guild of Colorado

I

By 1969, after three years of exposure in the national media and the emergent underground press, the new communes were attracting the attention of young professional people as well as stereotype hippies. In the cities and around college campuses there was a burgeoning of law collectives, free clinics, crash-pad services, and cooperatives of all description. For them what had begun to fade in Drop City and Haight-Ashbury by 1967 was still new and alive. For others, more alienated by the noise and frustration of the cities, the call to "get back to the land" was a siren song. It began to be news that year that stockbrokers were dropping out to become farmers and Ph.D.'s were becoming small-town craftsmen.

The Guild of Colorado was founded in April 1969 by two such families in their late twenties and early thirties who in more normal times would probably have been living in suburbs pursuing careers as teachers. Instead they were looking for more satisfying work as artisans and for a new degree of sharing and community in their lives. One husband wanted to be a carpenter, the other a welder. They met in the mountain town of Evergreen, some forty miles west of Denver, where both couples had dropped out of city life separately (but were still within commuting range). During the first six months of their relationship, they began to discuss the possibilities of communal living. Eventually this led to the Guild, an unincorporated legal entity composed of the two signatory families and based on shared property and autonomous work.

At first the Guild was to stay in Evergreen and consist of the two families' shared-but-separate dwellings and other buildings. But one couple, Tim and Susan, wanted to push forward to a more communal living arrangement. As they later explained,

> We wanted one big house for the community rather than several small ones. We believe in sharing as a philosophy, and that includes things like human feelings. Rather than this "every man's home is his castle" stuff, we wanted as many personal confrontations as possible, a situation where everybody would jump in, put themselves on the line, and work it out. We just weren't satisfied with the barriers around the usual marriage and that kind of nonsensical social life. We chose this place because we needed the experience of one roof over us.[1]

The Guild thus moved to a large two-story log house in a small middle-class village about twelve miles away. The house sat on about an acre of land at nine thousand feet and had once been some wealthy person's mountain retreat. Though there were serious heating and plumbing problems, it was still a beautiful old house which was soon well appointed with many valuable antiques from Susan's family. The Guild chose to cook on a wood stove and heat with wood, and the big old house took on all the rustic ambience of a mountain lodge—a romance of wood and smoke.

The mortgage on the house had been secured with trust stocks from Susan's family; nevertheless, the title was placed in the names of all four original adult members. All property except personal belongings (and personal bank accounts) was to be used communally. Each member was expected to contribute an equal share to the house payments and other expenses (totaling about $500 a month) and otherwise contribute to communal work sharing, but incomes would be pursued independently. Tim was to set up a wood shop, and Fred a welding shop.

This arrangement lasted for less than three months. By summer Fred and Cathy had moved out, later to dissolve their relationship to the Guild entirely. Tim and Susan's explanation a year afterwards was that Fred really wanted to go into business for himself, that Cathy was indecisive, that it would have been better if Fred's welding shop had worked out, and that Fred was somewhat jealous of Tim and/or his wood shop. The Guild retrenched to the one couple and their two children.

Over the course of the next year the Guild acquired three new adult members and two more children. It was a severe winter in the big house. The pipes froze continually as the fireplaces proved inadequate for heat. There was also harassment from certain of their village neighbors, led by the local deputy sheriff, who was very unhappy with the "Communists" in their midst and said so at village meetings. Guild members were assaulted twice in a nearby town by "drugstore cowboys."

For these reasons and others, the new members were all gone by the summer of 1970. For one member, John, the chronic household utility disasters were said to be the immediate cause of his decision to leave. As Tim put it, "The winter sort of separated the men from the boys." Tim and Susan also felt that John had what Susan called a "Freudian dominant-father thing" in his relationship with Tim. Tim and Susan's explanation for the departure of a member named Earleen was that she needed a man and more social involvement with the outside and that she found the Guild's chores too strenuous. The third adult, Diane, was expelled from the Guild (by Tim and Susan) for being a "bad mother to her children" and "just not ready to settle down and accept responsibilities."

In attracting and holding members, the Guild (or in effect Tim and Susan) faced the dilemma of being caught between two cultures. Their friends were mostly older and straighter, curious but noncommittal about communal living. Younger people became interested more readily but were discouraged by the requirements for income-producing skills, monthly payments, and other evidence of responsibility. In fact Tim and Susan made two trips to the commune scene around Taos and "each time we came back we felt less like calling ourselves a commune." Tim and Susan were not, at this point, considering going any farther back to the land than they already were. What they sought was simply acceptance of the Guild in a middle-class, single-family village. As Tim said:

> We're not interested in "dropping out," but dropping in, and opening up a basically suburban situation for people like us. In some ways our values are more like the deputy sheriff's than a hippie's, because we believe in the work ethic. I am a Western man, work is my trip. What we want is a work structure here at home where Susie and I can have a real family together. At the same time we want to explore how each one of us as individuals can fit into an extended family relationship with other people. We don't bother anybody else. Who has a right to say we can't live like this? If America is really what it says it is, this ought to be possible.[2]

II

By my visit in July 1970, Tim and Susan were back on their own once again. Their names alone were left on the Guild's property deed, and only their own children kept them company. Since there had been only the two of them six and twelve months earlier as well, 100 percent of the Guild's membership from these earlier periods was still in residence. To judge by this statistical artifact, the best way to have a stable commune was to keep it strictly in the family. A truer indication of the Guild's stability was its seasonal flux. Its smallest population in the preceding twelve months was only 33 percent of its largest population, which was average for the sample as a whole.

Despite the fact that the Guild was then no more than a family, Tim and Susan still thought of themselves as a commune, and they were still seeking new members. They were critical, though, of taking on new members who just wanted to try it out and had no clear purpose of their own. Tim was particularly interested in finding males who had their own scene going and did not relate to him as a father figure:

> Now we're looking for people not only with autonomous interests but with experience in doing what they talk about. A commune is based on equality, but equality implies mutual respect based on separate interests or vocations. We're looking for someone who has his *own* scene worked out but wants to do it communally, someone who's functional, strong, and capable of taking stimulus from the communal situation to grow from.[3]

Sacrifice The difficulties that the Guild had in gaining and keeping new members were, at first, something of a mystery. To judge from the number of commitment mechanisms used in its structure, it was not a particularly hard commune to enter. In fact, the total number of such mechanisms was almost exactly average for the sample as a whole. There was nothing unusual, for example, about the sacrifice mechanisms built into Guild life. The winters were harsher than most, and the members did without gas heat, but in terms of electricity, water supply, and sewage their lives were more comfortable than most. In furnishings and material resources, they were positively wealthy. And like most modern communes, members were not expected to make sacrifices by any form of personal abstinence.

Investment Likewise, the investment mechanisms at the Guild were milder than those in most communes in the sample. Housing for the group was preexisting and rather palatial. There were no fees or property signovers required to join, and in their most unusual departure from the practices of other groups, all other investments in the community except labor were scrupulously recorded and returned to defectors if they left. The only significant investment requirements at the Guild were the prohibition of nonresident members and the obligation to share in the monthly payments. The required house payments doubtlessly discouraged some potential members, but for value received the payments were still quite low.

Renunciation   The Guild was also below average in the level of expected renunciation of the outside world. In fact, of all the communes in the sample, the Guild was the least isolated geographically, since its nearest neighbor was only a few yards away and it was within commuting distance of the largest city in the Rocky Mountains. Similarly, it was the least insulated from outside media. The Guild had a television, a telephone, an expensive FM stereo, and an abundance of books, newspapers, and current magazines. The Guild was also low in its total of cross-boundary controls. The average member traveled outside daily, and there were no rules concerning visitation. The only significant contributor to the Guild's renunciation score was its screening controls over new members, including a brief probation period, a formal membership agreement, the unanimous acceptance of current members, and the fact that the Guild had previously used blackballing and eviction. But in sum the Guild did not require much renunciation from new members. The only commune in this study with a lower score on this count was Drop City.

Communion   The Guild's greatest departure from the norm was its intense use of communion commitment mechanisms, in which it had the highest total in the study. First, it required more communistic sharing than any other group. Second, the Guild had the highest degree of regularized group contact. Dwelling space and dining were all communal, there were no inviolable private places, there were official weekly group meetings, and the commune was located on an extremely small plot with a correspondingly high percentage of each day spent in contact with others. In addition, the Guild had the second greatest number of persecution experiences at the hands of outsiders. Communistic labor at the Guild was a legitimate and enforced expectation, though not a written rule. Finally, despite having the highest communion score overall, the Guild was one of only four communes in the study to have no ritual content to its life. For the Guild, high communion was something entirely secular rather than spiritual, a characteristic which later seemed as if it might have hurt the group as much as helped it.

Mortification   In its use of mortification mechanisms, the Guild was more average. On the one hand, it made mutual criticism and interpersonal encounter a greater part of its daily life than most communes. Tim and Susan both felt strongly that a constant attempt to bring things out in the open was a necessary part of living together so intensely. On the other hand, mechanisms of "spiritual differentiation" among the members, which have a similar humbling effect upon individual pride, were considered unacceptable. The Guild had no legitimized means to recognize those of higher and lower moral status, no formal probation period with limited privileges for new members, and no formal instruction in community doctrines.

Transcendence The Guild's score on transcendence mechanisms was likewise about average. The Guild's ideology was rather vague and unimposing, underpinned by no imputations of magic or miracles, backed by no traditions, and reinforced by no forms of behavioral programing. Potential members, nevertheless, had good reason to be somewhat awed by the prospect of joining, for power and authority at the Guild, while divided equally in theory, were divided very unequally in fact. The source of the Guild's rules, project initiatives, and collective decisions was most often a single person, Tim. By his own admission he was "full of messianic zeal" and "probably tried too much to take charge." Clearly Tim and Susan had far too much invested in the Guild to yield significant power in the group to other members. Although the Guild's transcendence score as a whole was not unusually high, these features were more typically found in authoritarian religious communes. The Guild, by contrast, was guided by a secular elite composed of a single family without religious underpinnings.

One possible explanation for the Guild's acquiring so few members was that Tim and Susan's leadership, without some form of ritual or religious sanctions, may have been perceived as illegitimate. It might also have been perceived as difficult to reach parity with them as Guild members because it was "their" house, "their" furniture, and so on. These factors, especially when combined with the Guild's intense use of communion mechanisms, could easily have been intimidating to prospective new members or made it harder for them to stay.

III

Over the next winter, Tim and Susan decided on a new course for the Guild. Life in the big house had been frustrating on several points: the hostility of their neighbors, the harshness of the mountain winters, social failures with old members, and the limited horizons of a community located on a one-acre plot. Tim and Susan had become even more disillusioned with cities and pessimistic in their outlook on American politics. At the same time, their long-standing interest in gardening, animals, homestead crafts, and other pleasures of rural life had far outgrown the boundaries of their mountain retreat. Consequently, they decided to put the big house up for sale and planned several trips to western Colorado to look for a ranch or farm, which seemed the answer to all their needs.

Meanwhile, anticipating a move to the country, they incorporated the Guild as "Magic Animal Farm," a nonprofit, educational organization. According to the articles of incorporation, "This corporation . . . shall undertake the creation and perpetuation of an experimental farm and self-sufficiency community which shall be its exclusive function." The board of trustees was to be "those members in permanent residence for six consecutive months on the facility . . . who have shown the existing Board of Trustees that they are sufficiently committed to and capable of providing for the aims and purposes of this Corporation."[4] Behind this syncretism of life-style and tax-exempt legal status, Tim and Susan would continue to pursue their elusive communal goals and perhaps start a school, using the farm as the campus, with demonstrations of organic farming and living as the curriculum.

By the summer of 1971, they found what they were looking for: a four-hundred-acre ranch in an isolated canyon in western Colorado. It was twenty-five miles from the nearest town; five of those miles constituted a rugged and rock-strewn "driveway" from the nearest pavement. It was impossible to drive up that tiny, twisted road without announcing one's presence at least twenty minutes in advance to anyone at the ranch, a feature which Tim noted approvingly. At the end of the road there was an orchard, some irrigated pastures, and a small house. There were no phone or electrical hookups in a place so remote, and Tim and Susan had never farmed before. Their nearest neighbor was five miles away. With this move, the Guild would go from being the least isolated rural commune I visited to being the most isolated by far in terms of human challenge as well as mileage.

The purchase of the ranch was made possible by the sale of the big house and the remainder of Susan's stocks. For income, they continued the existing lease on the pastures to a local rancher who grazed cattle there. They partially moved in during the summer of 1971 but decided they were unprepared for a ranch winter and returned east to the Denver area. Meanwhile, the Guild acquired a new member named Vaughn, who was to move in later but in fact never did. In the summer of 1972, it was just the family, as before, whose new life was just as precarious, for the most part, as it had been for the family who lived there fifty years earlier.

Over the next winter, a new person named Janis entered the picture as a result of a trip to Boulder that Tim made alone. By the spring of 1973, Susan had moved out and returned to the city to seek her fortune as a single working woman. Ambivalent between her dedication to Tim's ideas and the realities of her situation, she left the farm, leaving her assets in it uncontested. For the Guild, monogamy had triumphed once again over communalism. For the children, life spanned a metropolis and a wilderness in alternation.

Even so, Tim pressed on with the concept of Magic Animal Farm, which lay somewhere between a commune, a school, and a family business. In the spring of 1973, he published a twelve-page newsletter devoted primarily to a detailed organizational breakdown of the goings-on in the farm's seventeen "Areas of Responsibility" and who was in charge of them. In a way it was like a progress report from a promising new service organization. But to anyone who knew the family, it weakened the farm's credibility as either a commune or a school. "Electronics," for instance, was an area of responsibility assigned to Tim's nine-year-old son. "Organic Husbandry" was assigned to his twelve-year-old daughter. "Food Preservation and Preparation" had been assigned to his new ladyfriend, Janis. In all the other fourteen areas of responsibility, the "Person In Charge" was Tim, or "Peyote Cyote," as he now called himself.[5]

When I arrived on my last visit in August 1973, the fortunes of the Guild as a community, while shifting in personnel and location, had not otherwise changed much on balance. It had a vastly bigger plot of land and at last a garden, but the housing and utilities were of lower quality. There were no food animals (there had been rabbits at the big house), no growth of community industry, and no new buildings in progress. Moreover, there was no population increase. No new members had moved in, and only one potential recruit, another woman in contact through the mails, was then under consideration. Described by Tim as a "radical feminist," she never moved in either. While Tim was understandably anxious about the responsibilities of running virtually the entire farm himself, he either preferred it that way or else the Guild had become something that was keeping others away. It was a commune that never happened.

Perhaps the farm will one day succeed as a school, and Tim will find his *métier* once again as a teacher. Somehow it seems doubtful. Tim liked to joke of himself as "Big Daddy," and on one occasion referred to his family as "my disciples." His new mate was fifteen years younger than he, and he was "teaching" her, too. When I asked if she was teaching *him* anything, he took a long time to come up with this reply: "She's teaching me how to teach." For the most part, Tim has the skills to do as he dreams, but his record shows little stature as a guru. His charisma does not extend to spiritual inspiration, as perhaps it must for a leader who puts this much political distance between himself and his followers.

Factors like the geographical distance of the farm from urban areas also play a role. From anywhere recruits might be found, a major expedition is required just to visit the place. For most prospective members, the farm is far more isolated than anything they have ever known, or likely want. Magic Animal Farm stretches the outer acceptable limits of loneliness as well as patriarchal dominance. But as in so many communes, the farm's fate rests not so much on sociological variables as on the human drama enacted by the participants. In the end we can only predict its destiny with uncertain assumptions about character and motivation. Objectively, Tim came into personal and legal control of his estranged wife's estate. Subjectively, his *nom de guerre* would suggest a mocking self-identification with the legendary trickster of Navaho mythology. Should his former wife decide to continue her autonomous life in the city and sue to recover her abandoned resources, Magic Animal Farm could come to a legal as well as a social dead end.

Notes

1. Field notes of July 10, 1970.
2. Ibid.
3. Ibid.
4. Form D NP 1 registered in 1971 with the Colorado Secretary of State under the name "The Guild of Colorado, also known as Magic Animal Farm."
5. *The Eight-Penny Patriot*, 1 (Spring 1973).

5

Aristocrats of the Dharma:
The Lama Foundation

I

Unlike most of the new communal groups born in the 1960s, the gestation of what ultimately became the Lama Foundation was slow and deliberate, stretching over a period of almost four years. It began in New York in 1963 as an idea in the head of Steve Durkee and his wife Barbara, who had begun to experiment with communal living with their friends in the New York City art scene. Durkee himself claims inspiration from a letter he received that year advising that "the only place that one should live is where the heart is and where there is love, a radiance of love."

> Prior to that, I had only heard that from people in India. So it was obvious that one should find out who that person was, and we came to this area on a camping trip and met this man. He said that nothing was possible at the present due to the fact that the psychic vehicle was oscillating and spinning from the effect of drugs at too rapid a rate; in other words, that the only possibility for spiritual growth comes when your flame is burning steady. So he said, you know, "go on about your business." At the same time someone said that it was possible, if we found some land, to get it.[1]

The mysterious man Durkee referred to was Herman Rednick, a mystical painter who lived near Taos, New Mexico. In the summer of 1965, Durkee and his wife, then in their mid-twenties, began a series of trips across America to look for the place where their hearts felt at home and where they could found a new community based on spiritual, environmental, and back-to-basics values. Each time their search took them through New Mexico they would check in with Rednick:

> After many times of seeing him, the flame was beginning to burn steadier. You know, we drove transcontinentally back and forth and this is where we would always stop. And he'd like always tell you where your flame was at. . . . And we sort of narrowed it down to here. . . . So the last time . . . I came through, he said, "If you want to come back, go to New York and finish what you have to do." . . . It started on Mother's Day and ended on Father's Day [1966]. My father died the night we left. We left and that was the end. There was a decision reached that year by a number of us. Before that, we had always tried to fit ourselves into shells . . . it was the end of the shell period. And it was the beginning of trying to create something out of nothing, of furnishing our rooms.[2]

In late 1966 Durkee, his wife, and one other Lama founder set up a base camp near Taos and began looking for suitable property for sale. With guidance from Rednick, the search focused on the Sangre de Cristo Mountains north of Taos near the ancient village of San Cristobal. Both literally and figuratively, as Durkee recalled later, "We had to find a mountain."

> Well, New Year's Day was the first day we came up here, New Year's Day 1967. We had $4,000 in our pockets and we came to look at this land; but it wasn't this land, it was over on the other side of the mountains, same acreage but twice as much money. The person who had so kindly offered to help us was only into it for a certain amount, about half of what this other land was going to cost. In other words, that land was 44 [thousand]; this was 21—the number of the tarot and also very meaningful. But we had come with $4,000 in our pocket and were going to buy it, but this man said, "Don't do it." Now, that night an angel came to see this man, and the angel told him to see another guy, and when this man went to see this other guy, this other guy had only two weeks earlier decided to sell the land we've got now for exactly the sum that this very kind person had offered to begin this world. So boom! We clicked in and this was the place.[3]

The place thus selected was 115 acres of mountainside some twenty miles north of Taos at an elevation of nine thousand feet, a site commanding a sweeping view of the northern New Mexico *altiplano* and accessible only by twisting dirt roads. The land was purchased in June 1967, and in February 1968 the group was formally incorporated as the Lama Foundation, a nonprofit organization founded for educational, scientific, and religious purposes as "a center for basic studies . . . how to make an adobe brick, or learning how to plumb and how to carpenter, learning what's basic, learning what it is that people really need and what are their desires, and what is the relationship between needs and desires. And also . . . the relationship to the earth, to the sky, and to each other.''[4] The same year the founders applied for and received federal tax-exempt status and in addition a grant of some $7,500 from the Pastorale Foundation to begin construction of Lama's mountaintop facilities.

Over the course of the first year, several members of the original "unconscious community" from New York dropped out of the project as Lama came into conscious focus as a community with spiritual growth as its most important goal. "You see," said Durkee, "this is a very strange place, because what it actually is is a place for graduates, graduates of *high* school. That's what this is all about, when you really want to be high."

> The point was that we could see our way up, but it was obvious that if we were to go up by this path, we had to leave a lot of things behind us, like drugs and that whole world. . . . So we let go, but a lot of us who were originally involved didn't want to let go. They wanted to maintain it. So those of us who wanted to did let go, plus new people; that's why I say it's like graduation. . . . This is a new thing, a new grouping, a conglomeration of people who came out of a lot of different scenes . . . like this person over here, his head, his being, is rooted in the Tao and Chinese philosophy, and this person here comes out of the ethos of the eternal living God as manifest in human form, and another person comes of the world of the university, which is no longer alive. . . . In some way, all of these disparate things have to be woven into one seamless garment, and that's what this is an attempt to do.[5]

From the beginning the founders of Lama had organizational goals far clearer than those of most new communities. As Durkee explained in 1968:

> We have a five-year plan, and by the end of five years we hope to be financially independent. It's based on three different approaches: a school; the establishing of workshops, since a lot of us are artisans or artists; and publishing, because we're obliged to publish under our federal tax exemption. . . . Each year we hope to have a technical book, which is a help to people starting communities, and a spiritual book, one oriented towards growth. . . . As explorers we should bring back, you know, a map.[6]

Another dimension to the plan called for the "very slow growth" of Lama as a residential community. As Durkee put it:

The two things that really do communities in are rapid expansion and believing that you're further along than you are. . . . I still need my individuality and my privacy, let's say, and you need yours. Many groups say, well, if you're my brother and so forth and we're all one, let's live in a heap. But . . . it's not to be had by simply saying that I'm ready for that, because we know from experience, from having tried it, how far we are from it. It's like understanding all the time where you are and not trying to say that we're enlightened. . . .

Our ideal is no more than thirty people. . . . Let me make one thing clear. We have two levels going here. One is to establish a firm focal point on the physical plane, and to do that we're going to grow by about one family a year until we have eight families that live here all year. Those will be the building blocks. We want to do it slowly so that we can integrate things well. Then there's the summer thing [referring to the School for Basic Studies]. It's kind of like life: in the summer everything expands [that is, students] and in the winter things shrink back [to the permanent residents]. One of the screens we have against too rapid expansion is the rule that you cannot build any winter housing until you've spent one whole working season here—April to October, when all your energies are spent on the communal thing. It's just very natural.[7]

Yet another goal at Lama was to bring together the materialistic "brilliant mind thing" of the West with the spiritual teachers and disciplines of the East. A rigorous, if eclectic, spiritual discipline was a part of Lama community life from the first:

One of the things we'd like to do is to bring some of the people from the East here, because they have some brothers here and, in some way, we'd like to help them to get together. We don't know exactly how we're going to do this, but it's very clear that it has to be done. We will probably do it by becoming a center of attraction, the way people are drawn to India . . . not because people put up big banners saying: "Spiritual Life in Ten Easy Lessons . . ." If we are at all able to be what we're talking about, then it will happen.[8]

Remarkably, given the flood of fantasies and overreaching ambitions that swept through the counterculture in the late 1960s and largely went unrealized, it *did* happen, almost precisely on schedule.

Along with help from Rednick and the foundation grant, Lama also drew the support of architectural pioneer Steve Baer, who lived in Santa Fe and had been instrumental in the construction of America's first geodesic community at Drop City in 1965–1966. The result was the design and construction of what many seasoned communal travelers consider the most beautiful buildings to appear in the new rural underground.

The two most original combined the adobe-and-beam construction native to the area and the use of modern "zomes," which are a fusion of "zonal polyhedrons" and "domes" (the term was coined by Durkee). One was a two-story cooking and eating facility, with an octagonal kitchen on the first level and a circular dining hall on the second level, which in turn was topped with a many-windowed zome and connected to the kitchen by a dumbwaiter running down the building's center. The other main building, with an equally spectacular view of the valley below, began as a meeting hall of adobe topped with a zome pointing heavenward and then grew two flat-topped adobe extensions to either side. One led through a comfortable living area to an elaborate Japanese bath, the other to a library, work areas, and at its extremity, a semiunderground circular meditation room for group chanting and meditations. "Everything we do here," said Barbara Durkee, "is a kind of karma yoga. Chopping wood or carrying water, done in the right spirit, are meditation. Simple tasks keep me focused, centered on what's real. We praise God by building domes."[9] Or as her husband put it, "The essence of spirituality is practicality."

With this spirit of practicality, Lama made a significant change in its social life after the community's first year. In the beginning there was an encounter-style meeting every weeknight. "After a while," Barbara Durkee said, "we saw they weren't getting us anywhere, except deeper into neurosis and avoidance of the real, individual problems. Everyone became convinced that it did nothing to raise our level of consciousness. You can't get along with other people unless you're at peace inside."[10] What might appear as a flight from intimacy was thus fully consistent with their inward search for higher consciousness and individual responsibility and apparently more pragmatic for communal harmony as well. According to journalist Robert Houriet:

> Interpersonal conflicts became an individual concern. As they gained greater honesty, compassion and frankness, individuals were able to solve problems themselves without involving the entire community. "I've become much more honest with myself," Carolyn said. "When some people make me uptight, I look into myself to see why. I try to check the uptightness before it gets too far. Most problems are worked out one by one, as they happen."[11]

What had begun as an alienated critique of American culture therefore became introspective and meditative work on the self in an effort to root out bad habits, self-indulgences, and old emotional programing that blocked personal development. In Lama's language, which was much like that of Buddhism, the root cause of suffering is attachment and desire, and things like encounter groups were just enactments of "melodramas" that did not go to the root of the problem. For the most part, Lama's members had grown up with every material advantage and a high degree of opportunity to do whatever and be whoever they wanted—if they only had the personal focus to do so. The basic goal was to center in on a calm and unitary consciousness free of the overstimulation and fractionated identities of a privileged modern life and the pitfalls of ego:

> Now 99 percent of us, especially those who have dropped out of the drug or hip world, are still very undisciplined people, out of tune with ourselves and one another. . . . We have all found that there have been things in our life that we've wanted to do but found ourselves incapable of doing. We've lacked the necessary discipline to do them. We all admit that we're undisciplined in relation to the spiritual life, and we believe that through the centuries there have been very clear precepts for spiritual growth laid down that worked—at least they seem to have worked judging from people we have seen and met and learned about. . . . Why do we get up every morning at six-thirty? Why do we chant? It's not just to get up early. It's not just to chant. It's to begin accustoming ourselves to a new rhythm. A good word is tuning. The instrument is still being tuned, both in terms of the individual and the larger organism.[12]

By the spring of 1969, Lama had added two more permanent residents, had published its first book (Steve Baer's *Dome Cookbook*), and was ready to inaugurate the first session of its school that summer. As Lama's newsletter explained, "Building at Lama is our medium for teaching and learning many things on many levels: trust, care, practicality, tool skills and technics, structural realities, patience, craftsmanship, and the art of hard work."[13] In 1969, with help from its students, Lama built a barn and three new domes; finished seven A-frames for year-round use; completed the meeting house, dining hall, and library; and constructed a small experimental solar-heated greenhouse.

On the spiritual front, Lama continued to make a variety of religious exercises a prominent part of its daily life and was visited for a period by Samuel Lewis (Sufi Ahmed Chisti), who taught the members many of his Sufic dances and movements and whose body was buried at Lama when he died in 1971. It was an appropriate beginning for Lama's program of inviting outside spiritual teachers, since Sufism incorporates the dances and songs of all major religions. Like Lama itself, Sufism is based on a syncretic and ecumenical mysticism and is guided from within by a hierarchical progression of inner circles.

But even more important was a visit that year by Baba Ram

Dass, formerly Dr. Richard Alpert, Harvard psychology professor and LSD pioneer in the early 1960s with his colleague Timothy Leary. After his adventures with Leary at Milbrook and in Mexico, Alpert shared a house in California with the Durkees for eight months during the period they were searching for land. As Lama was getting under way, Alpert left for India in a mood of deep uncertainty about himself and the enigmas of psychedelics. While there, a strange series of events led him to the tiny old man living in the Himalayan foothills who became his guru. According to an account he published, "Our-Story Your-Story," Alpert's personal transformation took place following devastating evidence that the master could read his mind:

> The first thing that happened was that my mind raced faster and faster to try to get leverage—to get a hold on what he had just done. I went through every super CIA paranoia I've ever had. . . . None of it would jell. . . . Up until then I had two categories for "psychic experience." One was "they happened to somebody else and they haven't happened to me, and they were terribly interesting and we certainly had to keep an open mind about it." That was my social science approach. The other one was, "well, man, I'm high on LSD. Who knows how it really is?" . . . But neither of these categories applied in this situation, and my mind went faster and faster and then I felt like what happens when a computer is fed an insoluble problem; the bell rings and the red light goes on and the machine stops. And my mind just gave up. It burned out its circuitry . . . its zeal to have an explanation. I needed something to get closure at the rational level and there wasn't anything. There just wasn't a place I could hide in my head about this.
>
> And at the same moment, I felt this extremely violent pain in my chest and a tremendous wrenching feeling and I started to cry. And I cried and I cried and I cried. And I wasn't happy and I wasn't sad. It was not that kind of crying. The only thing I could say was it felt like I was home. Like the journey was over. Like I had finished.[14]

The story that is often repeated about Alpert's transformation happened the next morning, when at the master's insistence Alpert gave him a three-pill, 915-microgram dose of pure "White Lightning" (LSD):

> I see them go down. There's no doubt. And that little scientist in me says, "This is going to be very interesting!"
>
> All day long I'm there, and every now and then he twinkles at me and nothing—nothing happens! That was his answer to my question.[15]

Another anecdote Alpert relates shows that the master could read his thoughts about his friends back home at Lama as well as everything else:

I'd be at my temple. And I'd think about arranging for a beautiful lama in America to get some money, or something like that. Then I'd go to bed and pull the covers over my head and perhaps have a very worldly thought; I would think about what I'd do with all my powers when I got them; perhaps a sexual thought. Then when next I saw Maharaji he would tell me something like, "You want to give money to a lama in America." And I'd feel like I was such a beautiful guy. Then suddenly I'd be horrified with the realization that if he knew that thought, then he must know that one, too . . . ohhhhh . . . and that one, too! Then I'd look at the ground. And when I'd finally steal a glance at him, he'd be looking at me with such total love.[16]

For the next several months, Alpert lived near Maharaji and the temple or traveled about on foot with Bhagavan Das, an extraordinary young American who had lived in India for five years and had led Alpert to the guru they both revered. Although Alpert reportedly wanted to remain in India, his guru told him to return to America and publish a book to guide others. Arriving back in America as Baba Ram Dass, he found a great deal of respectful curiosity awaiting him and traveled extensively giving lectures. In the fall of 1969, he came to New Mexico and led Lama's first experimental ashram involving thirteen monks, seven karma yogis, and one teacher. As he later described the activities:

Each monk spent eighteen days in solitude, and each karma yogi nine days. In addition to the hermitages, communicants remained in silence, took daily vegetarian prasad together, did several hours karma yoga, shared readings, did asanas and pranyam as well as formal meditation sittings, chanted kirtan and mantra. There was one fast day a week and most participants fasted for periods up to nine days while in hermitage. . . . Without exception the participants reported that subjectively they felt as if they had profited by the experience.[17]

According to Barbara Durkee, the Ram Dass ashram "crystallized into a real experience all the different practices we had been experimenting with. It upped the level of Lama and helped us to withdraw from our own melodrama."[18] For Ram Dass and Lama, the association was generally very happy. Each supported the other's authenticity, and their goals meshed perfectly. Baba Ram Dass wanted to write a spiritual guidebook and help Lama, and Lama wanted to publish a spiritual guidebook and help Ram Dass. The result was a fascinating and evocative collaboration known as *Be Here Now*, which includes in four sections the story of Alpert's transformation, a guided conceptual and graphic tour of eastern mysticism in an American idiom, a "Cookbook for a Sacred Life" detailing a great variety of spiritual paths and practical religious exercises ("dedicated to those who wish to get on with it"), and a bibliography of spiritual books called "Painted Cakes" (from a saying of the Buddha that "painted cakes do not satisfy hunger"). Ram Dass raised $25,000 to publish the book and assigned all royalties to Lama. As it turned out, the book met with a reception exceeding all expectations and soon became financially successful, so successful, in fact, that it would underwrite Lama's future growth. For his part, Ram Dass of course received great respect and honor at Lama and a home whenever he wanted it. But while he was regarded as a legitimate teacher and a saintly man, he was not thereby the "Dalai Lama." "In other words," Steve Durkee had said, "we're antipriesthood."

> The world that makes sense is a world where each man and each woman lives out time and the cycles of the seasons, where no man is a priest and every man is a priest, and where the duty to maintain the cosmos is dependent on everybody instead of just a select few. . . . There are no priests here because everybody is a priest. There are none other than the elect.[19]

II

In more than one way, Lama's members were of the elect even before they began. They came from upper-middle-class backgrounds and to varying degrees were independently wealthy. They held degrees from the nation's best universities. Like the founders of Libre, they were older (late twenties and early thirties), experienced from years in the underground, and equipped with sophisticated skills for handling worldly realities. They were the quintessence of a generation with every advantage now facing the luxurious agony of deciding how to live. As explorers in inner space, like those in outer space, their missions depended in part on the prior existence of a launch and support system. But the design and fulfillment of their exploration was their own doing, and testimony to their competence and ingenuity at every level of organization building.

When I visited Lama in July 1970, the permanent membership had risen to a total of seven, including four men and three women. In addition were their seven children ("CHILDREN WELCOME!" stated Lama's 1970 brochure. "We feel that families with children are vital to the experience at Lama. Children of all ages [including infants] have been an important part of the community since its inception.") Also in residence at the time were twenty-three other adults as "active members" or "students," plus a few more children. Of the three categories of membership, the "permanents" lived there year-round, the "actives" for the work season of six months or so, and the "students" for periods of one to three months. Entry into the community and progress through the various levels of membership were carefully screened and coupled with one of the most elaborate rule structures found anywhere in the counterculture.

Altogether the adult population totaled thirty, the upper limit that Lama had deliberately set for itself. Using Lama's total population at that time as a base point, the community showed signs of instability: only five members (17 percent) had been there six months before, for example, and over one hundred students or other guests had passed through in the previous twelve months. But from the viewpoint of the core residential population, Lama had undergone the slow and stable accretion it had planned. The presence of children is one of the most accurate measures of communal stability, and here there was one child per permanent member, the highest ratio in this study. Unlike anarchical groups, Lama's population flow was guided and under control.

In its overall use of the various commitment mechanisms, Lama had the highest total of all communities in this study. Lama's nearest runners-up for this distinction, Ananda and Maharaj Ashram, were also highly disciplined, religious communities. The rationale for these structures was made explicit in Lama's "Cookbook for a Sacred Life":

> Many spiritual seekers have joined or started communities in order to provide a suitable environment for their inner work. Often they have been disillusioned by these experiments because of disorder, economic instability, ego struggles, and mixed motives on the part of the participants. Out of these early community experiments have evolved more structured attempts to provide the optimum environment for spiritual growth. These communities are usually less disciplined than traditional Eastern *ashrams* but more firmly structured than contemporary communes.[20]

But while Lama was easily the most structurally organized community in this study, it was still far from being a rigid monolith across the board, as the selectivity in its use of commitment mechanisms indicates.

Sacrifice   As we might expect from its spiritual goals, Lama was one of the few groups in this study to practice any oral or sexual abstinence. Alcohol, drugs, and tobacco were all prohibited. Coffee and meat (except occasional fish or fowl) were frowned upon but tolerated, whereas at Maharaj and Ananda these were completely prohibited. Lama was likewise more liberal in placing no unusual value on sexual continence apart from individual choice. In abstinence, then, Lama was more severe than most communities but less so than some. In austerity Lama was less distinctive still, about average for the sample as a whole. Although winters and other conditions of life are harsh at nine thousand feet, Lama's physical facilities and utilities were generally far better than those at most of the communes in this study. "A lot of people come here expecting some far-out community," Barbara Durkee had told Robert Houriet. "Actually, we're funky middle class."[21] Although austerity was a familiar and respected virtue at Lama and practiced from time to time with great intensity (as in the Ram Dass experimental ashram), its more rigorous applications were generally a matter of individual decision, to be applied with caution, as illustrated by these comments from the "Cookbook":

> The struggle that comes through imposing austerities upon oneself as a systematic part of one's *sadhana* is a powerful form of inner confrontation . . . if one is preoccupied with eating and oral gratifications, just fast. If one is obsessed with sexual concerns, just give up sex. And so on. This technique is known as tapasya or "straightening by fire." . . . But there are two warnings to be kept in mind with regard to any austerities:
> 1. Austerities can be performed in ways to enhance or strengthen the ego. Pride in how much one is suffering and masochism are two examples. . . .
> 2. Austerities that are excessive (in relation to the degree of spiritual development of the individual) are merely demonstrations of ego will and as such can harm the body or the mind in such a way as to make further *sadhana* in this lifetime difficult or even impossible.[22]

Investment Despite Lama's high overall use of commitment mechanisms, the degree to which some form of investment in the community was required was only about average. Previous requirements that new members pay a fee and build their own shelters had been dropped (except for student tuition). The only strict financial requirement was payment of a monthly share of Lama's expenses, which were closely budgeted and in the summer of 1970 assessed at a rate of $60 per member. (The annual budget that year was $12,000 to $15,000, a remarkable accomplishment in economical group living and still far plusher than most communal groups.) Otherwise Lama required no fees or property from prospective members and did not make entering or leaving Lama difficult on the material plane. The most extraordinary investment requirement at Lama was time. Lama employed a unique formula whereby a prospective permanent member must follow at least six months of living at Lama with six months *away* from it as an individual test of purpose and focus in desiring long-term occupancy. Another year of residence as an "active" member was typically required before the next annual consideration of new "Caretakers," as permanent members were called. In sum, the requirements totaled the equivalent of a two-year probation period. As such, it was probably the longest membership screening process of any community in the counterculture at that time.

Renunciation   Other requirements of Lama's detailed screening process included evidence of practical skills, a spiritual orientation of demonstrable sincerity (though not of any particular ideology or faith), reading a list of books covering Lama's various ecumenical bases, and taking ceremonial oaths of acceptance and responsibility. In considering prospective members, Lama gave preference to families with children. Unanimous acceptance by current members was required for a new member to be admitted to the community. Altogether it was the most complex as well as lengthy membership screen used by any group in this study.

There was a funnel-like character to the screen, too, which was unusual for its structured and ordered quality. Lengthy written applications at the mouth of the funnel were a screen for good students of maximal interest to the membership. The second level of the funnel brought good students through the participation process and therefore determined good prospective members. The third level of the screen was acceptance as an active member; the fourth was the time away to determine if the outside world was still tempting; and the fifth was the final distillation of those committed and qualified enough to accede to the status of Caretakers.

This approach to new members solved many of the chronic communal problems of identity and status within the organization and gave Lama far more control over its own development than the arbitrary policies of most communes of the era, which usually picked up new members fairly casually. Lama was also very fortunate—a fortune they themselves accomplished—in providing services of sufficient attraction to bring them an abundance of high-quality applicants. At any rate, Lama prospered under the arrangement. One reason the requirement that members build their own homes was dropped was that during the summers there would be students around eager to build whatever Lama wished, not for occupancy but for spiritual exercise—and as a chance to try the life without long-term involvement. It was a trade-off, in a way, between those who cultivated their impermanence and those who knew how to put it to good use.

Other dimensions of cross-boundary control at Lama were a relatively strict visitation policy (Sundays only with limits to where visitors should poke their noses) and a relatively relaxed view of trips outside by members (which averaged about once a week, as in most communes). Physically, Lama was situated with a high degree of insulation from the outside, at a mile's distance from the nearest neighbor, twenty miles from the nearest town over mostly unpaved mountain roads, and cut off from outside media like television, radio, newspapers, and telephones. Summing all these factors up as renunciation, Lama had the second highest score in the study after Ananda, also a religious community.

One of the most interesting uses of renunciation at Lama, though, is not covered by these indices, which relate only to barriers between the community and the outside world. At Lama renunciation was internal to the community too, underscoring the importance there of individual work on the self and freedom from attachment, including attachments to other members. The most potent such mechanism at Lama was the use of "hermitages," a practice introduced at the Ram Dass ashram and thereafter made an integral part of community life. "Each participant in the community spends a portion of his or her time in solitude in a hermitage. The amount of time spent by each individual is a function of the number of participants and the number of spaces. The minimum time for a hermitage visit is twenty-four hours. (The maximum we have worked with is three weeks.)" Usually an initial period of three to five days was considered a good "shake-down cruise." Only the "minimum requirements . . . useful to your specific *sadhana*" were to be taken along, and "the only reason to leave the hermitage room is for toileting and washing, both of which should be done without social interaction." Food was to be brought once a day by a member from the "Base Camp." Hermits were expected to spend a good deal of time in meditation and could communicate any special needs they had only by leaving a written note. "It is only under these minimal stimulus conditions that you can watch . . . your wild out-of-control mind 'do its thing.' "[23]

Another important practice in this vein was the use of silence, both individually and communally. An individual might start by remaining silent a few hours a day and then extend the practice to an entire day each week or even longer periods, perhaps aided by a small chalk board for writing only "the essence of the communication without all the redundancies and amplifications. With such a device, Hari Dass Baba has carried on much worldly work for fifteen years without speaking."[24] Still another use of silence was the practice of taking meals without speaking unless pragmatically necessary. Silent meals were normally both lunch and dinner. Still another was the proscription against "social conversations" in the meditation alcove. The importance of the meditation room at Lama is seen in the recommendation in the "Cookbook" to "create the center—the meditation room or alcove—*first*, before you get the kitchen and bedrooms in order. . . . Keep that area very special," advises the "Cookbook." "Try to build a natural ritual into your lives so that you use the space to share a daily moment when you transcend your ego games." Finally, the "Cookbook" recommends another Lama practice: performing some of the group work projects in silence, too. "Silence is an important part of the work. . . . Gossip, small talk, and hanging out . . . have a limited value in breaking through the illusion."[25]

Communion   On most of the variables taken here to define the degree of communion, Lama generally scored higher than any other group in the sample. In most aspects of its internal economic and social life, Lama was the most tightly organized community to be found in the counterculture. As such, Lama set the upper limits, so to speak, of the degree of communalization normally found in groups of its era.

In communistic sharing, for instance, Lama employed the typical pattern of communal ownership of land, all buildings and dwellings, and facilities like the garden and domestic animals, library, workshop, and equipment. Lama went a step further than most with its detailed accounting breakdown of expenses and its policy of expecting regular monthly payments from its members. But like practically every other communal group in America, it stopped short of expecting the signover of all personal property, bank accounts or income, or enforcing the communal use of personal possessions as a matter of course.

In communistic labor, Lama registered the highest score possible and developed several interesting devices for distributing its work. First, thirty hours of labor were required of each member each week, without compensation. For the most part this work was allocated by a detailed sign-up sheet listing all the community's work needs for the week. The sheet would be filled up on a first-come, voluntaristic basis until all the slots were signed and each responsibility was assumed. Overseeing this process was the "Hawk," also known as the "Abbot," a member of at least active status who functioned as Lama's work director. Being the Hawk was a role that Lama deliberately rotated each week to give each member a taste of the patience, power, managerial skills, and responsibility that running an organization requires. At Lama work was serious business, and it was up to the Hawk to see that it got done with adequate coordination and monitoring. It was an effective solution to several communal problems at once: everybody got to enjoy the experience and frustration of being a power tripper, everyone agreed that the Hawk was ceded legitimate authority, and the work got done.

> The abbot has the responsibility for making things run smoothly on the physical plane as well as for keeping the objectives of the community uppermost in everyone's mind. In order to fulfill such responsibilities, the abbot must spend much time meditating to keep his own spiritual center in order so that he does not become an agent of more confusion and illusion and power trips. . . . Unless there is a teacher in the group, leadership is risky. However, it is possible to rotate the duties of an abbot in the event that no teacher is available. . . . Perhaps the abbot could be the person who has just come out of the hermitage if rotation is required.[26]

Another important job was that of the "Janitor," Lama's mock-humble term for prayer leader. In keeping with Lama's participatory nature, this role was rotated daily to involve each person present in responsibility for the spiritual goals at Lama's center. The Janitor woke the community and marked the course of its day with bells and gongs, led morning and evening prayers or religious exercises, and attuned himself or herself to shepherding the community through the day. Other than the Caretakers, from whom these general policies emanated, the most long-term role at Lama was that of "Kitchen Master." The tenure of the Kitchen Master was the summer season, when there were many students and visitors to feed and continuity in the kitchen was essential.

In regularized group contact, Lama again had a high score. Dining was communal three times a day, there were scheduled group meetings two nights a week, and there was a fixed daily routine of great intricacy. A typical summer daily schedule written down for me by the Hawk on July 26, 1970, is reproduced below. It illustrates with a great wealth of detail the extent to which Lama was a comprehensively planned community. With this degree of organization, most members spent over 75 percent of their days with other members. Two members I spoke with hastened to point out, though, that this high level of life together was mostly either work time or "impersonal." The purpose of Lama, Steve Durkee had explained to reporters Hedgepeth and Stock, "is to awaken consciousness. We would sacrifice the community aspect of it before we would sacrifice that."[27]

TYPICAL SUMMER DAILY SCHEDULE
(six hours work)

5:00   First gong, optional meditation.
6:00   Second gong.
6:15   Final gong.

6:30   Morning meeting announced by hand bell outside meditation/ prayer room.
First 10 minutes Essene prayer chanting Ah Nu Ta Ra Hum (E W N S Center).
Second 10 minutes, silence opened by Essene prayer of the day.
Third 10 minutes, chant or reading of the day, chosen by Janitor.

7:00   Sometimes Sufi dancing. Breakfast; milk animals. Do whatever you want—yoga, tai chi, exercises, rapping, caring for children.

8:15   Bell announcing that work starts in 15 minutes. Work until lunch.

12:15   Warning bell—15 minutes until lunch. 12:25, five-minute warning.

12:30   Lunch. Hold hands first, silence, often grace.

1:15   Class (15-minute warning bell).

3:15   Go back to work until 5:30 bell.

6:00   Dinner (15-minute and 5-minute bells). Hold hands, silence, sometimes grace.

8:30   Evening meetings (bell 8:15). All evening meetings open with daily evening Essene prayer and 10-minute silence. Close with 10 minutes chanting AUM.

Monday	Prayer meeting, 8:30–9:30.
Tuesday	Teachers' meeting or impersonal eye meditation or prayer meeting.
Wednesday	Business meeting, Only Room (living room).
Thursday	Singing in prayer room, spontaneous (mostly) as they come out.
Friday	Business meeting.

No meetings Saturday or Sunday.

WEEKLY SCHEDULE

Monday–Friday	As above.
Saturday	Morning meeting (meditation). Process—next week's work. Clean up. Lunch. "Free" afternoon.
Sunday	"Free" except for caring for visitors.

This muting of idle chitchat and encounter was one of several accommodations that Lama made to personal privacy as part of its quest to fit the needs of the inward search with the needs of social organization. Others included the sanctity of private dwellings (even if only temporarily occupied and never individually owned) and a scattered residence pattern by couples, families, and singles on the wooded mountainside. Lama never went through a communal dwelling or group-marriage phase, though some individual members had. Lama recognized minimal privacy needs from the beginning, and accepted the nuclear family and coupling instinct as natural or even necessary in the interests of organizational stability.

As the typical summer daily schedule shows, the ritual content of Lama's life was quite extensive, and Lama had the maximum score on this dimension of communion, too. On the negative side of communion, Lama had experienced only one instance of harassment, an attempt by the county health officials "to red-tag every commune around Taos," according to one member. (It failed on legal grounds of discrimination.) In general, Lama was one of the groups in this study which got along best with their surrounding neighbors, most of whom were at a great distance anyway. Lama's high score on communion was internally generated and did not reflect any significant outside persecution.

Mortification   The function of mortification mechanisms is to subordinate the private ego to the norms and processes of group functioning. In Lama's early phase, this involved regular meetings devoted to mutual criticism and personal encounter in addition to community business. As time went on, the deliberate use of encounter and criticism was dropped as needlessly debilitating and fruitless. Although the drama of encounter was obviously still an informal part of the twice-weekly business meetings or sometimes even prayer meetings, in general Lama shifted the onus of criticism and confession to the self through meditation and attempted to keep it at an abstract or impersonal level when it had to be discussed socially. Members generally agreed that this way of dealing with garden-variety frictions was the most valid spiritually and least disruptive socially. It dovetailed smoothly with Lama's overriding goal of personal self-awakening, which was, after all, the *raison d'être* of each individual's participation. What with all the screening processes, it was difficult in any case to advance toward Lama's center without commitment to organizational ascendancy over private gripes. In effect, the very legitimacy of private gripes was denied. As one member put it, "It's your karma, man."

With the goals of the group effort holding this kind of primacy over individual egos (the group goal being to get rid of egos), not surprisingly some Lama members were distinguished from others on moral or spiritual grounds, relative to the purity of their zeal for the religious life, their tenure of service at Lama, the nature of their spiritual and practical contributions, and so on. These processes of spiritual differentiation were reinforced by practices like lengthy probation periods, formal instruction in community doctrines, and initiation into the highly important ceremonial aspects of community life. Even a visitor to Lama could tell fairly readily who was a newcomer and who was an old hand. Like the visitor, the newcomers did not know the songs, chants, or postures with much proficiency. The fear of embarrassment is a strong socializing influence even (or perhaps particularly) in a community seeking enlightenment.

Likewise those toward the center of the organization (particularly visiting teachers and gurus) were generally regarded as spiritually advanced people of unusual wisdom, character, and energy. The tripartite nature of membership reflected these differences, although there was little structured deference to members of higher moral status observable in daily life (for example, Caretakers could be addressed on an ordinary informal basis by students or challenged as equals in meetings by active members). Only visiting teachers were treated to terms of special respect or endearment; only they were thought pure enough to deserve them. But with these men as models, it was clear that Lama rested atop a moral hierarchy of selfless service and spiritual purification. Thus Lama had the highest total of mortification mechanisms in the study, even though there were other communes where spiritual differentiation was equally evident and even more pronounced (Ananda and Maharaj).

Transcendence Lama's use of this variety of commitment mechanisms was generally strong but less so than the study's other two communities of religious discipline, Ananda and Maharaj. All three, but particularly Lama, had elaborate and precise ideologies governing daily life, a reputation for magical people and events, and a powerful mystique about them to awe the newcomer. The main distinction was the fact that Lama incorporated many schools of thought instead of cultivating a single tradition, leaving plenty of room for ideological individualism under an umbrella of general agreement about first principles:

> We have a basic core belief in God—Christ, Meher Baba, the Buddha, Mohammed—and in the transitory illusive nature of life: the fact that you can only work on yourself, no one can do it for you; and that there is no meaningful goal other than enlightenment.[28]

At the more secular level of power and authority, Lama likewise differed from Ananda and Maharaj by the lack of any single person embodying the community. Structurally Lama was governed by the central committee of Caretakers, which made every effort to involve the entire active membership in decision making but reserved for itself the ultimate right to set basic policy, make the most crucial decisions, and incorporate new members into its ranks. Authority at Lama could be described as benevolently aristocratic. Interestingly, though, the status of Caretaker had to be renewed annually by vow. It was not a landed aristocracy but a spiritual one, and not even this was permanent. This requirement was a way of both insuring updated commitment and providing an honorable way out if an impasse or ambition made a Caretaker's leaving necessary.

Other transcendence factors on which Lama scored high were "programing," which as we have seen was complex and comprehensive, and "ideological conversion," which as we have also seen was tested in many ways before full membership was extended. In all, Lama followed only the study's two other religious groups, Ananda and Maharaj, in the strength of its transcendence mechanisms. On this dimension in particular, Lama, Ananda, and Maharaj were markedly distinct from the other groups in the study, which by and large were secular anarchies to whom questions of programing, power, and authority were obnoxious. Yet despite the hierarchical nature of things at Lama, its political affairs were on balance as equalitarian as several anarchical groups and more equalitarian than other religious groups. Most decisions at Lama were reached in open business meetings on the principle of unanimous consensus with equal participation by men and women. It was true that a distinct minority held sway over the community's long-range policies and most important decisions, but there were patriarchal elements in almost all communes. The difference was that at Lama the influential minority was formally recognized as legitimate, a legitimacy based on a higher-order moral imperative. The Caretakers who wrote the "Cookbook" were talking about their own legitimacy as well as the success of spiritual communities in general when they set down these three "Things Which Make It Work":

1. The nature of the contract must be explicit. That is, each person participating in the experiment must understand the form, schedule, and objectives. . . . The experiment cannot work properly if the group has many ideas of "how it should be done. . . ." In traditional *ashrams* there is usually a guru or teacher who leads the way . . . or a traditional structure which is known to every one who seeks to participate.

2. All members of the community . . . have consciously and freely chosen to participate in the experiment. . . . In the most rigid selection

procedures, if one partner of a couple does not wish to fully participate in the experiment, then neither will participate. . . . It takes very few people who do not share the desire to work on themselves in this way to destroy the effectiveness of a spiritual community.

3. All participants in the community (with the exception of smaller children) spend time in the hermitage as well as the base camp and share base camp activities and responsibilities.[29]

Fortified with this legitimacy, Lama's elite governed almost invisibly, leaving the heavy hand to personal religious humility. Basic agreement with Lama's organizational goals was built in by the Caretakers' screening procedures. Although that agreement did not necessarily exempt Lama from internal disputes, there was a practical device for dealing with them, too. When conflict emerged in meetings and threatened to get out of hand, a quiet "AUM" chant would be initiated until things calmed down into perspective. Quoting the "Cookbook" again:

Interpersonal matters are dealt with only to the extent that they are disruptive (i.e., capture the consciousness of the group or some participants). Such matters can be dealt with at group meeting if necessary . . . but the moment the group gets bogged down in heavy melodrama . . . it is well to call a meditation interlude until everyone can find a center again. Melodrama sucks us in again and again, but diminishes in power if actively thwarted.[30]

The system was effective but altogether uncommon in 1970 or even today. Despite the recent growth of spiritual communities following the decline of secular ones, Lama still stands alone. As far as I know, Lama is unique in its peculiar combination of rigorous religious discipline, elite management, democratic participation, and rational-legal administration. One interesting contrast that comes to mind is Twin Oaks, a secular community based on B. F. Skinner's behavioralist principles, which is somewhat like Lama except for religion. But without the binding force of religious transcendence, Twin Oaks suffered chronic battles over authority and legitimacy and experienced many defections as it slowly came into focus as an organizational entity.[31] At Lama, comparatively speaking, these problems were only minor blinks in God's eye.

III

On my return visit in 1973, Lama showed signs of continued growth and prosperity. Buildings standing or in progress in 1970 were completed and well maintained, and new buildings (notably a large dormitory for students) were under construction (with student labor). There had been improvements in the community's utilities and growth in Lama's principal cottage industry, the production of prayer flags and Tibetan-style shirts and dresses. But the most important development over the three-year interval between my visits was the success of Lama's publishing efforts, particularly the Ram Dass collaboration *Be Here Now*. By January 1975 the book had gone through fifteen printings totaling 473,000 copies. With fifty-one cents of each sale going to the Lama Foundation Reservoir Fund ("used to support the Lama Foundation and to water the spiritual garden around the world"), the community had made a quarter of a million (tax-free) dollars from this one project. In 1970 Lama had produced less than 25 percent of its own income needs and remained dependent on donations, monthly payments, and tuition from the school. By 1973 it was entirely self-supporting and itself supported two Taos-area schools. Lama's own school now hosted thirty students out of many times that number of applicants. With this success, it was perhaps understandable that Lama no longer maintained livestock or put much energy into its garden—the only evidence I saw of community decline.

In addition to *Be Here Now*, Lama published a number of other volumes by recognized spiritual teachers (for example, *The Yellow Book* by Hari Dass Baba and *Buddha Is the Center of Gravity* by Joshu Saski Roshi). Lama had also organized the Bountiful Lord's Delivery Service, a subscription series of some of these and other publications. There was little question that Lama's financial future was secure.

Along with the success came a number of relaxations in Lama's strict rules. The ban on tobacco had been lifted, and discreet drug use was tolerated on an individual basis. The regular monthly payments were no longer required beyond the first month, after which they became irregular depending on individual choice and circumstance. Attendance was no longer required at meetings and meditation gatherings, though these were still well attended. The probation period had been shortened, and the Sundays-only visitation rule was no longer as rigidly enforced. All in all, Lama had passed through the early trials of scarcity and organizational survival and could now allow more expression of individual predilections. Otherwise Lama's policy, scheduling, and activities remained the same.

One of the most interesting aspects of Lama's continuity was that the social composition of the membership had changed considerably while the organization itself remained stable and intact. In July 1973 Lama had twenty-nine members, only one less than three years before, but of the thirty members in 1970, only five remained in 1973. There were now twelve Caretakers, but only one of them had been an original member from 1967. The Durkees, their five-year plan a complete success, had gone on to other things and left the community in the hands of the new Caretakers they had so carefully recruited into responsibility. In short, 79 percent of the total 1970 membership had left, though not necessarily permanently. But 71 percent of the Caretakers had remained, and this figure rather than the others was perhaps the most important.

Despite this success, life had not been easy within the inner circle, which attempted to be a group of equals and was therefore subject to the same conflicts as any other. The 1973 edition of *Be Here Now* included this "current note" on the Lama Foundation: "Honest experimentation in the evolution of economic, social, and spiritual forms for communities of seekers is exceedingly difficult, and the moments of love and trust and consciousness are interspersed by periods of paranoia and struggle. Through honesty we grow, and the beings who work, pray, and live together at Lama are no exception."[32] But unlike most other communes, Lama had a conscious social design that took ample account of both the needs of the members and the needs of organizational integrity.

But social design is only one dimension of Lama's story. "If a pickpocket meets a saint," says Hari Dass Baba, one of Alpert's teachers, "he sees only his pockets." Behind the social design was a clarity and authenticity of purpose without which Lama could not have attracted the many contributions, leaders, students, teachers, or the other factors that made it all work. "In regard to every action," Gandhi once said, "one must know the result that is expected to follow, the means thereto, and the capacity for it. He, who being thus equipped, is without desire for the result, and is yet wholly engrossed in the due fulfillment of the task before him, is said to have renounced the fruits of his action."[33] So it was at Lama.

What will happen remains to be seen, now that those who escaped from an excess of material advantage have come full circle through an ideology of self-denial and created prosperity all over again. Yet even as Lama waxes fat, it still fasts, at work on a freedom that lies beyond both poverty and prosperity. If dropping out was all there was to it, Lama would probably be just another spiritualist movement of jaded aristocrats of the sort that dot the side rails of history. Instead it became the single most influential spiritual community of its time, and clearly Lama could not have accomplished what it did as a mere collection of privileged neurotics and psychedelic cripples desperately groping for one messiah after another. I prefer to think of Lama as an attempt to push beyond future shock and existential despair into new realms of personal peace, creativity, and social responsibility. Where, after all, are human beings to go when all their basic material needs are met and they acquire an almost unlimited capacity for self-stimulation? In modern America, this question is of the highest relevance.

Notes

1. Steve Durkee, "Steve Durky [*sic*] and the Development of Lama," in Richard Fairfield, *Communes U.S.A.: A Personal Tour* (Baltimore: Penguin Books, 1972), pp. 116–122.
2. Ibid., p. 117.
3. Ibid., pp. 117–118.
4. Ibid., p. 119.
5. Ibid., p. 118.
6. Ibid., pp. 119–120.
7. Ibid., p. 121.
8. Ibid., p. 122.
9. Quoted in Robert Houriet, *Getting Back Together* (New York: Avon Books, 1972), p. 366.
10. Ibid., p. 364.
11. Ibid., p. 368.
12. Quoted in Fairfield, *Communes U.S.A.*, p. 122.
13. "Lama Foundation 1969" (San Cristobal, N.Mex.: The Lama Foundation, 1969). Broadside.
14. Baba Ram Dass, "JOURNEY" or "The Transformation: Dr. Richard Alpert, Ph.D., into Baba Ram Dass," Book One of Baba Ram Dass et al., *Be Here Now* (San Cristobal, N.Mex.: The Lama Foundation, 1971).
15. Ibid.
16. Ibid.
17. "Lama Foundation 1969." Some definitions from the "Cookbook" published two years later (see note 20 below): Karma Yoga is "realization through action; selfless service;" Asanas are "comfortable postures" in yoga; Pranayama is "control of life energy through control of breathing;" Prasad is "consecrated food;" Kirtan means "repetition in song of the Names of God;" and Mantra are "words, syllables or phrases manifested to effect psychic states by sounding the psychic energy vortices in the body."
18. Quoted in Houriet, *Getting Back Together*, p. 368.
19. Quoted in Fairfield, *Communes U.S.A.*, p. 119.
20. "Cookbook for a Sacred Life," Book Three of Ram Dass et al., *Be Here Now* (San Cristobal, N.Mex.: The Lama Foundation, 1971), p. 104.
21. Quoted in Houriet, *Getting Back Together*, p. 364.
22. "Cookbook," p. 11.
23. Ibid., pp. 106–107.
24. Ibid., pp. 12–13.
25. Ibid., pp. 105–106.
26. Ibid., p. 107.
27. Quoted in William Hedgepeth and Dennis Stock, *The Alternative* (New York: Collier Books, 1970), p. 162.
28. Barbara Durkee, quoted in Houriet, *Getting Back Together*, p. 363.
29. "Cookbook," pp. 104–105.
30. Ibid., p. 106.
31. See Kathleen Kinkade, *A Walden Two Experiment: The First Five Years of Twin Oaks Community* (New York: Morrow, 1973).
32. "Cookbook," p. 121.
33. Ibid., p. 70.

6

From Hobbitland to Subdivision: LILA

I

Like several other communes in the Taos area, the Lorien Institute for Life Arts, or "LILA" as the members called it, was made possible by a wealthy hip benefactor. LILA's patron was an idealistic young Philadelphia poet named Charles ("Chick") Lonsdale, who had dropped out to Taos with a sizable portfolio of inherited IBM stock. On the Taos scene, he was preceded and deeply influenced by other communal benefactors like Rick Kline (New Buffalo, Libre), Herman Rednick (Lama Foundation), and Michael Duncan (Morning Star East, Reality). Inspired by these examples, Lonsdale put his resources to work in support of a number of hip service projects in Taos. His private foundation, Lorien Enterprises, Inc., funded a free clinic, an information service for transient hippies, and a general store selling low-cost dried foodstuffs, back-to-the-land books, and a variety of tools and local craft wares. Though he was a relative newcomer to the Taos underground, he quickly became one of its most prominent pillars.

In early 1969 Lonsdale's generosity extended to his own land, a beautiful, wooded fifty-acre plot adjacent to what later became LILA, some thirty-five miles north of Taos on the arid plain abutting the Sangre de Cristo Mountains. Like his foundation, the new commune was called "Lorien," a name taken from the magic elfin forest in Tolkien's *The Hobbit*. And like Duncan's Morning Star East, which had opened three months earlier, Lonsdale enforced no restrictions on who could come and live at Lorien. According to Hedgepeth and

Stock, apparently the only reporters to visit Lorien in its first year, Lorien's shifting population of some thirty-five members was extremely young (average age about twenty) and inexperienced (except for a few migrants from Morning Star and Wheeler's Ranch in California). "Until they become agriculturally productive and self-sufficient," wrote Hedgepeth, "they'll continue living, chiefly, off Chick's largess." As for Lonsdale himself:

> He . . . seems content to live in his tiny wood hut, writing bad poems and generally allowing all earthly things the chance to happen in their own way. "We're trying for a unity thing," he smiles. "Like, not everybody's into a work-trip just yet. It takes time."[1]

But personally, Lonsdale was moving in a more specific direction. He had become very interested in yoga and was beginning to gravitate toward the influence of Herman Rednick, the artist who had been so instrumental in the creation of the Lama Foundation. Over the course of Lorien's first year, tension began to develop between those members who shared Lonsdale's religious concerns and those who did not, or as Lonsdale himself put it three years later, "between those who do Hatha Yoga and those who do Tokay wine, those who greet the sun in the morning and those who drum to the moon." Moreover, this was the year that *Easy Rider* was released and thousands of hip vagrants brought Haight-Ashbury–style chaos to Taos.

Lonsdale's reaction to these developments was to begin planning the creation of a new commune, LILA, which took as a model the energetic, successful Lama Foundation. Like Lama, there would be no dope or alcohol, and visitors would be restricted to one day a week. LILA would be a nonprofit corporation governed by a board of trustees, consisting initially of sympathetic outside advisors but eventually controlled by the resident membership. Lonsdale's Lorien Enterprises would provide seed money for a down payment on the site and some basic construction materials. The balance of the land payments were to be assumed by the members once they got on their feet. A tract of 550 acres was purchased near Lorien, and in January 1970 LILA's initial membership of ten people, several of whom were Lorien veterans, began construction of their new home.

In the meantime, Lonsdale maintained his residence at Lorien and patiently continued to subsidize it as an open-land community with only two basic rules: "Respect the land" and "Respect other people's rights." But the differences between the yoga faction and the tokay faction continued to sharpen, exacerbated by Lonsdale's preference and greater trust for the former. When he went on a vacation in March 1970, for instance, he left $5,000 and managerial authority at

Lorien to one of his lieutenants from the yoga faction. The resentful tokay faction took advantage of Lonsdale's absence to stage a rebellion, and the split in Lorien's membership came to a conclusion that is unparalleled in modern communal history for its ugliness and violence. It started as an argument over where to plant fruit trees. It ended in a brawling gun battle which put six people in the hospital and resulted in the issuance of arrest warrants for six others.[2] For Lonsdale the fight was the last straw for "open land" and redoubled his conviction that LILA would be built upon spirituality and hard work.

II

By the time I visited LILA, it was August 1970 and a Saturday, since only on Saturdays were visitors allowed. The commune was situated inconspicuously off the highway leading north from Taos to Questa. From all appearances it was just another sheep ranch or farmstead off in the distance toward the mountains. There was nothing to mark its presence as a community. It was not even well known around Taos, since it discouraged visitors. LILA was tightly closed within itself as a result of the transient hippie crunch of 1969 and the tragedies at Lorien a few months earlier. By August most of the remaining yoga faction at Lorien had moved to LILA, and Charles Lonsdale had begun construction of a luxurious private home on his original fifty acres.

Physically, LILA was arid, barren sagebrush country, with limited irrigation rights two days a week. It had little promise for agriculture, and the two or three acres that LILA had under cultivation, mostly in scraggly pinto beans, showed equally limited promise for feeding a community that had now grown to twelve men, ten women, and eight children. LILA's buildings consisted of some old sheds, a small ranch house that had been converted to a communal kitchen and living room, and a dozen or so small cabins spread out behind the house in a semicircle opening to the west. The cabins had been hastily built that winter to meet the new community's pressing need for shelter. They were all tiny, square, and identically constructed of unpainted rough lumber, with perhaps 150 square feet of interior living area. Despite the wide open spaces at LILA, all the buildings were clustered within one acre, and the curious array of little boxes made of ticky-tacky gave the community the appearance of a seedy motel. In the middle of the yard between cabins and ranch house stood the community's old windmill, which now pumped LILA's water in a blaze of psychedelic colors.

Sacrifice But psychedelia at LILA was limited to colors. All such drugs were forbidden, as was alcohol. This placed LILA among only four groups in the sample to practice any form of abstinence, though unlike the three others, which were all very religious, LILA's ban did not extend to tobacco, coffee, or meat. LILA had "gone beyond drugs" but not quite all the way. It was one of many compromises at LILA between individualism and group solidarity. In its daily practice, LILA was a hybrid of the self-indulgent anarchies and the disciplined monasticism of the ashrams and religious retreats. In overall degree of communal sacrifice, LILA was exactly average for the sample as a whole.

Over the first six months of LILA's existence, the population had initially swollen to fifty members during the cold weather and then tapered back down to its current size of twenty-two adults with the arrival of warm weather and the continuing efforts of Lonsdale and the founding members to arrive at more communal discipline. In the summer of 1970, the average LILA member was between twenty-five and thirty years old, with a few around twenty-one and several over thirty; about two-thirds of them had been to college. With few exceptions the population was distributed by monogamous couples among the little cabins, and the cabins were considered private, though not privately owned. Since LILA's housing was communal and individual simultaneously, occupancy was determined by informal seniority rights rather than property rights.

At its center LILA showed a fair measure of stability, for nine of the ten founding members were still present after six months. On the outer perimeters, however, forty or fifty ex-members and prospective members had passed through the community in that period of time. Most of them were not as interested in emulating the Lama Foundation as the founding nucleus. For this reason and others, LILA had made little progress toward its stated goal of hosting spiritual workshops and other Lama-style functions. Even the founders had not known each other well before joining, and social life at LILA was preoccupied with seeking collective agreements where very few had existed before. Formal community meetings took place three nights a week. Since unanimous consensus was required on all major decisions—and for a new community there were many to be made— these meetings were often intense, circular, and riddled with personal conflicts. Looming in the future and casting a pall over the proceedings was the problem of making the $10,000 payment on the land in November. It was generally agreed that each member would be responsible for a $500 share of it. For the time being, contributions to the community from outside income or savings were voluntary.

Investment   In other respects, the investment pattern at LILA was identical to Libre's. New members were expected to build their own shelters, nonresident members were prohibited, and defectors were not reimbursed for any contributions of money or property. On the other hand, there were no requirements for paying an admission fee, turning over property to the group, or donating personal income. LILA was navigating in the archetypal gray zone between private ownership and communal use, with very little actual signover of property. Its use of investment mechanisms was again average for this study, or light, compared to the outside world. In its use of other commitment mechanisms, LILA had some features which were shared mostly with more serious and religious groups and others that were more akin to political anarchies. In more ways than one, LILA was a community betwixt and between.

Renunciation   LILA was above average for the communes in its degree of renunciation of the outside world, but only slightly so. LILA had no electronic media connecting it with events elsewhere. Geographically it was not particularly isolated, and the average member traveled outside at least weekly. The rules concerning visitation were strict. Visitors were normally allowed on Saturdays only, and any stays beyond that were deliberately limited, requiring sponsorship from some member of the community and payment of a $2 daily fee. Becoming a new member involved a probation period varying from a week to a month, unanimous acceptance by the existing membership, and a formal oath to abide by the rules. But unlike more stable or religious communities, little effort was made to evaluate prospective members in terms of their skills, beliefs, or family situation. Although LILA had blackballed one prospective member (who "thought he was a guru" and "was indifferent to work"), it had never ejected an existing member.

Communion   Here again LILA was a hybrid. In its degree of communistic sharing, it was identical to Drop City. What was voluntarily donated was shared. Without requirements for turning over property or income, LILA was impoverished, and Charles Lonsdale was not nearly as interested in subsidizing LILA as he might have been a year earlier. Communistic labor at LILA mainly took the form of two hours of required work a day and the rotation of kitchen duties via a sign-up sheet, in addition to whatever income-producing jobs members might have otherwise. Monetarily, the community was largely supported by eight members who took temporary or part-time jobs on the outside, an inequality that reflected markedly different

levels of commitment among the membership, sign-up sheets notwithstanding. Regularized group contact among the members was high,
with daily communal meals, thrice-weekly scheduled meetings, the
Drop City–like concentration of living quarters, and the Lama-like
practice of announcing demarcations in the daily routine with a gong.
LILA also imitated Lama in its ritual life, with daily (voluntary) meditation, mealtime prayers, and, more infrequently, group singing and
dancing. LILA did not, however, enjoy the homogeneity and long
acquaintances of Lama's membership. Comparatively speaking, it
was a community of strangers. LILA's rituals seemed more an effort
to make up for that than a natural extension of community life, as if it
were obligatory to manufacture anew what had been so shockingly
destroyed at Lorien. Indeed it *was* obligatory, for the performance of
religious service functions was one of the conditions of Lonsdale's
patronage. Finally, and perhaps most interestingly, LILA members
reported no harassment, discrimination, or significant negative reaction locally, despite the guarded nature of the community and the
Chicano horror stories echoing out of Taos from 1969. Their symbolic
enemies were instead people like themselves.

Mortification   One of the most important differences between
LILA and its nominal model, Lama, was the absence at LILA of any
distinctions among members of such a nature that some sort of legitimate leadership might emerge. Unlike more authentic religious or
tribal communities, LILA observed no gradations in spiritual or moral
status, even informally. On the other hand, the pressures to find a
group identity (and make the land payment) made the laissez-faire
approach of anarchistic communes inadequate to the community's
needs. The encounters and mutual criticism that took place at group
meetings, in consequence, were more a corrosive to interpersonal
relations that a force to bind member loyalty through ego-loss. As
communes everywhere eventually discovered, the educated American
middle-class ego needs more than a little consideration.

Transcendence   Similarly, LILA's religious ideology was eclectic and incompletely shared by the membership. Religion was important to some members but not nearly so pervasive a part of community life as it was at Lama, where it was the very *raison d'être*, where
magical powers were imputed to the community, and where specific
spiritual teachers were attended with great importance. Likewise,
power and authority were diffuse and equalitarian at LILA, more like
an anarchistic group than Lama. The original founding core of more
committed and religious members formed a kind of leadership clique,
four of whom were accepted on LILA's board of trustees, but authority hierarchies were anathema to the group at large. Leadership initia-

tive was under constant challenge by other members and usually forced into compromise or confusion. A voluntaristic committee system was established in order to deal with routine issues like food purchases, community finances, making up a community brochure, and auto maintenance, but all such committee decisions were subject to validation or rejection by the membership as a whole. LILA did not trust the emergent patriarchal leadership of anarchies, but neither did it permit the exercise of any real authority as in religious groups like Lama or Ananda.

Politically, LILA made up for a certain hollowness in its religious underpinnings with a democratization of its daily life that was almost compulsive. Committee meetings in the afternoons, community meetings three nights a week, sign-up sheets and gongs regulating daily life, unanimous consensus required on all issues, job rotation—in these respects LILA was one of the most equalitarian communities in this study. Lama did just the same but had legitimate, even revered, leaders. The crucial test of LILA's leaderless system would be its capacity to meet the $10,000 land payment some three months later. Lonsdale and Lorien Enterprises, Inc., had put LILA on notice that they were on their own now and that there would be no more subsidies.

III

The sum total of LILA's use of commitment mechanisms had been almost exactly average for the study as a whole. Several communes survived with fewer such mechanisms but with one critical difference. In each commune which survived with a weaker commitment structure than LILA's, the land had been purchased free and clear in advance of founding. In short, they were not stuck with a weighty mortgage.

Revisiting LILA in 1973, I heard that it had failed, and I paid a call on Charles Lonsdale. In discussions with him and two ex-LILA members, I was able to learn more about the group's fate. Lonsdale called the LILA episode "an idea that came after its time." Of the twenty-seven communes he said were active in Taos County in 1969, he could count only four which were still alive and reasonably well in 1973. "Much was learned by many people about sharing, love, and trust," he told me, "but it was all too far in advance of our skills in human relations and understanding."

Technically, LILA's failure was economic. Lonsdale, and the membership, too, had felt it was not unrealistic to expect each member to be able to contribute $500 a year to the land payment, but it had not worked out that way. Five hundred dollars proved the measure of commitment. As the November deadline approached, according to Lonsdale, "the members all drifted away, and those who went out in search of jobs to make their share of the money didn't come back if they found one." When the time to make the payment arrived, Lonsdale was left holding the bag as he had so many times before, and apparently it put an end to his idealism about communes once and for all. According to Tom, an ex-member, the real problem was spiritual: "LILA had no center, no soul, no draw, nothing to pull people together with the kind of energy and focus to make the payment."

Further discussions revealed that absolute democracy was an inadequate substitute for genuine collective goals and positive motivation. The strain of reaching unanimous decisions was sometimes so tiresome that some members went along just to get things over with, only to feel later that they had been bullied into a mistake. Others, more obstinate, managed to block decisions for meeting after meeting. But most important was the constant atmosphere of debate. Committee meetings every day and group meetings three nights a week left everyone tattered and frayed. In a way, some LILA members came to have a peculiar addictive dependency on these meetings, storing up their petty social frustrations for council instead of resolving them person to person, thus unnecessarily making private issues into more problems for the group. It was as if the mere existence of continual meetings to resolve conflict made conflict more inevitable.

The fact that leaders were explicitly disallowed did little to help, for LILA was thereby left with no dependable, legitimate source of guidance and direction. The members had not known each other very well in the beginning, and little effort was made to screen out contrary goals apart from agreeing not to take drugs. The decision-making system had no real way to accommodate such conflict once it emerged. And since it was so often difficult to reach unanimous decisions, some members took to acting on their own, thus creating resentment among those who abided by the group processes. LILA's complex democracy stood between members as much as it brought them together, locking the community into contradictions it could not resolve. If LILA had a realistic economic future, perhaps its politics would have become more realistic too. When utopia goes begging for $500, its prospects must have been poor indeed.

In 1972 Lonsdale bought LILA's land himself and made of it a legal subdivision with five- and ten-acre lots, scenically and conveniently located between Highway 3 and the Sangre de Cristo Mountains. Lonsdale, the ex-savior, was now a devotee of Herman Rednick and a commercial real estate developer. He had supported a total of three communal failures, including the Taos Family, which ran his general store and chronically looted the till.[3]

The Family went on to become the personal bodyguards for *Easy Rider* director Dennis Hopper, who moved to Taos after filming *The Last Picture Show* in South America, reportedly with mixed feelings of retreat, atonement, and defiance to accusations that he helped bring the hippie flood of 1969. He hired the Family to protect him when he was beaten up by Taos Chicanos. Though they were contemporaries, in a way Hopper was Lonsdale's successor in propping up the eroding mystique of northern New Mexico, as if he were starring now in a movie called *The Last Padrone*. Lonsdale just wanted enough money back from his "real estate hustle" to clear his debts and pay for his home, which is a delightful little goat-and-vegetable farm graced with a babbling brook and a luxurious adobe *hacienda* well appointed with modern conveniences. The homemade goat's milk cheese there is excellent.

By the summer of 1973, all but two of Lonsdale's lots had been sold, and a total of twenty-two private dwellings had been built and occupied. Even though Lonsdale's lots were available to anyone who wanted to purchase them, he kept his advertising local, and among the buyers were some of the old LILA members. "The concept," said one of them, "is now community rather than commune." Apart from a legal compact with Lonsdale specifying various zoning and land-use regulations, each individual family was on its own. There was talk that LILA might someday be a town, with businesses on the roadside lots. But for certain differences in life-style and costume, then, LILA had become a kind of middle-class suburb. But, joked Tom, "at least it hasn't reached wife swapping yet!"

Notes

1. William Hedgepeth and Dennis Stock, *The Alternative* (New York: Collier Books, 1970), p. 82.
2. Robert Houriet includes a thirdhand but accurate account of this incident in *Getting Back Together* (New York: Avon Books, 1972), pp. 189–190.
3. This charge was corroborated by a man at New Buffalo called Sun Dog who professed to know and like the Family well. For a sympathetic, honest, and moving account of one encounter with the Family, see Elia Katz, *Armed Love* (New York: Holt, Rinehart and Winston, 1971). Katz's book began as a cynical New York street boy's con game and turned out as one of the most alert and straightforward reports written on the counterculture circa 1970.

7

Love and Hate on Duncan's Mesa: Morning Star East and the Reality Construction Company

I

Sometime around 1967, a wealthy young heir named Michael Duncan purchased 750 acres of desert mesa north of Taos, about three miles into the wilderness from the little roadside town of Arroyo Hondo. At the time it was unreachable by vehicles, and after taking possession, one of the first things Duncan had to do was dynamite a precarious road up the side of the mesa. To the north and east the mesa merged into the Sangre de Cristo Mountains and national forest land. To the south it fell off steeply into the arroyo, and to the west it overlooked a dusty landscape rolling off in the distance to the gorge of the Rio Grande. It was harsh terrain but an ideal retreat, almost a natural fortress. With proper irrigation and hard work, it had some potential for agriculture. Duncan certainly had no intention of starting a commune or supporting transient hippies, although he, too, was a dropout from the cities and drawn to Taos for the same reasons they were. In another time he might have been just another wealthy eccentric of the sort that Taos had attracted for decades. But that was before he met Lou Gottlieb.

As the chapter on Wheeler Ranch describes in more detail, Lou Gottlieb was the benefactor of the original Morning Star commune in Sonoma County, California, in 1966. When the commune became overrun with human fallout from Haight-Ashbury in 1967, Gottlieb's experiment in "open land" and "voluntary primitivism" began to draw the wrath of local officials and property owners. Arrests and raids began in July 1967 and continued for the next three years, including the bulldozing of dwellings and a permanent injunction against anyone living at Morning Star except Lou Gottlieb. Gottlieb steadfastly stuck by his people and ideology of open land, but by the fall of 1968, after over $15,000 in fines and mass arrests of his friends, he knew that Morning Star was doomed to prolonged harassment if not outright extinction. But by then open land had become his personal religion, and like a good shepherd persecuted by the philistines, he wondered where his flock could go while he stayed on to fight for what Morning Star represented. Brilliant, voluble, utterly charming, and most likely holy, Gottlieb carried the Morning Star mixture of faith and politics— land access to which no one is denied—wherever he went.

Thus it happened that on a trip through New Mexico, Gottlieb was introduced to Duncan by a mutual acquaintance and persuaded him to consider the plight of his California communards and the importance of "free zones" and "lawless sanctuaries" like Morning Star. Under an agreement that was apparently not very clear, Lou returned to California and told the besieged residents of Morning Star about the availability of Duncan's mesa. As the "Open Land Manifesto" related two years later, "The dispersion of the Morning Star tribe seeded the western and southwestern states with young folks eager to continue the Open Land discovery."[1] Outside California the most direct result of this seeding was Morning Star East, where fifteen ex–Morning Star residents traveled early in 1969 to squat on the mesa with Duncan's sympathetic but somewhat reluctant consent.

Gottlieb, however, was not the only influence on Duncan. There were also the examples of Duncan's wealthy young peers around Taos itself—men like Rick Kline and Charles Lonsdale, who were at the time supporting communal projects of their own in the area. The other major thread in the story of Duncan's mesa came from the nearby New Buffalo commune that Kline had patronized (with $50,000) and lived in for a while in 1967. Several of New Buffalo's original members had left within a year of the group's founding, including Kline himself (to a mountain estate near the Lama Foundation about fifteen miles north). Another defector was founding member Max Finstein, a beat poet from New York whose wife had left him for still another of New Buffalo's original members. It would be Finstein, then in his late thirties or so, who would organize the second commune on Duncan's mesa, the Reality Construction Company, by recruiting a band of young revolutionaries from New York and San Francisco and other disaffiliates from around Taos itself.

Finstein left New Buffalo in 1968. That summer, a year before the founding of Reality, Finstein was interviewed by Edmund Helminski about his experiences at New Buffalo and the thoughts he drew from it. In the excerpts that follow are distinct foreshadowings of the closed off, disciplined work ethic that he would institute at Reality and the ambiguities that this would involve for middle-class communards who had never really known scarcity.

> I believe that working together is the way. Trying to think up love doesn't work. Love is a very physical thing, it's not a head thing. It comes out of any kind of discipline you can find to make it become real. And by spending eight or ten or twelve hours a day working with a bunch of people you can really get something. Even that kind of love which includes fighting amongst the kin.
>
> I think that a strict work discipline is very necessary, but you have to find a way to make it human, to allow for twentieth-century people— there has to be some way to temper that old work discipline with humanity. If it were possible to just let people walk around . . . *if it were possible,* then that's the ideal. . . . If anybody doesn't work, then the community is as much at fault for not giving them what they want. And then it's for everyone to straighten their heads out about whether they want to be there or not. If not, get out.
>
> You see, what I think the difficulty in a contemporary communal scene is is that all the communities that have existed before were created because of an intense need on the part of the people involved, you know, out of necessity. And now we have a huge body of people who really don't have to put up with much and whose background tells them, "Well, if it gets hard, just go somewhere else." With the extreme mobility that people have today, where most people that are poor are poor out of *choice* (I mean that most of the people involved in this thing are from the middle class), they don't have any background of intense want or deprivation.
>
> . . . I really think that a communal situation will not really exist until there is a situation of necessity. Of course, in this country, we're probably approaching that situation already.[2]

The object of Finstein's recruiting was to locate those who *did* feel that necessity, that is, political radicals so alienated from the system and so convinced that fascism was coming down from all directions that the idea of a survival-oriented retreat into the New Mexico hinterlands seemed strategically sound and appealing. Come the revolution they would be prepared: self-sufficient, mountain fastness at their backs and natural fortifications in front, able to fight back, able to survive in the wastelands and pick up the pieces when it was all over—and in the meantime escape America's cities for a rugged pastoralism that was preferable anyway.

The feeling of necessity that Finstein sought in 1969 was found among those who had been through the campus wars, who were in utter despair that the system could be salvaged, and who believed that Armageddon could not be far off. But along with these somber feelings went the romance of building your own house and growing your own food that motivated the back-to-the-land movement as a whole. The difference at Reality was mainly the quality of political refinement to their cynicism about modern America. A common criticism on the left in those days was that communes were a cop-out from the real struggle in the cities. The Reality Construction Company would therefore be an attempt to fuse, through disciplined work, the apocalyptic critique of the urban radicals with the gentler goals of building back-to-the-land alternatives represented by the hippies.

Nevertheless it was the pacific squatters of Morning Star East, not the radicals, who opened the way onto the mesa where all this could happen. The former was founded in April and Reality in June 1969. In effect the founders of Morning Star East simply appropriated a section of the mesa. Out of the urgency of their need and the righteousness of their cause, they persuaded Duncan to allow them to stay. "A man has to have a home," said one of the founders. "The land belongs to God." Or as Lou Gottlieb put it, "Exclusive ownership of land is original sin." Against these arguments, the manifest presence of the people making them, and the example of his peers, together with his own positive ideals, Duncan's reservations were morally outnumbered. Having gone along with Morning Star East, Duncan went along with Reality, too.

But clearly Duncan did not exactly "liberate" the land as the rumors of the time suggested. According to residents of Morning Star East who were there from the beginning, Duncan originally thought he was just providing a home for a small number of people who would in effect be sharecroppers. For bookkeeping purposes he set up the "Institute for Organic Living" and leased thirty-five acres to Morning Star East and twenty to Reality. The rent of $1,000 a year asked from each, I was told, was "plausible" enough to absolve him of any liability for what the groups did, as a nominal $1-a-year rent might not. At first, it was even plausible that he might collect it.

In any case Duncan did not follow his exemplars Gottlieb and Kline by subsidizing the two new communities beyond making the land available to them. One long-time Morning Star resident remarked to me years later that all Duncan ever gave Morning Star was two wheelbarrows. "But I like Michael," added my informant, "and in all fairness to him he didn't realize that what he was getting into was a strung-out crash pad for hundreds of people."

The first summer was a time of high energy and enthusiastic

building for both groups. It was the classic honeymoon period that all communes seem to go through when the simple urgencies of building shelter against the winter create a sense of collective purpose bordering on euphoria. At Morning Star East some two thousand adobe bricks were made each month that summer, while at Reality some eighty-five tons of earth were reportedly moved in similar construction efforts. Morning Star East's main projects were an adobe quadrangle divided into small rooms and an underground kiva behind that for ceremonies and sleeping quarters for transients. At Reality housing quarters were built with a communal kitchen in the middle and private rooms extending out in angular wings, with workshop and garage wings attached to the rear. In between the two communities, which were separated by perhaps half a mile, were the cooperatively farmed fields and the house of the man in the middle himself, Michael Duncan.

Of the two groups, Reality was decidedly the more industrious. During that first summer, Reality did all the plowing and planting on the mesa and in addition raised a growing population of goats, chickens, pigs, and work animals, including two mules and a horse. Although Morning Star East was influenced by Reality's zeal, they themselves raised no animals or produce that year and were naturally more inclined to let God provide (God manifesting Himself or Herself, as at Drop City, mostly in the form of sympathetic visitors with extra resources). According to reporter Robert Houriet, Reality was also the more conscientious in their use of the mesa's resources, which sometimes led to bad feelings between the groups:

> The original understanding was that Reality and Morning Star would cooperatively farm the land. Last summer [1969], when Morning Star didn't get around to planting its side, Reality appropriated it. Later in the season, Morning Star people began to rip off Reality's corn, and Reality reacted by driving off poachers with rifle fire aimed a few inches above the corn silk. Reality accused Morning Star of wasting water from the common irrigation ditch and of needlessly cutting down the mesa's few piñon trees for firewood. Reality gathered its wood from the national forest to preserve the trees on the mesa for The Revolution. Jasper explained, "When we don't have any gas to get out, that's when we'll need the piñon to stay alive."[3]

Episodes like this miniwar over the corn crop soon brought Reality a reputation as a cadre of wild-eyed guerrillas with blood lust in their hearts. They were even reputed to have shot at a policeman who came poking around on the mesa, and *Newsweek* ran a story that year about Reality's "gun-toting hippies" that curdled the blood of hip and straight alike. Though I later found these rumors to be exaggerated, they were not entirely without substance, at least on the level of bluff and bluster, as former *Look* editor William Hedgepeth found out when he went to see for himself:

> About five miles south of here, and straight up a winding, impossible road, lies a broad mesa ringed with mean, shiny barbed wire. Silhouetted against the sky along the gentle slope of the land, distant figures of boys chop the ground with hoes. This is Reality Construction Company. It's a commune, but it looks more like a prison work farm.
>
> When Dennis Stock and I arrived at Reality we didn't get even as far as the heavy wood-and-barbed-wire gate before the doors of a tiny hut burst open and out boiled two blacks, one wearing a helmet and looking like a dropout from the Biafran army and the other aiming a rifle from hip level and hollering, as he ran toward us, "We don't want it." When they reached the gate, the guntoter took more deliberate aim and said, "Whatever it is, we don't want it." We didn't either. Up along the ridge, the other boys continued their solemn hoeing. None so much as bothered to look up.[4]

In the meantime, Morning Star East carried on the traditions begun three years earlier on the West Coast. The basic tenet of the Morning Star faith was "Open Heart, Open Land," with an abiding belief that "the land selects the people" rather than the other way around. The gates at Morning Star East—in literal fact there were none—were always open, and no one who felt he or she belonged there was made to leave. Philosophically the two communes seemed as far apart as night and day. "Nowhere had I found such diametrically different communes so close together," wrote Robert Houriet. "On the north end was Morning Star: mystics, winos, runaways and hermits. At the south was Reality: Weathermen and outlaws who warned visitors away with rifleshot. The two communes represented the extremes with which the movement had begun. . . . Overall, Morning Star's joy and disorder appealed to me only slightly more than Reality's grim paranoia."[5] But as we shall see, the similarities were ultimately more important than the differences.

II

One such similarity, at least in the first year, was a high degree of flux and turnover in both groups. At Morning Star East, which grew to a population of seventy within six months and within a year had experienced hundreds of temporary residents, this was rather predictable. At Reality it was more of a surprise, but when cold weather came the first winter, the original population of twenty had doubled with transients having no other place to go. According to one Reality member reporting in *The Modern Utopian* in 1970, this growth led to the "establishment of regulatory factors such as—setting and maintaining a stable population of stable individuals—meetings of forty and fifty people around a table built to seat twenty-five comfortably to decide who will have to leave—very unnatural—but necessary."

> We do not play any games of friendliness, unity, one humanity, cosmic cowboy bullshit—we all know that! We inform our brothers of the possibilities available to them elsewhere and encourage them to move on. This we all agree is the right thing to do. . . .
>
> The land we are established on is specifically designated for cultivation and game preservation. There is no room for more dwelling structures. The land has told us it cannot feed more people.[6]

By the time I arrived on the mesa in late July 1970, both groups had experienced a flux of 75 percent or more in their memberships over the previous year. At Morning Star East the only constant was the continued presence of the original fifteen squatters from California in the center of a shifting adult population that then numbered sixty: forty-five men, fifteen women, and ten children. At Reality there were only nine members who had been there twelve months earlier, somewhat less than half of the original members. From a peak population of forty that winter, the membership had dropped by July to a total of twelve: seven men and five women, plus two children. One of the defectors was none other than Max Finstein, Reality's original founder, who had left the previous March after less than a year in residence. Robert Houriet, who was visiting at that time, explained the situation as a collapse of Finstein's belief in Reality as a revolutionary vanguard:

> In one great leap forward, the commune was built. But the revolution didn't come. Moreover, they were rebuffed by local Chicano members of the Alianza Federal de Mercedes, the revolutionary movement intent on reclaiming thousands of acres of federal land in New Mexico, who assert that the land belonged to their ancestors before the Mexican War of 1846–1848. In the face of this, Max decided to split to Israel, where he hoped to find a truly revolutionary movement in the kibbutzim. "American youth are too soft," he later told me at his going-away party. "They're not prepared to make the necessary sacrifices."[7]

Sacrifice   On one point, at least, Finstein was correct about this lack of preparation for sacrifice. Like Morning Star East, Reality practiced no forms of oral or sexual abstinence. There were no proscriptions in either community against the use of meat, alcohol, tobacco, or other drugs. Although Morning Star East had much the greater reputation for drug use, dope smoking was a daily affair at Reality, too. There were marijuana plants growing openly in front of the community pueblo. It was true, though, that the use of harder drugs like speed and peyote was more common at the Morning Star East end of the mesa.

But Finstein was surely incorrect to the extent that sacrifice entailed living in an austere setting with the minimum of conveniences. Both groups had to build their own crude housing, and neither Reality nor Morning Star East had any electricity, gas heating, or reliable water supply (even a well Duncan eventually drilled was not dependable). Wood was a scarce commodity, and its procurement required driving many miles. The winters on the mesa were severe, too. Just getting in and out on the tortuous roads could be a major undertaking. Sanitation was limited to an outhouse at Reality and at Morning Star East was nonexistent. Morning Star had no community kitchen, and food, of which there was seldom enough, was prepared on wood-burning stoves outdoors. Even the use of food stamps was considered by some members of the two groups to be too much of a concession to the society they had left behind. "We should get off those fucking stamps," said one person at Reality, "they just tie us to the system." "Not until I get used to beans for breakfast, for lunch, and for dinner," was the reply. "I go farting around all day as it is."[8] At Morning Star, where hunger and dysentery were a part of everyday life, I recorded the following exchange in my notebook:

> And then another guy comes over. "You making some coffee, man?"
> "Yes. You want some?"
> "Far out." Pause. "Is that a loaf of Roman Meal Bread in there, man?"
> "Yeah. You want some?"
> "Far out." He takes the coffee and the bread.
> "You want some sugar in your coffee?"
> "Is that brown sugar, man?"
> "Yes."
> "Far out. Can I put some on my bread?"
> "On your bread? Sure, if you want." Heaping an enormous quantity of sugar on the bread, he eats, drinks, and departs without another word.

Altogether the conditions of life at both Reality and Morning Star East were the most primitive and harsh of any of the groups in this study. Compared to American society at large, this was sacrifice indeed, Finstein notwithstanding. Only Maharaj Ashram, which practiced abstinence and continence in addition to living in a physically austere setting, had a higher score in this respect.

Investment Another similarity between the two groups was the lack of any financial investment being required to live in either and the irreversibility of any investments that were made. Like almost all communes in which the land was provided by a patron, contributions of money to the group effort were strictly voluntary and hence tended to amount to no more than the minimum necessary to eat and survive, if even that. The one difference between the two groups in this respect was that at Reality, at least, an investment in the form of actual live-in participation was required. Anyone who left was very unlikely to be readmitted. At Morning Star East, though, membership was more like a state of mind. Anyone there was free to leave and return for any length of time whenever he or she wanted.

Renunciation The biggest difference between the two groups, at least in the terms used in this study, was their relative degrees of renunciation of the outside world. This separation had nothing to do with their isolation in terms of geography or communications media, since both were similarly situated physically, and neither paid attention to modern media (being unable to receive them anyway). Nor did they differ in the extent to which their members came and went on forays of one sort or another to the outside, which averaged about once a week in both cases. The difference instead was the gulf separating the two in their respective policies toward outside visitors and prospective new members. At Morning Star East there were no rules whatever on these matters, and in essence there was not even a very clear distinction between "visitors" and "members." Like Drop City, in fact, the group economy at Morning Star East was almost entirely dependent on the bounties of serendipity brought by visitors. Any rules restricting entry would have not only been contrary to the community's philosophy but also seriously damaging to the gross domestic product. Somehow, by a kind of divinely guided magic, whatever was most crucially needed would just appear:

> Everything here happens seemingly by accident, you see, but it's *supposed* to happen that way. . . . Today, two visitors showed up and laid money on us to buy a truck. They said, "God bless you," and split. We're not uptight about visitors. Most of them go away without being told. Some can't hack living out here . . . where there's no corner drugstore. Only those who have a real reason stick.[9]

At Reality, by contrast, there were limits to visitors' numbers (five) and how long they could stay (one day). A certain attitude or purpose justifying their presence was expected, and there was also a requirement that they put in a full day's work to be allowed to stay overnight:

> What more do we need to offer a visiting brother but a good day's work, three good meals and a good night's sleep and that's all! This is a way of life, not a scenic wonderland—a bridge, not the water flowing under it. Visitors are encouraged to find a family for themselves in another state and begin themselves elsewhere. Plainly, frankly, openly and honestly—begin for yourself. It is a sin to step in another's gain.[10]

Exceptions to this rule were made (as in my case), but only under the mercurial sufferance of unanimous consent and only when the visitor displayed an unflagging interest in helping with community labor. In actual fact, few visitors had to be turned away since Reality's fearsome reputation kept most of them—even those who stayed on the same mesa at Morning Star—from ever showing up in the first place. In the summer of 1970, Reality averaged only one or two visitors a week, usually friends of existing members, compared to Morning Star's twenty or more, even though they were only a half mile apart.

Screening new members was likewise a completely different process at the two communes. At Morning Star East it was entirely a process of self-selection. At Reality, on the other hand, it required a sponsor among existing members, a period of probation (one week), some sort of useful skill, a revolutionary outlook, unanimous group consent, and preferably a family situation with children to encourage stability. In addition, Reality had a history of blackballing prospective members and ejecting existing ones. At Morning Star a few might be told by the informal "cops" of the community they weren't cool and weren't wanted, but nobody was ever forced out. It should be added, though, that while Reality had the strictest screening policy of any of the secular or anarchistic groups (sharing this distinction with Libre), it was still not as strict as the policies of the three religious communities in the study.

Communion   Another dimension of commitment in which Reality scored higher than Morning Star East was the homogeneity of its membership. Most members had known each other longer (one to two years on the average) at Reality, and with the departure of Finstein, no member appeared to be more than ten years older than any other. At Morning Star East, as at Reality, most members were around twenty-five, but with the exception of the inner circle of California emigrants, most had not known each other longer than a few weeks. At Morning Star East members ranged in age from sixteen-year-old runaways to dropout professionals over thirty and ex-junkies over fifty. On the other hand, Reality was one of the few communes anywhere in America where young blacks and Chicanos formed any significant portion of the membership along with the usual middle-class whites. The two groups had in common, however, a tendency to attract a number of people at odds with the law for one reason or another. Duncan's mesa was an ideal hideout for fugitives as well as a retreat for the alienated.

Another measure on which Reality scored higher was the degree of communistic labor, particularly on construction and the communal gardens (five acres at Morning Star, seven at Reality). Daily group work efforts were common at both communities, but at Reality communal labor was unequivocally required of all members five or six days a week. At Morning Star there were seldom more than half the members working on any given day, usually the longer-standing and more committed core group from California, with a sprinkling of the more enthusiastic newcomers. At Reality work was of the essence, while at Morning Star there were always many people stretched out in a bored and listless torpor. On one occasion I observed a Morning Star member chiding another for being a "lazy motherfucker" and not working. To which the other replied, "Shit yeah, I'm lazy. . . . I didn't become a hippie so I could do no fuckin' work, man. I *hate* to work." End of encounter.

But on other dimensions of communion, Morning Star scored the higher of the two. One was regularized group contact. At Reality there were no truly communal living quarters, while at Morning Star the setup was mixed. At Morning Star communal dining took place twice or more each day (when there was food) but only once each day at Reality. Even then several members cooked and ate in their private rooms. At Morning Star the members spent the great majority of their day with others, while daily life at Reality was more individualistic and privatized. The only indicator favoring Reality in this respect was a policy of having group business meetings every couple of weeks or so, while at Morning Star there were none, except for informal consultations among the more tenured members.

One dimension of group communion favoring Morning Star was the ritual and ceremonial content of its life, which contrasted with the relative absence of such events at Reality. At Morning Star voluntaristic group religious ceremonies, including peyote meetings in connection with the Native American Church, took place about weekly, and group singing and dancing took place informally several times a month. At Reality ceremonial life was more reminiscent of the "tokay faction" at Lorien, the precursor of LILA, where some members would occasionally get together to drink wine and "drum to the moon." There was usually a similar faction in residence at Morning Star too, of course, but generally drug use and ceremonial practice there was of a more psychedelic and religious nature.

One of the most pronounced communion factors distinguishing the two groups was the much higher incidence at Morning Star of persecution experiences at the hands of outsiders and law enforcement officials. Both groups had experienced unsympathetic visits by local health authorities, though nothing much came of them. The big difference was in visits by the police. At Morning Star the FBI and local police were continually checking for the presence of felons, drug dealers, AWOLs, and runaways—who were often, indeed, there but usually had sufficient warning to hide. But virtually none of this ever happened at Reality. On one occasion when the police did visit Reality, they soon retreated after observing a man semihiding with a gun. Not a shot was fired. Although there were wanted persons at Reality throughout its existence, the police were simply afraid to press their luck against Reality's fierce reputation and strategic advantage of terrain, preferring instead to try to nab their targets if and when they ventured into town. Ironically, for all Reality's paranoia, they were seldom bothered, while at Morning Star, which welcomed even the cops, there were continual attempts to make busts. There appeared to be even more hostility among Taos-area ranchers and Chicanos toward Morning Star than Reality, not so much because they were more criminal but because they were so much more open and better known and hence more notoriously emblematic of all that the local people considered wrong about the "hippie invasion" of Taos.

The roots of this hostility were never more clearly explained to me than by one of Reality's own members, a young Chicano who called himself Indio. His people's reaction to the hippies, he said, was based on their ancestral memory of what had happened in the region one hundred years previously when the first invasion of white men, with beards and long hair then as now, came into the Taos area and bought up much of the choice land. "Every time a white hippie comes in and buys a Chicano's land to escape the fuckin' city," Indio said, "he sends that Chicano *to* the city to go through what he's trying to escape *from,* can you dig it? What can you do with that bread out here, man? Nothing. Then when that money's gone, see, the Chicano has to *stay* in the city, cause now he ain't got no land to come back to. He's stuck, and the hippie's free. That's why they don't dig the fuckin' hippies, man."

Mortification   But the similarities between Reality and Morning Star East were once again apparent in the degree to which they subordinated individual egos to the group; that is, little or not at all. In neither group were there meetings devoted to encounter or mutual criticism among members. Even informally it was uncommon. At Morning Star such matters concerned only the individual and his or her interpretation of God or the Morning Star faith. At Reality they were considered "bullshit" and subsumed under the overweening importance of work. In neither case were personal issues and interpersonal complaints considered to be of very much importance. What there was of it at Morning Star was essentially a matter of personal karma. Those with personal conflicts either spread out or left without involving the group as a whole. At Reality a certain measure of bravado and abrasive behavior was simply accepted as normal and seldom taken seriously. Indeed, it was taken as a sign of weakness to let it get to you, so strong was the emphasis on personal toughness and self-sufficiency.

Still, there was a certain degree of spiritual differentiation in both groups, though in neither case was it embodied in formal structures of deference, initiation, or doctrinal instruction. At Morning Star East there was, despite the daily confusion, an ethic of selfless sharing and spontaneous self-initiated work against which certain members rose to a kind of spiritual prominence, notably those who had been there longest, were older, or assumed more responsibility. At Reality the legacy of Max Finstein lived on in the greater moral authority informally ceded to the hardest workers and in particular to the commune's two black males, whose revolutionary aspirations were considered to be more firmly rooted and authentic. But compared to most other communes in this study, particularly the religious ones, both groups were basically anarchies in which personal mortification was anathema. Spiritual and human-relations values were irrelevant at Reality and too eclectic to have any greater binding force at Morning Star East. Structurally they were much the same, though for different reasons.

Transcendence   Both communities were likewise lacking in any significant degree of institutional development that might have served to deepen member loyalties. In both of them the power of ideology was vague and diffuse. Reality's ideology was one of grim resentment toward straight or "honky" culture and the system giving it form. But it was almost totally lacking in the sophisticated concepts of radical social thinkers and equally lacking in implications for innovative social organization. Morning Star's ideology, on the other hand, was the injunction "Do thy own thing and leave others alone," which chronically undermined the group's potential for social organization beyond individual voluntarism. Coercion was the deadliest sin, as anyone who pulled a power trip at Morning Star was soon told one way or another.

In terms of actual power and authority, the differences were more pronounced. Morning Star East had a mild patriarchal quality about it in that the leaders—more precisely those who initiated action that inspired others to follow—exercised a fair amount of persuasion over others by virtue of their moral example. But the higher morality was never to coerce, and hence there was no true authority hierarchy. The majority of members, who were mostly transient, were only too happy to let the oldtimers make what few decisions there were, like buying a truck, in the best interests of all. Had they any personal investment in the matter, it might have been different, but most did not.

At Reality, on the other hand, the authority structure was more tangible, though still elusive, since authority was just as illegitimate as at Morning Star. Still it was there, partly by virtue of merit and competence and partly by virtue of ethnicity. The organization of work proceeded by skill or by individual initiative, but the organization of emotions and policy at Reality was dominated by its two black males, Chuck and Bill, the men reporter Hedgepeth observed "boiling out" to shoo him away with Reality's .22 rifle (the sum total of its arsenal). Up close they were not so fearsome, but there was no question that they basically spoke for the group and contributed disproportionately to its atmosphere. The ideology of Reality was described to me—not by them—as "Third World Revolution," which neatly summed up the behaviors I observed. It was clear who the exponents of the Third World were, and it was equally clear who was in moral command. Nevertheless Bill and Chuck did not have any other special perquisites that I could determine. The shadow they cast, though, was long.

With other transcendence factors figured in—the fixed work routine, the political ideology, and the new-member screen at Reality— clearly Reality had the stronger commitment structure in this respect. But Reality appeared strong only in comparison to Morning Star. Compared to the other communes in this study, it was only average. Reality was moderately more structured than Morning Star, but not by much. Altogether the two communes were not nearly as far apart as an anecdotal sketch of their beliefs and attitudes might suggest. Contrasting the two shows a tendency for Reality to make more use of internal power structures and rejection of the outside world, where Morning Star East preferred to accentuate the positive by its greater openness and communalism. But in both groups, actual decisions were made by a *de facto* minority; community tasks were voluntary rather than rotated or delegated; the only participation of women was in traditional housekeeping roles; and most important of all, both communities were subject to intervention in their affairs by their mutual benefactor.

III

When I returned to Duncan's mesa in July 1973, I found that both communes had vanished. In their place I observed about one hundred acres of irrigated alfalfa and a new home that Duncan had built for his family. Surrounding the house was a deep ditch, apparently dug to receive the foundation of a large wall. From the depth of the ditch it would be strong and high enough to withstand a military assault, which given my reception as I called hello from outside the moat, was the way the Duncans must have felt by then about uninvited visitors to their estate. After identifying myself to a woman's challenge from inside the house, her answer came back in an angry, tremulous shout. "Go away! I don't want to talk to you! Just get out of here!" As I walked back to my truck, three young children came out of the house and set up a frightening chorus of venom for ones so tiny: "Hey, I'm gonna get my gun and blow your head off"; "Hey, you, come back here and I'll shoot your ass"; and so on, even as I was two hundred yards away and driving back down the arroyo. Whatever the righteousness of their parents' feelings about hippies, sociologists, and journalists, it was devastating to hear them echoing from the mouths of babes. I would rather have faced Reality's rifle.

From other sources in the area, including ex-residents of the mesa, I finally pieced the story together as one of deepening disgust on Duncan's part with the goings-on around him and the appeals continually being made—even though he disclaimed responsibility—for his time, energy, and resources. By 1972 he made it clear he wanted nothing further to do with Reality or Morning Star East and that if they did not leave voluntarily, he would evict them. With the arrival of cold weather that fall, Reality had been abandoned, but when Morning Star members started drifting over and occupying Reality's pueblo as their own, Duncan decided to take the ultimate step. In December 1972 all but a few who desperately pleaded to stay temporarily were evicted. Shortly thereafter Duncan demolished the communal buildings at Reality and Morning Star to erase forever the fixtures of an experiment in patronage that had proved, for him, a bitter mistake. From the beginning, I was told at Morning Star in 1970, Duncan had been "half sympathetic and half pissed off." After almost four years of tolerance all sympathy had finally left him.

The experiences of Morning Star East, like those of Drop City and Wheeler's Ranch, make it abundantly clear that free and open land will always find takers, even under the most primitive imaginable conditions, even in modern America. How to assess such communities depends on one's point of view. It would be easy to see Morning Star East, for instance, as a place where the criminal and cynical preyed on the labors of an idealistic minority, who themselves were parasites dependent on patronage and the largess of impressionable visitors. On the other hand, Morning Star East could be seen as a saintly kind of therapeutic community where ex-junkies could dry out, where the casualties of injustice could hide, where adolescents and fortyish dropouts alike could find freedom from social pressures and oppressive work for the first time in their lives, and where the elemental goodness of it all—despite the poverty, filth, and disease—always seemed to attract contributions from outsiders who apparently felt their own lives to be corrupt by comparison. Such were the contradictions of Morning Star East and the moral agony that plagued Michael Duncan for so long. Had he not kicked them out, they would still be there doing exactly the same things. Small wonder that by the time he did evict them they had become the huge personal threat that I met at the moat.

As for the Reality Construction Company, it was apparently crumbling under its own internal tensions even as Duncan was preparing to boot the residents out. "We're a strange bunch," a prescient member calling himself Jasper Blowsnake told Robert Houriet in 1970. "Most of us are outlaws. But the whole West was settled by outlaws. We're strong individuals. . . . But we don't feel as angry as when we first came up here. . . . And the less political we get, the more our anger gets turned against one another."[11] According to my informants, Reality became ever more intense as time went on, and by "intensity" they meant ethnic and racial conflict. Sometime in 1971 or early 1972, young Indio brought in two of his *amigos,* giving Reality a total of at least five militant "Third-World revolutionaries" in an atmosphere of increasing domination over the group's whites. "The liberals," I was told, "your Berkeley campus politico types, split pretty soon after that." The last to leave were the two blacks, Chuck and Bill.

In retrospect it was all rather like a parable of the failure of radical politics over that period to cross the barriers of class background and cultural heritage and fuse them together into some kind of common aim for the future. Like most of the small number of blacks who found their way into the commune movement of the late 1960s, Bill and Chuck had been to college, and both had been artists at one time, giving them considerable experience in living among *simpático* young whites. They had known each other for a long time. When they were united, which was usually the case, there was no comparable force among Reality's "white liberals" to countermand them. At times their disdain was obvious, as when a sycophantic white newcomer told Chuck, "I'm really glad you let me into Reality," and Chuck replied with a sneer. On another occasion, when a young white named Dave was leading a timber-cutting expedition by virtue of his sheer competence at the task and knowledge of the tools, Bill and Chuck had an irrepressible desire to tease him continually and spoof his skills, not to interfere with his functioning, but sufficiently to retain moral command of the group.

On the other hand, their joking and jiving was almost the sum total of the spirit that this otherwise sober and serious group had going for it. Chuck and Bill seemed unable to decide completely whether to lead their companions or just toy with them. White deference brought black scorn, but somehow Chuck and Bill could not surrender the status they so obviously enjoyed and let it be otherwise—and the whites weren't going to tell them differently. It was a curious vicious circle of communal segregation that was probably never resolved.

At the heart of the problem, though, were different objectives. For the whites the experience was not exactly a lark, but they obviously had other options should their experience at Reality fall through. Thus there was a special irony in Jasper Blowsnake's remark in his letter to *The Modern Utopian* that "It is a sin to step in another's gain," which is precisely what Reality itself was doing to Michael Duncan. Underlying the white mentality at Reality was a sense of guilt about their privileged backgrounds that they buried in compulsive work and in their deference to Chuck and Bill. For Bill and Chuck, on the other hand—who vilified Morning Star's hippies and expressed respect only for Lama among all other Taos-area communes "because at least they're *doing* something"—what was being attempted at Reality was serious business. Compared to the whites, who were downwardly mobile by choice, it was no surprise that they were the last to give up. Chuck was the only person I met in all my travels who talked of a commune as a "chance to get ahead."

Of all the communes that had once blossomed around Arroyo Hondo from 1967 to 1972—altogether at least a dozen within as many miles—only Lama and New Buffalo were still surviving in 1973. Lama we have already discussed. An excellent account of New Buffalo's first three years can be found in Houriet's *Getting Back Together,* and though he only takes the story up to 1970, nothing but the faces ever really changed thereafter. One of its members in 1973 told me that the reason New Buffalo had survived was that it sought a middle ground between the "intensity" of Reality and the "looseness" of Morning Star East. Houriet's book echoes this sentiment, but in retrospect it is probably not true. For most of its history, New Buffalo has been just as loosely organized as Morning Star, and I can testify from personal experience that it was no less intense than Reality, at least in 1970. It was the only commune I ever felt forced to leave for fear of my safety, after a night spent in a sweat-filled sleeping bag while one of several psychopathic personalities in residence at the time walked around in the dark randomly shooting a rifle at targets unknown, some not very far from my head.

The secret of New Buffalo's success was instead that Rick Kline's money had been used to secure the land free and clear of debt from the first. In the years that followed, New Buffalo was a revolving door like most Taos communes, but unlike most, it had free land from the beginning. Like Reality, New Buffalo evolved a culture of hard work, but it has yet to rise above poverty on its own efforts. And like Morning Star, it could never firmly close the gate. Either of these factors would have doomed, and did doom, most of the other communes in the area. But unlike Reality and Morning Star East, New Buffalo's subsidy could not be retracted.

Notes

1. Louis Gottlieb et al., "Open Land: A Manifesto" (Bodega Bay, Calif.: Wheeler Ranch Defense Fund, 1970), p. 5.

2. Quoted in Richard Fairfield, *Communes U.S.A.: A Personal Tour* (Baltimore: Penguin Books, 1972), pp. 195–197.

3. Robert Houriet, *Getting Back Together* (New York: Avon Books, 1972), pp. 197–198.

4. William Hedgepeth and Dennis Stock, *The Alternative* (New York: Collier Books, 1970), p. 80.

5. Houriet, *Getting Back Together*, pp. 197, 199.

6. Jasper Blowsnake [pseud.], "Reality Construction Co.," *The Modern Utopian*, 4 (Summer–Fall 1970), 15.

7. Houriet, *Getting Back Together*, p. 196.

8. Ibid.

9. Ibid., p. 199.

10. Blowsnake, "Reality Construction Co."

11. Houriet, *Getting Back Together*, p. 197.

8

God and Woman: Maharaj Ashram

I

The founding of Maharaj Ashram in 1969 was the result of a very singular meeting between East and West at the Summer Solstice Festival that year in Santa Fe, New Mexico. Earlier that spring a young dropout construction worker named Dawson, then working in Santa Fe, purchased twelve acres a few miles south of town with the intention of starting a commune. Exactly what kind of commune was unclear, and seeking an oracle, Dawson consulted the *I Ching*. The hexagram Dawson threw told him to "prepare to meet your master." Having no particular idea of what was coming, Dawson, nonetheless, prepared himself by fasting for four days and then attended the solstice affair, where various spiritual teachers were scheduled to appear as part of the celebration. With this much preparation and receptivity, it may have been inevitable that Dawson *would* meet his master as the *I Ching* foretold. In any case he did. When Dawson first saw Yogi Bhajan, he later told me, he knew immediately that this was the man.

Siri Singh Sahib Yogi Bhajan had come from India just a few months earlier on a "mission to Canada and the United States to teach the secrets of the ancient and evolved science of yoga to all capable of receiving them," and in particular "to cleanse people of their negativity and to train teachers."[1] According to one of the yogi's printed handouts:

> He brings with him twenty-two years of study and devotion to the search for truth. His knowledge of the esoteric wisdom of India, his

humility and power as a yogi, and his worldly experience eminently fit him as a teacher for the West. He bears on his person and in his action the markings of a Master. In recent years he became the leading disciple of Swami Dhrindraji who, as head of the Vishwayatan Yoga Ashram, is considered to be India's Raj Rishi. Among the latter's students were Prime Minister Indira Gandhi and the late Pundit Jawaharlal Nehru.[2]

As the "Singh" in his full title indicates, Yogi Bhajan is a Sikh, born and raised in that energetic and relatively prosperous group in Indian society which is centered in the Punjab and better known in the West as "the Indians who wear turbans" (and in pure forms the five "kakas" of uncut hair, underwear, curved sword, bracelet, and comb). Sikhism dates from the early sixteenth century as a blend of the Hindu tradition of Bhakti devotionalism and Sufi mysticism as embodied in its founder, Guru Nanak, and the collected teachings of Sikhism known as the *Adi Granth*. The original Sikhs, one of many such groups in India at the time, rejected the caste system and the concept of temples in favor of direct devotional communion with God. In response to the persecution and chaos of the sixteenth century, the Sikhs became a highly militarized warrior society at the same time that they sought to sustain the devotional life. Over the centuries their original quietist communities evolved through political turmoil into an ethnic group which made a living as merchants, travelers, and in the modern era, parts suppliers and taxi drivers. They number about 7 million in India today. Somewhat like the Jews of the West, they have developed a reputation for business acumen in peacetime, ferocity in war, and a pragmatic leaning to worldliness in between. For missionary and entrepreneur alike, America in the late 1960s was a new frontier for Eastern ideas.[3]

After leaving India in 1968, Yogi Bhajan first traveled to Canada, where he established followings in Ottawa, Toronto, and Vancouver. He then went to Los Angeles, where he founded what he called "3HO," which stood for "Healthy-Happy-Holy Organization," symbolized by a triangle enclosed in a circle. On February 8, 1969, he released this statement from his Los Angeles headquarters to the teachers he was training and other prospective converts:

> After meditating at the Lotus Feet of my Master, who has granted me liberation from the time cycle and the cycle of Karma, oh my sweet student teacher of the day, I disclose to you the secret of the Nam. If you care to listen to me this day and will practice you will be liberated like me.
>
> I have seen the God. It is a light equal to millions and billions of rays of sunlight. It is the cosmic energy which is the brightest of the bright-

est and most beautiful of the beautiful. Nothing beyond this can be said. It is the greatest of the great. When the Master, through his blessing blesses you, you will realize this within you. . . .

Thus the Master meditated and became one with the Lord and gave the Mantra EK ONG KAR SAT NAM SIRI WHA GURU, which has eight vibrations and describes the Glory of the Lord. Thus said the Master, "In the Time period two and a half hours before the rising of the Sun when the channels are most clear, if the Mantra is sung in sweet harmony you will be one with the Lord. . . ."

All Mantras are good, they are all for the awakening of the Divine but this Mantra is effective and is the Mantra for this time, so my lovely student, at the will of my Master I teach you the greatest Divine Key which has eight levers and this key can open the lock of the time which is eight in figure (wheel over wheel). Therefore, when this Mantra is sung in the neck lock, at the point where Prana and Apana meet Sushumana, this vibration opens the lock and thus one becomes one with the Divine.[4]

Along with this mantra, Yogi Bhajan offered training in kundalini yoga, one of several yogic paths or schools which deals in particular with "energy channeled from the base of the spine; aroused like a serpent by various yoga exercises to light the chakra lamps of consciousness."[5] "He is a spiritual revolutionary," stated one of his handouts, "aware that the science of yoga has been abstracted and polluted in the Western world and he has come to teach correct methods of physical and mental conditioning which will allow students to experience a real contact with the Divine Forces within." Just as his mantra was implied to be the most effective, so too was his yoga presented as encompassing competing yogas:

The Kundalini Yoga which Yogi Bhajan teaches incorporates the disciplines of Hatha, Laya, Bhakti and Raja Yogas. *Kundalini Yoga is the Yoga of Awareness.* It brings Control of the Senses and Awareness of the Consciousness of an individual so that he may be Aware of the causes leading to effects and he will be able, through conscious control, not to cause that cause which will have a negative effect. . . .

To put this in modern terms, it may be said that the individual is in automatic control of awareness regarding his projected personalities, and therefore he can withdraw all causes which could lead to unhappiness or which could make him subject to his lower nature and the subsequent downgrading of his spiritual personality.

Thus a native can reach a higher consciousness for which the tuning up of the physical apparatus is required. The Kundalini Yoga technique utilized involves uncoiling the coiled energy under the navel point, raising it through the spinal column and injecting this energy into the pineal gland, which has been described as "the seat of the soul."[6]

As a "spiritual revolutionary" against the abstractions and pollutions of the Western world, Yogi Bhajan was fully aware of the idioms and problems of life in modern America, particularly among the young. A key point in his approach, which gave him heightened legitimacy in the eyes of both hip and straight, was his challenge to drug use with the promise of something better and healthier. "This ancient wisdom," continued his flyer, "is particularly attractive to the young people of America because it is simple and practical. It results in withdrawing them from the temporary states achieved through drugs which ultimately would take them toward weakness and insanity. It provides them with valid spiritual experiences of a permanent, positive nature."[7]

To those on the outer fringes of attraction to his message, Yogi Bhajan may have appeared as just another guru offering enlightenment the easy way. Those who came closer discovered that it was not in fact so easy. "The effort and the sincerity necessary to purify the self must be offered by the student in order to bring a new age of enlightenment into being."[8] Those coming in still closer discovered that sustaining "valid spiritual experiences of a permanent, positive nature" involved joining or establishing new ashram communities under the yogi's overall direction, which in turn were to be connected together through the corporate umbrella of the 3HO. The yogi's basic approach to organization building was to find dedicated and competent lieutenants at different locales who would create or lead these communities; hence his early emphasis on training teachers. These teachers would in turn lead the activities of the local ashrams under general guidance from above as official delegates of the yogi's charisma and authority.

By the time he arrived in New Mexico in June 1969, Yogi Bhajan had established "3HO North" in the San Francisco area as well as his headquarters in Los Angeles. What then became Maharaj Ashram, or "3HO South," was born of the yogi's encounter with Dawson that month in Santa Fe. Soon after meeting the yogi, Dawson offered his twelve acres to his new guru as an ashram site and immediately underwent an intensive two-week training session preparing him to lead it. Under the direction of Dawson, an able young man in his late twenties with a charisma of his own, Maharaj became the third key link in the yogi's new chain of communities in the United States.

II

At the founding of Maharaj there were just two members, Dawson and his wife. That summer, though, the new community attracted several dozen prospective members. At one point the population reached a total of fifty. Entering the ashram was easy, requiring only a $2-a-day fee as a share of the general expenses. But as many prospects soon found out, to stay required firm acceptance of the ashram life, a regimen which began at 3 A.M. each morning and continued with strict organization throughout most of the day. Some had just drifted away, but a number had been expelled by Dawson for "insufficient adherence to discipline," as he told me later. Over the 1969–1970 winter, some six months after the community's founding, the population of Maharaj had dropped back to only four members. By the summer of 1970, it had grown slowly back to thirteen: eight men and five women; there were no children. At first it was not easy for Dawson to kick people out—it never was in any commune—but to hold the ashram in focus, he knew it was necessary. With his sense of responsibility tinged with a sense of humor, he soon came to terms with himself as the community's "benevolent despot."

Maharaj Ashram was located about seven miles south of Santa Fe and a further half mile or so down a dirt road into the area's gently rolling, arid hills. When I arrived in August 1970 (on the condition that I would "get behind the discipline"), Maharaj consisted of a trailer home serving as office and living quarters for Dawson and his wife, a large wall tent serving as a gathering place for ceremonies and yoga instruction, and a number of smaller tents variously shared by the other members. There were no permanent structures on the land and no immediate plans to build any except a water storage system then under construction. Most of the ashram's work time was instead directed toward opening a natural foods restaurant in Santa Fe, by which the community hoped to become financially self-supporting. The restaurant opened some months later under the name of "Nanak's Conscious Cookery," in honor of the first guru of Sikhism. But even though construction at Maharaj seemed of secondary importance, Dawson considered the ashram there to stay. Its twelve acres had been blessed by many holy men and could never be sold or used for any other purpose. "This is sacred ground," Dawson said. "Many strange things have happened here."

One strange thing, at least to me, was the extent of the yogi's influence over the members, who ranged in age from fifteen to twenty-five. Most were college dropouts. In talks with various members I was told that the yogi knew everything that was happening, that he could read a person at a glance, and that he had "engaged" several of his disciples to other followers as future husbands and wives, including Michaelin, who at fifteen was Maharaj's youngest member. I was also told that the yogi had taken forty thousand people off drugs (in what would have then been one and a half years). To the membership at large, both Yogi Bhajan and Dawson were considered egoless, "pure channels of God's will." The ashramers therefore accepted their directives without question, in complete trust. With Dawson this most often meant the assignment of chores and control over daily affairs. For the yogi the time frame could be as large as a marriage. For what it is worth, the members of Maharaj seemed relaxed and happy. To them the peace of the discipline obviously was preferable to whatever had gone before, such as alienated schooling, unhappy, middle-class families, or downward spirals of drug use and sloppy, directionless living. Although I never met the yogi, it was easy enough to understand their deference to Dawson, who looked like a blond Jesus, moved with the grace of a dancer, and whose authoritative presence was softened in individual relationships by a quiet voice and a distinct twinkling around the eyes.

A typical day at Maharaj began at 3 A.M. with the tinkle of small bells. After brief ablutions, the membership gathered in the large wall tent for yoga exercises. Following these the community chanted for a period of about thirty minutes with deep breathing and expulsions of breath in a vigorous "hah-hah-hah-hah-hah." Then came readings and meditation. All these ceremonies were led by Dawson, who in turn followed the belief of Yogi Bhajan (and many other Eastern spiritual teachers, including Chinese Buddhists) that the best time to connect with divine forces is very early in the morning. Anyone who lives in large American cities would probably agree.

After the morning services, a vegetarian breakfast was served. On a summer day work began about 7 A.M. and generally continued until noon or early afternoon. While I was there, the men spent their time working on putting the restaurant in Santa Fe into shape while the women remained at the ashram with conventional domestic chores. There was no lunch, or only a light one, since partial fasts were thought to be purifying. Depending on the course of the work, the members usually had free time in the afternoons until dinner at 4:30, which was again vegetarian, usually some combination of rice, nuts, and vegetables. After dinner came more free time or chores, depending on Dawson's assignments. At 7 P.M. classes were held to expand the members' (and visitors') knowledge of yoga techniques and concepts.

A typical evening class might begin with a series of exercises lifting the arms and legs while prone on the back—first the left and right of each, then the right and left, and then parallel—together with deep breathing and intervals for relaxation. The leader, in this case a twenty-one-year-old woman named Krishna, then showed us how to arch our stomachs upward from the back position and form a "cosmic bridge of energy." We were instructed to direct healing energy to areas of our bodies that pained us and to deep-breathe out the poisons: "Inhale *sat*, exhale *nam;* inhale truth, exhale lies; inhale love, exhale joy." "God is vibration," Yogi Bhajan had said. "The Divinity in you is in the control of the breath." Throughout the presentation, though, were the metaphors of the electronic age. Our forebrains were to be "channels" for God's will, our hair "antennae" for the divine energy. We were to make our very bodies into arcs for the current to flow, empty but for pure white light.

After these exercises might come a period of guided, sequential relaxation: first the toes, then the heels, calfs, knees, and eventually the internal organs—intestines, spleen, stomach, diaphragm, even the pancreas—and on up the body to the very tips of our "energy antennae." Then into the "easy" pose of the lotus position, chanting a simple mantra and trying to become "pyramids of pure light." Depending on one's subjective readiness for these experiences, they are entirely real if one allows them to be real, if one is willing to enter the realm of magic, hypnosis, and metaprograming of the self. I view it as entirely an inadequacy on my part that I was not able to complete the concluding exercise, which was to leave our bodies and float around the tent.

Sacrifice In its overall use of structural commitment mechanisms, Maharaj was the second most tightly organized group in the study, only slightly behind the Lama Foundation. It ranked a great deal higher than Lama, though, and higher than any other commune in the study, in its degree of sacrifice expected of members. Along with the predictable prohibitions against smoking, meat, drinking, and doping, Maharaj also expected sexual continence of its members. The guidelines were once a month for unmarried members, and twice a month for married ones (all but Dawson and his wife were then single). I was told, however, that this did not represent antisexuality, but rather that sex became something much more meaningful and holy if savored only occasionally. In Eastern mysticism, sexual and psychic energy are usually thought to come from the same source, and it is commonly believed that the former is best stored in service of the latter. At Maharaj the compromise tended to favor legal marriage.

Maharaj's living conditions also demanded a high degree of sacrifice of its members. The winters were not as severe there as in the mountains at Lama, but neither were the shelters as substantial. Maharaj had no electricity, only a gas-powered well pump for water with no pipes or storage, no heat but bottled gas for the kitchen, and no food stamps.

Investment Maharaj's investment requirements, though, were more typical of the average commune elsewhere. No fee or property turnover was required for admission, nor was there any requirement that a member provide his or her own shelter. The only financial requirement was payment of $2 a day or $60 a month to meet daily expenses. On the other hand, nonresident members were not allowed, and communal labor was required. Although community records were kept of contributions of money and property, it was understood that none would be returned to those leaving the group.

Renunciation   In its degree of renunciation of the outside world, Maharaj was somewhat but not much above average for other communes. It was not very isolated geographically, being only seven miles from town and perhaps only a hundred yards from its nearest neighbor in a terrain not very conducive to privacy. Its insulation from modern media was complete, though, except for a telephone. In terms of comings and goings over the boundaries of the community, Maharaj combined easy exit policies with making the group hard to enter. With work on the Santa Fe restaurant, most members went into town every day, as they were free to do anyway during their afternoons off. But visitors were screened for their attitude and their willingness to respect the discipline. They were charged a fee and were required to have the personal okay of Dawson. For new member prospects there were even more requirements, including a probationary period of two weeks to a month, various texts to study, evidence of sincere belief in Yogi Bhajan's teachings, and a formal agreement to adhere to the discipline. Most importantly, they had to secure the approval of Dawson, who had turned away new members or expelled existing ones several times in the past.

Communion   On the many variables indicating the level of communion, Maharaj was again about average overall. Most members had not known each other six months previously, and the community was not particularly homogeneous apart from the common orientation to Yogi Bhajan. In communistic sharing Maharaj followed the usual pattern of communal ownership of land, dwellings, and certain tools and equipment but not personal property. Maharaj shared more than some communes by requiring an equal apportionment of operating expenses, but less so than others in the absence of any communal garden or livestock. In addition, the land title remained in Dawson's name as an individual, though he said he intended to make Maharaj a nonprofit corporation soon.

Roughly thirty hours of communal work were required weekly of each member, usually apportioned by experience and voluntary preference, although Dawson made assignments where necessary to fill gaps. Under this system, women and men workers generally gravitated toward a traditional division of labor without the need for direct assignments. Regularized group contact was fairly high, due to the partial use of shared dwellings, communal dining twice daily, the structured daily routine, and the rather small spatial setting. Attendance at both morning and evening ceremonies was required. But there were no regular meetings concerning the conduct of community business. These matters were Dawson's province, and he was not obliged to defend his decisions or share them with others, although he did hold irregular meetings about every two weeks to deal with complaints. The ritual content of Maharaj's daily life, of course, was intense and added much to the group's degree of communion. On the other hand, there was no negative input into the group's communal identity. They had experienced no forms of harassment and felt that any bad feelings about them locally were either trivial or nonexistent.

Mortification Apart from the biweekly meeting where Dawson adjudicated complaints among the members, there were no other forms of mutual criticism among the members. As at Lama, such behavior was considered bad form and unbecoming of someone pursuing the spiritual path. Still, Maharaj scored high on mortification mechanisms because of the clear lines of spiritual differentiation observed between members, particularly with respect to Dawson but to a lesser extent between older, more evolved or practiced members and newer ones.

Transcendence The greatest departure of Maharaj from the average of the other groups was its unusually high use of transcendence mechanisms, in which it scored highest in the sample and indeed made the highest possible score. Ideologically, Maharaj was based on a complete and detailed philosophical system related specifically to Yogi Bhajan's teachings. In addition, magical powers were imputed both to the community and to certain members, and remaining in the community meant respect for and acceptance of these phenomena as valid realities. Maharaj likewise employed a full range of overbearing power and authority relationships, including a sacred authority hierarchy topped by a single person, special prerogatives and a special residence for him, and no provisions for replacing him from below or advancing upward in community responsibility or initiative without his approval. Maharaj also used rigorous tests for ideological conversion and a high degree of social programing and was linked with a long religious tradition which justified these various codes of behavior. On all the measures of political equality used in this study Maharaj registered a complete zero, and the community easily ranked as the least anarchical group of them all.

In summary, Maharaj was most unusual for its intense levels of sacrifice and transcendence. Given Maharaj's level of population flux over the previous year, which was as high as Drop City's (and that is as high as it went), one might suspect that these were not easy adjustments to make, despite the legitimacy of shared religious beliefs. Once made, of course, Maharaj could become a smoothly oiled social organism comparatively free of the conflicts experienced at most communes, where institutional programing was almost nonexistent and everything was open to question. The problem with Maharaj's organizational arrangement was not its lack of democracy, for such communities would not exist were not their people happy to be led, but instead with the special importance of leadership, and therefore the special burdens of responsibility confronting those who lead.

III

For Dawson these burdens proved to be too much. In the fall of 1971, Maharaj was dismantled, the "sacred land" was sold, and Dawson and his wife left the 3HO organization. The restaurant and most Maharaj members, however, remained in the fold. A new ashram was founded north of Santa Fe near the town of Espanola, and at least six former Maharaj members were there in 1973. A new teacher was brought in by Yogi Bhajan to lead the new ashram and to direct Nanak's Conscious Cookery, which continued in operation in Santa Fe at a new and bigger location. Despite the defection of Maharaj's leader, then, most members were sufficiently committed to Yogi Bhajan and 3HO to simply transfer their loyalties to a new teacher and location and continue as before.

Exactly why Dawson left remains something of a mystery. According to those who stayed within the organization, the reason was his wife, who was put through "heavy changes" by the discipline and "freaked out" in opposition to it. It is said that other members of 3HO around the country, who were very fond of Dawson, wrote hundreds of letters to him encouraging him not to be swayed and to stay on, but that his wife intercepted these letters and tore them up. Thus, unaware of this support (which 3HO members assume would have made a crucial difference in his thinking), Dawson opted for continuing his marriage rather than his ashram. Another version of the story holds that Yogi Bhajan was consciously testing Dawson's capacity for leadership and commitment under stress and that he failed to live up to expectations.

In either case, Dawson was portrayed as very hesitant to leave 3HO and is said to have parted with it on good terms. Needless to say, these stories are transmitted within a powerful continuing belief system and avoid any implication that Dawson's defection represented negativity toward the organization or Yogi Bhajan. Personally I accept this with little suspicion. As one of Dawson's fellow teachers told me later, "The Sikh *dharma* is the hardest discipline there is because it requires you to stay in the world as a householder, to be in the Maya [illusion] but still radiate God-consciousness with all your being every day all day."

But more interesting than Dawson's defection itself was his substitutability as a leader and the ready transfer of his followers to another entity within the 3HO network. What Maharaj Ashram represented, then, was not so much a community as a way of life defined by new institutional identities rather than specific locations or particular group leaders. Although Yogi Bhajan initially presented himself only as a mystic and yoga master, what he actually brought to America could be more accurately described as the culture of Sikhism. In 1970 the members of Maharaj retained their English names and did not wear turbans or the other symbols of Sikh identity, but by 1973, as a perusal of 3HO's magazine *Beads of Truth* makes clear, the movement traced its lineage to Guru Nanak and Guru Govind Singh, the first and last gurus of Sikhism, and had by then adopted the Sikh costume, saints, ceremonies, texts, and life-style virtually in their entirety. Most devotees had also taken new Sikh names:

> Never before in the history of America have there been so many "Singhs" and "Kaurs" . . . and we are experiencing the psychological and emotional changes that new names stimulate . . . not only in ourselves, but in others. A new name helps us to forget the past and all of its unpleasant associations, and enables us to really feel like "new" people, who *can* respond to life's challenges on a new basis. With a new name we are no longer limited and forced to counteract the vibrations of preconceived ideas about us in other people's minds which are always summoned up by the repetition of the old name. A new name is a new birth.[9]

It is important to note, though, that traditional Sikhism in general has no necessary relationship to either kundalini yoga or living in monastic communities. By some accounts the teachings of Guru Nanak actually prohibit yoga of any kind. By 3HO's interpretation it has always been a small, secret, but powerful tradition within Sikhism, so powerful in fact that it is extremely dangerous, and hence anyone teaching it publicly would die within a year. The legend within 3HO today is that Yogi Bhajan himself became gravely ill in 1969 for daring to be an iconoclast (iconoclasm itself being a Sikh tradition) and was saved only by the great outpouring of prayers from his students. Yogi

Bhajan's yoga and Sikhism were thus knit together with the imprint of his own personal charisma. In 3HO, kundalini yoga practice became an ideal way of learning to distribute one's energy in the enactment of a godlike life, and Sikh *dharma* became an ideal way of "channeling *kundalini*."

Likewise, living in ashrams under autocratic discipline was an important but quite limited tradition within Sikhism which Yogi Bhajan reinterpreted as the central feature of his teachings for America and the backbone of the social movement he inspired here. Yogi Bhajan teaches that the route to God-consciousness is first through individual consciousness and then through group consciousness. In the idiom of one of his student teachers, "There's no way to talk to God if you can't talk to your brother." In this and many other ways, Yogi Bhajan correctly read the pulse of the time in America and put it together with the requirements for organization building. In 1975 there were said to be over a hundred 3HO ashrams in America with up to one hundred members each and an additional estimated 200,000 lay followers doing their *sadhana* on the fringes of these groups.

Taken together these people represent a modern American version of the Khalsa, or "Brotherhood of the Pure Ones," which dates from the death in 1609 of the tenth guru of Sikhism, Govind Singh, who declared that the texts were written, that the guruship was ended, and that the faithful would henceforth be guided by the brotherhood. At this point in their history the Sikhs were a warrior society embroiled in wars of persecution and retribution, and the old reputation for holy soldiery lingers on today in the gentle words Yogi Bhajan spoke to the Khalsa initiation in 1973:

> Under all environments, the life of the Khalsa is the life of a soldier and a saint together, blended in one way of life. Sometimes, in this country especially, we do not understand the significance of a saint, neither do we understand the significance of a soldier. My feeling was, and other things may have given you the idea that a soldier is one who kills. Well, if a soldier is one who kills, then you are the soldiers who are going to kill all the negativity and should live righteously in the light of God-consciousness to proceed on your path.[10]

Quoting further from the initiation ceremony:

> And you are entering into a brotherhood, so serve each other, love each other, stand for each other. . . . It is a question of one family, where Guru is your Guru, God is your God and we are all One in that oneness. . . . We definitely have to keep our holy relationship within our family so that the purity of this creed may go unto our children. And

you have to avoid people who live negatively, have negative means to
live, and have negative desires to achieve. Basically, you have come
into a life of purity.[11]

For Dawson the struggle came down to his identity in the
brotherhood versus the existence of his marriage. For the other members it just meant finding other places within an organization that was
expanding coast to coast. The fate of Maharaj thus shows the vulnerability of religious communities whose destinies follow the destiny of
single leaders, but it also shows the flexibility of such communities
when they are organized within a larger belief system and a network
linking different groups of believers together as a supracommunity.
Maharaj may have failed but 3HO did not, for by the time Dawson
pulled out he was but one of many lieutenants in a sophisticated
corporate structure.

The invisible but key person in this drama of leadership, God-
consciousness, and brotherhood was, of course, Dawson's wife. Perhaps it was partly because of her that the "Grace of God Movement
of the Women of America" was organized within 3HO in response to
the challenges of modern women's liberation, which had criticized the
inferior status of women in movements like Yogi Bhajan's. "Our aim
and our ideal," said a spokesperson for the Grace of God Movement,
"is to restore woman to her rightful status . . . where woman will
once again be known as the living goddess and put back on her
pedestal in the hearts of all men and all mankind the world over."[12]

For Dawson's wife the role of pampered menial, even if ceremonially romanticized as goddess, must have arrived either too late or
with too little substance. For Dawson the experience must have
meant discovering his personal limitations within the sacred charge he
held to be husband, disciple, teacher, God-conscious despot, and
business executive all at once. Together they moved to Denver and
opened a health-food restaurant. In the midst of all the exotica theirs
was somehow a very American story.

Notes

1. "Yogi Bhajan, Master of Kundalini Yoga" (Los Angeles: Healthy-Happy-
Holy Organization, 1970). Flyer.
2. Ibid.
3. See Khushwant Singh, *The History of the Sikhs*, 2 vols. (Princeton, N.J.:
Princeton University Press, 1963 and 1966), for a good general introduction to Sikhism.
4. Untitled flyer published in "Los Angeles, California, February 8, 1969, 8
A.M."

5. "Cookbook for a Sacred Life," in Baba Ram Dass et al., *Be Here Now* (San Cristobal, N.Mex.: The Lama Foundation, 1971), p. 118.

6. "Yogi Bhajan, Master of Kundalini Yoga."

7. Ibid.

8. Ibid.

9. Shakti Parwha Kaur, "What's in a Name?" *Beads of Truth,* #18 (Los Angeles: 3HO Publications, 1973).

10. "Drinking the Amrit (Nectar of God)," *Beads of Truth,* #18 (Los Angeles: 3HO Publications, 1973), pp. 43–44.

11. Ibid., p. 45.

12. Krishna Kaur Jenson (Pink Krishna), "Shakti Yagna: The Celebration and Preservation of Women's Purity and Innocence," *Beads of Truth,* #18 (Los Angeles: 3HO Publications, 1973), pp. 24–25.

9

The War of Sonoma County:
Wheeler Ranch

I

Rural Sonoma County, California, is a picturesque ranching, tourist, and retirement community about an hour's drive over the Golden Gate Bridge from San Francisco. Geographically, it is just a short hop from the birthplace of the hippie, the bay city's Haight-Ashbury district. Philosophically and politically, it is more like a giant step to the moon. Staid, prosperous, and thoroughly middle class, Sonoma County was the scene of one of the most intense confrontations between hip and straight to occur anywhere in rural America during the communal era of the 1960s and 1970s.

The story began in 1962 when Dr. Louis Gottlieb, musicologist, composer, and bass player of the Limelighters, a folk group then coming off the peak of its success, bought a 31.7-acre farm near the little Sonoma County village of Occidental. At first his idea was to use it as a vacation home for himself and possibly as a site for a real estate development. But over the next four years, the old jive-talking hustler in Gottlieb gave way to a new interest in LSD, Indian mysticism, and cooperative living. Inspired by his friend Ramon Sender—another musician, dropped out son of a Berkeley professor, and an early associate of Ken Kesey's "Merry Pranksters"—Gottlieb decided in 1966 to convert his acres to a commune called Morning Star, to which anyone could come and stay as long as he or she liked.

As its name implied, Morning Star was devoted to a new vision of humanity: gentle, noncompetitive, spontaneous, loving, and free. It was to be governed by only one (somewhat ungrammatical) law:

"Land access to which is denied no one." The assumption was that with no rules and no organization and with the selection of the people who belonged there left to the land, a new kind of human society would emerge where people lived in harmony with each other and with the earth, without the conflicts, tensions, and pollution endemic to American culture. Sender dubbed this new life-style "voluntary primitivism," and the key to bringing it about was creating sanctuaries of "open land." Morning Star, in Gottlieb's words, would be an experiment in a "community style of life suited to the needs of a society in which cybernation will have rendered leisure compulsory."[1] It was the hippies, Gottlieb felt, who were instinctively pioneering these new evolutionary concepts.

In the first year of its existence, Morning Star's population was small, hovering between fifteen and twenty. Inconspicuous though it was at first, an inexorable chain of events began to unfold on two fronts. One was Morning Star's connections with the Diggers and related hip service groups in San Francisco, where the word passed along the grapevine that Gottlieb's land was open to all comers. The other was a rising tide of complaints from Morning Star's neighbors about the nudity visible from the road or the homes next door—for Gottlieb's land was scarcely isolated even if rural—and about the sex and drug orgies thought to take place there.

These two trends converged in 1967, on the eve of the death of hippie in Haight-Ashbury, when Morning Star began to be inundated by a flood of homeless flower children, weekend dropouts, wine-guzzling wastrels, motorcycle toughs, and diffident ghetto blacks. Simultaneously, Morning Star began to be visited by health and sanitation officials, building inspectors, police officers, fire safety authorities, and an appalled sociologist named Lewis Yablonsky, who wrote a chapter in his book *The Hippie Trip* called "The Morningstar Bummer."[2] To the good citizens of Sonoma County, it was a veritable invasion of degenerates. To Morning Star, what had begun as a yogic ashram of a dozen souls now found itself sitting down to dinner with up to three hundred strangers and a series of official orders to clean up its act or else.

The authorities were most galled, apparently, by Morning Star's belief that the fertility of Mother Earth was served well by defecating openly and naturally. Other complaints were filed about the shacks, tree houses, and tents erected by some residents and the crowding of others into buildings not designed as human dwellings. In July 1967 Gottlieb was arrested for running an "organized camp" in violation of the applicable building and health codes. Thus began Lou Gottlieb's new career in lay jurisprudence. "If you can find any traces of 'organization' here," he told the judge, "let me know and I'll destroy them immediately." But the judge was not amused by Gottlieb's disarmingly comic explanations. "We're not here to discuss your philosophy," said Judge Mahan. "We're here to discuss toilets."

In the meantime, one of Gottlieb's neighbors organized a petition drive which collected 396 signatures to have Morning Star closed down as a public nuisance. Gottlieb was ordered to clear his land of those unrelated to him, told he would be fined $500 for every day an inspection revealed he had failed to do so, and ordered to tear down the community kitchen and dining hall which were judged unsafe. On September 12, 1967, official notice was served on Morning Star that the land was contaminated, that it was a public health hazard, and that all present but Gottlieb had to vacate within twenty-four hours. On September 13, Morning Star had a party instead, including the Steve Miller and Allman Joy bands, five hundred hits of acid, hundreds of people, and lots of "grass," love, and sunshine. The police dropped in but were given flowers, and there were no busts that day.

But the grace period lasted only a month, until early October, when Gottlieb was brought into court and ordered once again either to clear the land or construct facilities conforming with local codes. A day or two later fifteen Morning Star members voluntarily went to jail. The women were bailed out that night, but the men stayed in for ten days, fasting and singing "Hare Krishna" until they were finally released and the charges were dropped. The first round in the War of Sonoma County was a draw, and Gottlieb had won a kind of moral victory. But he found himself continually in and out of court for the next several months—and years—on contempt charges, code violations, and appeals. He built an outhouse and brought the mess hall up to code, "but still it didn't stop," he told me in 1970. "After that I became aware it never would." Within a matter of months his fines totaled $15,000.

A year later, in September 1968, Morning Star was served with a permanent injunction forbidding anyone but Gottlieb to live there. "Needless to say, people have been ignoring the injunction ever since it was instituted," Gottlieb said in 1971, "and in the great American tradition of civil disobedience, there have always been people living at Morning Star Ranch."[3] On May 7, 1969, Gottlieb tried a new approach and took jurisprudence into the uncertain realm of divine law by deeding his land to God:

> Now the principal advantage, it seems to me, for having a deed naming God as the grantee is that we raise the question of jurisdiction. It seems to me that in these days, to mount demonstrations . . . is really like trying to cut off the head of Medusa. What I think is . . . that if land is deeded to God, you have what is, in effect, a statute-free sanctuary.

Now obviously we couldn't declare that all over the world, all over the country, that'd be anarchy . . . people would freak out! But there is need for statute-free sanctuary in the country today. If we are as we say, one nation under God, then whose statutes prevail on God's land? The minute anybody trained in the law begins to meditate on the question of God as landowner, the question of jurisdiction immediately presents itself. And most lawyers of the straight variety give a little dry cough, consult their watch, and immediately find that they are 15 minutes late to a very important engagement. But I believe there will come a time when it will be seen that the history of jurisprudence has an important watershed; the history before God is recognized as the legal owner of land and the time after.[4]

That summer Gottlieb found himself in court again under a "show cause" order to explain why the buildings on the property that were not up to code should not be torn down:

Hippies had moved in and built up structures, and naturally the neighbors had complained. . . . We made the defense that I was no longer the real party of interest, because, since May of 1969, I contend that Morning Star Ranch has been the property of God. It was a deed made over naming God as the grantee, and it was recorded in the hall of records in Sonoma County. This was the first time that we had a chance to go into court and make this particular contention. Judge Eiman [Eymann] of the superior court took it under advisement and came out with a decision which is practically famous now, in which he said that the deed naming God as the grantee was not a valid conveyance because—I'll quote the sentence verbatim—"Whatever the nature of the Deity, God is not a person, natural or artificial, in existence at time of conveyance and capable of taking title."[5]

In short, the judge ruled that God did not exist as a legal entity and that Gottlieb was still the responsible party for what went on at Morning Star. The court thus empowered the county to remove the offending structures. In August 1969 the county government brought in a bulldozer and did just that. This was not the final round in the battle, which continued for another two years of appeals, legal struggles, and more bulldozing, but it was the decisive one for Morning Star Ranch. By this time the War of Sonoma County had shifted to another front. To set the scene for this shift we have to back up a few years.

In 1963 a young man named Bill Wheeler bought the old Sheep Ridge Ranch about eight miles away with a family inheritance that was then, at least, large enough to afford him a comfortable living for the rest of his years. Wheeler sought a quiet life as a painter, and the 320 acres he purchased, set off from the county road by a mile of deeply rutted and nearly impassable jeep trail, was just the sort of peaceful isolation he was looking for. He built a sunny studio-home for his family and his art, and for four years he lived and worked undisturbed. The doings at Morning Star, however, soon caught his interest. In the aftermath of the mass arrests at Morning Star in September 1967, they also took hold of his sympathies. In early 1968 a few people who had previously been at Morning Star—including Ramon Sender—asked if they could move to his ranch. Wheeler said yes, and by March he was inspired to go all the way and open up his land as Gottlieb had done:

> As far as The Ridge went and what happened, it was a real leap of faith to open the land. Originally, my wife and myself were living on The Ridge, and that was it. Then Morning Star started getting closed down. I admired Lou and I believed what he was saying. I didn't particularly want the gig, but I didn't have the choice in the matter. The land was there. . . .[6]

Within six months the new open-land community had about twenty residents scattered about Wheeler's acreage, mostly in tents and hastily constructed shacks well hidden from view. In the meantime, the county district attorney's office went to court asking for an injunction to close Wheeler's Ranch for flagrant violations of building codes and health laws. Concurrently, a suit was filed against Wheeler by a neighboring rancher named Kelly to deny Wheeler the access road, which crossed Kelly's land. Since Wheeler had the resources to hire legal help, he was able to delay these moves for the next couple of years, but the attacks continued from other directions even as the population was steadily growing. Those who parked their cars on the county road and walked to Wheeler's sometimes returned to find their tires slashed or deflated or their car full of bullet holes or pushed down a ravine. On a technical building code violation, Wheeler was even forced to move out of his own home and use it only as a studio.

In July 1969 the district attorney filed an action asking that the court order the destruction of all Wheeler Ranch dwellings. In September of that year, county officials rezoned the land to forestall a move by Wheeler to escape county inspections as a "labor camp." In the early morning of October 31, within two weeks of the bulldozing of Morning Star, a total of twenty-five police and FBI agents raided the ranch without a warrant, ostensibly to look for runaways and AWOLs. Under dubious circumstances which later resulted in a hung jury, Wheeler and his brother-in-law were arrested for assaulting a sheriff. Five in all went to jail. Like Gottlieb's, Wheeler's life became a running legal battle that never let up for more than a week or two at a time.

In the wake of all this, Wheeler and his colleagues at Morning Star published an "Open Land Manifesto" stating their case and appealing for contributions to fight back with a major suit against the county. Like Gottlieb, the deeper Wheeler got in, the more committed he became, and the more he began to see the idea of open land as revolutionary. "When you give free land," Lou Gottlieb said, "you pull the carpet out from under the capitalist system. Once a piece of land is freed, 'no trespassing' signs pop up all along the adjoining roads."[7] "The more I view the situation," Gottlieb told interviewer Dick Fairfield on another occasion, "the only hope I see for the future is open land. The only hope ecologically. The only hope sociologically. The only hope in any number of areas. . . . If open land is not the future, there isn't any."[8] For Bill Wheeler, the language became even more radical:

> We are very much like the Vietcong. We're an underground movement. We're going to take some very hard blows for sure. It's not inconceivable that the county will succeed in tearing down all the buildings on The Ranch. . . . We'd hate to see the place torn down and we'll actually fight to our dying breath to prevent it. But we are a form of guerrilla warfare and we're going to take our losses. People have said that The Ranch is the most revolutionary place in the United States.[9]

It was a measure of Wheeler's maturity that he realized the inevitability of the opposition and even welcomed it:

> There's this supervisor in Sonoma County—I oddly enough met him at the tax window a couple of years ago. He's actually a fairly nice guy, and he's fairly friendly to me. And he said a very wise thing. He said, "You know, we've *got* to fight against you. Every revolution that's ever happened has had resistance against it, and if you think this one's going to be any different, you're crazy." I thought about it. And he's right—we need it. It's got to happen that way. For us to come together we've got to fight for what we believe in.[10]

II

Despite this grim litany of oppression and struggle that marked the early history of Wheeler Ranch, I found when I visited in 1970 that above all others in my study it was the most serene, easygoing, and relaxed. "On the land," as the expression went, these hassles were like a distant and forgotten memory that nobody except Bill Wheeler thought much about in the slow and easy motion of everyday affairs. Wheeler explained this serenity in terms of the physical and psychological distance set between the ranch and the outside world:

> The reason we've been as successful as we have is because we're isolated. Appropriately isolated from straight society. Whereas Morning Star is so close and so exposed, it's like a raw nerve. This is one of the reasons why they've had such a hard time. Tourists in general are very debilitating to a community. I think most places have found this and it's really a drag. People coming in with cameras and people getting uptight. The reason we don't have to get uptight is because we're isolated enough that anyone who cares enough to walk in that far is cool. Also, if a person is uncool, there's enough of us and so few of them that we're protected. And they know it. . . . Very rarely do we ever get any really bad trouble, in terms of drunks coming in and stuff like that.[11]

While what he said was true, equal emphasis should be given to the sheer spaciousness and diversity of the land itself. Falling off to either side of the ridge that ran through the center of the Ranch were 320 acres of timber, knolls, meadows, shrubby hillsides, and steep little valleys. In short, there was ample room for hundreds of people to spread out and do their thing as openly or as privately as they wished. Without rules or strains to create something communal, the residents of Wheeler's chose to spread out, pitching tents or building crude shelters as individuals, couples, or small affinity groups at widely dispersed and even concealed locations.

The social life of the community, for the most part, was equally dispersed. At the time of my visit, there were about seventy-five people in residence, but seldom could one observe any more than a few of them together at any one time, apart from a cluster of newcomers and visitors who hung around the gate. From the gate there was little to be seen except junk cars and a wild forest—scant reason to stick around or press on for those with no business there. Still, there were many visitors at Wheeler's who might have been unwanted had the immensity of the land not swallowed them up, permitting anyone who didn't wish to deal with them enough room to ignore their comings and goings—or even their staying. Despite its isolation, the ranch had many visitors, an average of twenty a week in the summer and as many as fifty a week in the winter, more than any other group in this study.

The spaciousness of the land also helps in explaining the good vibes internally. Unlike Drop City or Morning Star, Wheeler's Ranch had plenty of room to spread out away from other members as well as visitors. And unlike Morning Star East, atop its desert mesa, there was no practical need to huddle together, since the climate is so much

milder in Sonoma than in Taos. Like these other open-land communes, though, Wheeler's had a high turnover in population; only 40
percent had been there six months earlier, only 20 percent twelve
months earlier. But unlike the others, there was no pragmatic need to
find a social center. With turnover this high, the climate this mild, it
was pragmatic instead to build small, dispersed, temporary shelters.
In many respects Wheeler's was more a campground than a commune, but the more interesting point is that it was one of the very few
places that *thought* of itself communally which had room enough to
give territoriality and privacy their full spontaneous due. Since Bill
Wheeler's form of patronage did not make it necessary to be communal, the ranch community that grew up around him was almost a pure
test of exactly *how* communal its inhabitants really wanted to be. As
The Modern Utopian put it:

> Other than a Sunday feast once a week and a community garden that
> is worked in a fairly casual way, there are no structures to bind the
> community together. The felt need for anarchy is more real than the
> need for community. People are not opposed to living communally,
> but they're not pushing it either. If it comes, they want it to come
> naturally.[12]

Sacrifice   Since the very essence of open land was free and
uncensored behavior, it was, of course, predictable that there were no
forms of abstinence expected of the membership either sexually or
orally. On the contrary, nudity, casual sex, and drug use were almost
as common as the burghers of Sonoma County imagined them to be.
The only form of abstinence practiced at large was the informal norm
against eating meat, which made sense in the absence of refrigeration
if for no other reason. But refrigeration was not the only modern
amenity that was missing at Wheeler's, for the only utilities present
were a single hand-operated water pump and a few chemical toilets
scattered about the premises (required by law but seldom used).
Otherwise it was voluntary primitivism all the way. Some, like Ramon Sender, chose to live on the land entirely without shelter. But
despite its relatively high score on austerity, the climate at Wheeler's
was warmed by year-round, offshore breezes from the Pacific Ocean
only a few miles away. Although most of the dwellings at Wheeler's
were small, flimsy structures built out of scrap lumber, discarded
window frames, and plastic tarps, they were fully adequate shelters
throughout the year except for a brief rainy season in the winter.
"Nature is very gentle in California, and for at least six months of the
year a roofless tree house would be all you need," stated the Open
Land Manifesto. "For the winter rains buckle the roof on, stock up

on firewood and let it pour! So it falls down in the first windstorm.
The second one won't."[13] In view of the mild climate, there was
justice in Wheeler's complaints against forced adherence to building
codes:

> Two-by-fours sixteen inches on center just does not make any sense to
> us. As California and the whole country is progressively filling up with
> plastic architecture, impersonal and cold plus prohibitively expensive,
> we feel we must present a viable alternative of free and happy homes
> that everyone joins in and builds. One of the most significant aspects of
> Wheeler Ranch has been this evolution and practice of this philosophy
> of architecture.[14]

Just as the climate was gentler in California, so too were the
welfare services. Several members drew unemployment checks, Aid
to Dependent Children (ADC), or food stamps. The income was not
enough to make things much less primitive, but it was enough to help
keep things going. There was little visible economic production on the
land itself. Wheeler's response to criticism on this point frequently
included references to the support of the Israeli government for the
kibbutzim, especially in their early years, or to the support the United
States government gives to farmers and business in general:

> I feel that the welfare trip which goes on at The Ranch is really just a
> subsidy from the government to help us get going. Because agriculture
> things take years and years and years to get going. Home industries
> take a long time to get going—to support themselves. Most people *want*
> to support themselves. . . . But it's going to take time for us young
> people to find out where we're at, to know exactly what we want to do.
> The energies are there. There's *no* doubt in my mind about that.[15]

Investment   Financially, there were no requirements whatever
for living at Wheeler's. Although Wheeler could be counted on for
favors in serious situations, like a medical emergency, he did not
otherwise make his money available to other members or spend it on
their daily needs. "As Lou Gottlieb says," wrote Wheeler, " 'open
land is open land and nothing else.' "[16] It was up to each individual
or family to provide for themselves. The bare facts of survival were
expected to separate those who could pull their own weight from
those who could not. In actual fact, though, most stays on the land
were temporary. In the absence of any permanent system of land
tenure, there was little incentive to invest anything in the ranch
among the members at large, and few did. The only investment factor
of any significance was that members should provide their own
shelter. Given the climate and the liberty of each member to dis-

mantle the home and take it along on leaving, there were virtually no forms of investment at all.

Renunciation   In its renunciation of the outside world, Wheeler's was below the average of other communes on all factors except for the total absence of media connections with the outside and the infrequency of members' trips into town (about every two weeks on the average). Surprisingly, given the importance Wheeler himself ascribed to the community's isolation, the ranch was not actually as far from centers of straight civilization as most communes in this study. The ruggedness of Wheeler's access road made it seem so rather than true remoteness, for the town of Occidental was within walking distance and San Francisco itself was only an hour away by car.

In its social isolation, Wheeler's was insulated only by the choice of outsiders not to come. There were no visitation rules except a vague respect for private dwellings, and the only screen against undesirable members was that Wheeler might take it upon himself to throw them out. Since eviction ran counter to the norms of the community, their behavior had to be outrageous and almost universally unpopular before Wheeler would take this step. To my knowledge he did so only twice, in one case for chronic thievery and in the other for compulsive vandalism and destruction.

Communion   Were it not for the unusually high number of negative persecution experiences at Wheeler's, which included refusals of service from several local merchants, this would easily have been the least communal group in this study on the measures used here. As a whole, the community assembled only once a week. The festivities included a potluck dinner (with pot), sauna baths, singing and dancing, and perhaps a meeting to discuss community issues like fire prevention, legal hassles, or other matters of concern to all. Otherwise it was a disparate group averaging about twenty-five years old but varying widely in age, prior acquaintance, and background. Communal work efforts were infrequent and entirely voluntary, and all forms of sharing were a matter of individual conscience and discretion. There was no group routine, and there were few group dwellings (beyond a small group marriage or two). Very little of an average day was spent in groups larger than two or three. The ritual content of the community was limited to whatever happened at the Sunday meetings, which were seldom programed, and to community births, which were widely attended (there had been eight by 1970) as the high points of community life. There was definitely fraternal feeling, but there were very few ways in which these feelings were built into any kind of observable group structures which might have fostered personal commitment. When Wheeler residents addressed each other as "brother" (as they commonly did), it was often a prelude to asking a favor from a "member" they did not know.

Mortification   Similarly, there was little by way of group processes at Wheeler's which might have subordinated individual egos to the group whole. Mutual criticism was usually limited to individual encounters on the periphery of group life. Generally speaking, the need for it was obviated by the distance that one member could put between himself and another he did not like. There was absolutely no need to have anything to do with someone who might precipitate a conflict. The only visible mortification factor was the shining example set by community patriarchs like Bill Wheeler or Ramon Sender, who were clearly (but not universally) distinguished from most other members for behavior on an unusually high moral and spiritual plane. "Don't worry," one Wheeler member told reporter Sara Davidson when her car got stuck on the torturous access road, "Bill's saved people who've given up hope, lost all confidence."[17] In any community discussions or decisions, this moral elite was accorded considerable deference befitting their status (not to mention Wheeler's ownership of the land). But mortifying anybody else's ego was the farthest thing from their minds.

Transcendence   For Wheeler, exercising power was another matter. He was not apologetic about keeping the land in his name, and he was not, at that time anyway, interested in surrendering his control by forming a nonprofit corporation of some sort. Despite the open-land concept, he did not hesitate to make rules where he thought they were essential. He had an absolute rule against dogs, for instance, since earlier in ranch history dogs had formed deer-killing packs and chased the neighbor's sheep. "We've had more hassles and lost more friendships over dogs than any other thing," he told me. Another rule he strictly enforced was one prohibiting open fires in the summer, when California vegetation is extremely dry and flammable; a fire in 1968 had cost him substantial timber losses. Still another rule was that all vehicles (except his own) were to be parked by the gate and not driven through the land. The communal truck was available only with Bill's permission, which would be denied to someone he did not trust. Similar rules applied later in the group's history to things like the use of a community workshop, kept closed and locked with the combination known only to Wheeler and a few others. There were other rules as well, which are perhaps less important than the fact that Wheeler instituted them unilaterally.

Altogether Wheeler's authority at the ranch paralleled that of the leaders of religious groups like Maharaj and Ananda, except in its lack of sacred underpinnings. Wheeler himself embodied the community on all matters requiring unequivocal decisions. He could not be impeached, he had special prerogatives, and he functioned as the community's central figure in all dealings with the outside. He was rather like a feudal baron who extended his protection and lands to those who served under him but for the fact that he expected so little of them in return. This authority hierarchy, comprised of Wheeler and his most trusted lieutenants, combined with the ideology and tradition of the Morning Star faith, gave the ranch an above-average score on the dimension of transcendence even though it was otherwise a perfect anarchy. Instead of necessarily boosting the group's strength, however, Wheeler's hegemony tended to make the ranch vulnerable to the same weakness that had emerged at Dawson's Maharaj Ashram in New Mexico. Whenever a group is this dependent on the strength and resources of a single leader, it may find in a crisis that it is no stronger than he is.

III

Over the next year or so the ranch flourished despite all efforts at the Sonoma County courthouse to dislodge it. The population grew to about two hundred, and slowly but surely the community began to acquire more signs of organization. The gardens were expanded and a "food conspiracy," or wholesale buying cooperative, was established to supplement them. A small dam and windmill were erected to augment the water supply, a craft shop was built, a cooperative kiln/ bread oven was constructed, and a nursery was formed among the mothers—all but the last made possible by Wheeler's money, which he spent on the community despite himself. Wheeler also bought an old school bus, and "community runs" were instituted twice weekly for shopping, laundry, mail trips, and community excursions. Weekly trash runs were made in the community's (formerly Wheeler's) flatbed truck, which brought back manure for the gardens by arrangement with a neighbor who needed his barns cleaned.

> As time has gone on . . . people . . . have adjusted to the open-land concept and have become dedicated to it. They've also found their own niche . . . what they do on the Ranch. We have one person who takes care of the water. We have one person who will do a community run of some kind or another, and we have another person who takes care of the livestock. Each person seems to have found a thing. It's really an incredible thing just to watch it happen, sort of unfold before your eyes.[18]

In view of this progress, Wheeler decided to surrender direct control and in the fall of 1971 incorporated the Ahimsa Church as the governing entity of ranch life (Ahimsa is the Indian philosophy of nonviolence to all living things). The deed to the land was transferred to the church, and a board of five directors was elected to handle the financial, legal, and secretarial duties of the corporation. Meetings of the church were to take place on Sundays as extensions of the community feast, and all the residents were to be heard.

But on the legal front the battles continued unabated. That same year, the district attorney succeeded in obtaining an injunction against the ranch as a public nuisance and health hazard, thereafter forbidding any new structures. Wheeler countered with an appeal and attempted to redefine the ranch legally, first as a "campground" and then as a "trailer court."

"With the county government's lack of success at eliminating us," Wheeler wrote in early 1972, "their frustration has built up. Finally in desperation and in an attempt to really get us, they staged this latest raid. . . . This time they were prepared to give us the real whammo—with 150 pigs in a predawn assault. Many people were awakened staring up the barrel of a gun . . . not too nice a way to start the day. . . . Some seventeen people were arrested on drug charges alone, mostly for cultivation of marijuana. One person got arrested for ginseng root in a capsule, another for vitamin pills." The warrant was later quashed for illegally obtained evidence, and some of those arrested were acquitted. Predictably, the county appealed, and the war went on. Wheeler's lawyer filed a suit against the county charging harassment and violation of the community's civil rights, but it brought no relief.

By the winter of 1972–1973, Wheeler's resources to continue the struggle were fast being exhausted. It became clear that the county was fighting a war of attrition they would inevitably win, and most of the residents left and moved elsewhere. The suit filed by Wheeler's neighbor Mr. Kelly over the access road resulted in a restriction of traffic to Wheeler himself and a "limited guest list"—providing that properly certified housing was established. Entrance through the Kellys' gate was limited to Wheeler's personal vehicles and excluded towed vehicles and trailers. All legal efforts to get the ranch exempted from enforcement of the building codes failed, as did Wheeler's appeal of the superior court order. In the early spring of 1973, the county brought in the bulldozers, and the buildings at the ranch were destroyed. In anguish and despair, Wheeler himself burned the remaining rubble late one night.

The last cataclysm in this drama came in early July 1973 when Wheeler wanted to tow a trailer home into his land but the Kellys refused him access. Wheeler announced publicly that he was going in anyway. At the gate he was met by Mrs. Kelly and a number of Sonoma County deputies standing by. True to his word, Wheeler crashed through the locked gate and unintentionally sent it flying into Mrs. Kelly. Mrs. Kelly went to the hospital and Bill Wheeler went to jail. The gate to Wheeler's Ranch was repaired, locked with heavy chains, and covered with "no trespassing" signs when last I visited. Over at Morning Star the only thing left standing was a rose trellis in full bloom. The War of Sonoma County was over, and the brief era of open land was a thing of the past—or of the future, perhaps, too far ahead of its own time. Some of the former residents of Wheeler's had formed a new community nearby called Star Mountain, but this time it was private, secret, and closed to outsiders and crashers.

Could it have possibly turned out any differently? Perhaps, for many of the frailties of other open anarchies were not problems at Wheeler's. Unlike Drop City and the original Morning Star, Wheeler's had plenty of space and was not nearly so exposed or cramped. Unlike Morning Star East, Reality, or LILA, the ranch had a committed benefactor who stuck with the group, gave up his personal control, and fought for the community until the end. Like Libre, which did succeed, the ranch had plenty of space and made full provision for territoriality. And while it began as an exercise in pure individualism, it showed signs of a slowly evolving internal organization and gradually increasing levels of personal commitment. Other things equal, Wheeler's Ranch would have made it, since instability was largely irrelevant to the community's continuation as a social entity. Presumably new institutions would have continued evolving. One day, perhaps, there might have come a time when the acreage was saturated, the community was stabilized, and the Ahimsa Church turned away from its origins and closed itself off to new settlers.

The most obvious reason for the group's failure, of course, was the setting. Sonoma County is one of the wealthiest rural areas in America. Land values there are high, and only rich people can afford to buy in on any scale, as Gottlieb and Wheeler themselves demonstrated. Not surprisingly, then, the county is extremely conservative. Its status as a bastion of middle-class propriety is perhaps best expressed by its reputation as a colony for police officers who work in the cities to the south and move there to raise their families or retire. In a sense, then, the fate of Wheeler's Ranch was written into the deed the day that Wheeler bought it. Had the community been located in Colorado's Huerfano Valley, southwestern Oregon, or even Taos—all poor areas which never mounted any decisive, organized resistance to the communes in their midst—it might have worked out differently. It is impossible, of course, to gainsay history or the actors who find their way onto its stage. In any other setting Bill Wheeler would probably never have met Lou Gottlieb or taken up his cause.

It would be equally futile to point out in retrospect that the community might have changed and adapted better to its circumstances. It may have been impossible in any case to satisfy the Sonoma County building inspectors, but few members of Wheeler's Ranch had either the resources or the incentive to try. It was nobody's fight as much as Wheeler's, and unlike the *kibbutzim* he so often referred to, nobody's back was really to the wall but his own. For the story to have come out differently, the whole cast of characters would have to have been different from what it was.

"I believe one of the major problems of our time is to teach people to do nothing," Lou Gottlieb had said. "Americans are all karma yogis, people who literally can't sit still. My mother, if she came upon a catatonic schizoid, would scream at him to get busy. I got that until it absolutely deformed my childhood. It was never enough just to sit still and scratch your balls, enjoying yourself."[19] At Wheeler's Ranch it was enough for personal therapy but not for a community of permanent homes. That, which might have been worth fighting for, would have taken more than Bill Wheeler's determination to keep it going and more than the vibrations of the land to protect it.

Notes

1. Joe David Brown, ed., *The Hippies* (New York: Time-Life Books, 1967), p. 64.

2. Lewis Yablonsky, *The Hippie Trip* (New York: Pegasus, 1968), pp. 181–198. What appalled Yablonsky most was an encounter with a dirty, hungry, and untended child whose mother was off somewhere on an acid trip. He also feared for his safety at the hands of some blacks who were temporarily occupying one of Morning Star's buildings. The bad vibes he felt were at least partly attributable to the tape recorder he carried in his briefcase.

3. Quoted in Richard Fairfield, *Communes U.S.A.: A Personal Tour* (Baltimore: Penguin Books, 1972), p. 254. Fairfield conducted interviews with both Gottlieb and Bill Wheeler in February 1971.

4. Ibid., p. 257. Four days after Gottlieb deeded his land to God, a story about it appeared in the *Oakland Tribune*. An Oakland legal secretary named Betty Penrose filed suit against God for mismanagement of the universe by causing lightning to strike her house in 1960. As partial payment for her damages she asked for title to God's new ranch in Sonoma County. This particular case got lost in the cobwebs of history when one Paul Yerkes Bechtel of Tamal, California, stepped forth proclaiming that since he was God, he should be the defendant.

5. Ibid., p. 255.

6. Ibid., p. 282.

7. Quoted in Sara Davidson, "Open Land: Getting Back to the Communal Garden," *Harper's Magazine,* 240 (June 1970). Reprinted as "Hippie Families on Open

Land" in *Communes: Creating and Managing the Collective Life,* ed. Rosabeth M. Kanter (New York: Harper & Row, 1973), pp. 338–339.

8. Quoted in Fairfield, *Communes U.S.A.,* pp. 260, 257.

9. Ibid., p. 281.

10. Ibid., p. 283.

11. Ibid., p. 278.

12. Jim Sosenski, "Wheeler Ranch," *The Modern Utopian,* 4 (Spring 1970), 17.

13. Louis Gottlieb et al., "Open Land: A Manifesto" (Bodega Bay, Calif.: Wheeler Ranch Defense Fund, 1970), p. 9.

14. Bill Wheeler, "Wheeler Ranch," *Communitarian,* 1 (March/April 1972), p. 53. The *Communitarian* was a short-lived (one issue) magazine that merged into *Communities,* which is still publishing today.

15. Quoted in Fairfield, *Communes U.S.A.,* p. 280.

16. Wheeler, "Wheeler Ranch," p. 52.

17. Davidson, "Open Land," p. 336.

18. Quoted in Fairfield, *Communes U.S.A.,* p. 275.

19. Quoted in Keith Melville, *Communes in the Counter-Culture: Origins, Theories, Styles of Life* (New York: Morrow, 1972), pp. 127–128.

10

The Spirit of Free Enterprise: Ananda Cooperative Village

I

At one time in California history, between the discovery of gold in 1848 and the Civil War, the most populous community in the state was a town called Nevada City some one hundred miles northeast of Sacramento. It was a boom town brought into existence by gold, feeding and supplying the thousands of prospectors who poured into the Sierras, and in turn being fed by them. When the gold petered out, in part because of the invention of a new kind of hydraulic mining that ravaged the landscape but was very efficient in removing the precious metal quickly, the Motherlode Country settled once again into obscurity.

In recent years, though, the rural counties of the area—Nevada, Sierra, Yuba—have experienced a new kind of gold rush, this time for land. Located about equidistant from San Francisco and Reno and an easy drive from Sacramento, the region has become one of the most popular vacation and second-home areas of northern California. Its appeal has become equally great for those seeking to escape city life more permanently, however, since the founding of Ananda Cooperative Village there in 1967. "A surprisingly large number of people," says Swami Kriyananda, the village's founder, "have moved to Nevada County as a direct consequence of our being here. All in all, Ananda has been good for local business."[1] Today, Ananda is widely known among those who follow such matters as one of the most prosperous and exemplary new intentional communities in rural America.

In Sanskrit, the word "ananda" means "bliss." In essence the community is the culmination of the life work of its founder, Kriyananda, an American who for three decades has been a disciple of the teachings of Paramahansa Yogananda, author of *Autobiography of a Yogi*. In his last years, according to Kriyananda, the great teacher spoke often of what he thought was destined to become a basic social pattern for the new age: the formation of self-realization communities, or "World Brotherhood Colonies." "The day will come," Kriyananda quotes him as saying, "when this idea will spread through the world like wildfire. Gather together, those of you who share high ideals. Pool your resources. Buy land in the country. A simple life will bring you inner freedom. Harmony with nature will bring you a happiness known to few city dwellers. In the company of other truth seekers it will be easier for you to meditate and to think of God."[2] This was not the central point of his teachings, Kriyananda says, and other disciples showed little interest in it. "It was a keen interest of mine, however, long before I met him. His words only fanned an existing flame."[3]

In the introduction to his book *Cooperative Communities: How to Start Them, and Why,* Kriyananda traces this flame back to World War II, when he was only fifteen and attempted to write a utopian novel about a group of people "skilled in various civilized disciplines" who retreat to South America "to keep the lamp of civilization burning brightly through the Dark Ages to come." "Unfortunately," he writes, "my imagination proved unequal to the task. Or perhaps I was already beginning to sense the absurdity of trying to perfect anything so inherently unstable as human society. . . . My future study of the subject, and finally the writing of this book, was guided always by a search merely for *better* alternatives, not for perfect ones."[4] In college after the war, Kriyananda became convinced that the key to real social change was personal transformation. "Social uplift, I now saw, must come from the inner consciousness of individuals; it cannot be inspired by outward legislation, nor by any mass approach to human problems. A widespread transformation of consciousness was, I felt, more likely to be initiated in small communities . . . than in large, heterogeneous urban communities."[5]

In 1948 Kriyananda met Paramahansa Yogananda personally and became his disciple. For the next fourteen years he spent his time living in his guru's monasteries in India and America and mulling over his ideas about communal living. In monastic life, too, he was an early starter. "At an early stage of my life there I was placed in charge of the other monks, and came thereby to learn at first hand many of the problems to be faced in coordinating such a community."[6] But for the most part, his dream of founding such a community was dormant over these years.

Its "more active beginnings" date from 1962, when the Self-Realization Fellowship, the religious organization founded by Yogananda in which Kriyananda had risen to the position of first vice-president, abruptly dismissed him "with stern warnings never to return." "My belief in decentralization, wherever possible, as a vital factor in spreading the work had brought me under suspicion of being a potential schismatic."[7] It was a crushing blow. "I felt for a long time that I had lost my reason for living. There was simply no imaginable disaster for me that could be greater than this one."[8] His one desire then became "to find a place where I might remain quiet and alone, to pray deeply for new directions."[9]

Between the years 1962 and 1967, Kriyananda searched throughout the West and even Mexico for a place of retreat without finding what he wanted. In any case, he had little money. All of his adult life, in fact, he had been living on a monk's monthly allowance of $20. But during this period he began working as a lecturer and yoga instructor, and over the years he acquired something of a reputation, many new friends, and finally, as he came to terms with charging fees for his services, "a sudden spurt" in his income. In 1967 a chance encounter—with overtones of being foreordained—brought him into a land deal with poets Gary Snyder and Allen Ginsberg and Zen Buddhist Dick Baker, all of whom were interested in buying land for personal retreats of a spiritual nature. For $6,000 Kriyananda bought a twenty-four-acre parcel adjacent to the others. That summer, with little thought of forming a community, he set out to build a geodesic dome for his own use. The shape had long fascinated him as seemingly ideal for meditation. But three times he built it, and three times it blew down within a matter of days. To Kriyananda "It was a sign that I would not be able to have my own home until I had built a temple, and perhaps even a community, for the benefit of others."[10]

With his funds exhausted by his land purchase and house-building failures, Kriyananda went back to teaching classes. In January 1968 an opportunity arose to buy two other twenty-four-acre parcels in the original total of seven. Indeed, somebody had to buy them or the deal would have fallen through. Since the other partners in the land purchase had no immediate plans to build there themselves, it was agreed that Kriyananda could buy the extra parcels for his new community if he would move it somewhere else in two or three years. With money offered by an old friend, Kriyananda bought the two additional parcels and now had seventy-two acres for his retreat. Soon after that, he called a formal meeting in San Francisco to discuss his plans for a new community. "My own enthusiasm," he writes, "had led me to expect a quick, positive response from anyone to whom I described my ideas. I had overlooked the many years it had taken me to grow into these ideas myself." In short, the response of the meeting was "How do we know you're on the level?"[11]

Kriyananda's reaction to this skepticism was twofold. First, he gathered up his notes and wrote a loose-leaf version of what later became his book, expressing the urgency, desirability, and proposed design of such a community. Secondly, he decided that potentially interested persons "needed not only enough time to reflect on these ideas, but also the reassurance of seeing something already solidly accomplished. . . . No one, I decided, could accuse me of black motives if I built a meditation retreat. It was a project about which little theorizing was necessary, and it would attract active participation. Slowly out of this group labor, the seeds were to sprout that would grow in time to become the cooperative community."[12]

With money from his teaching, from friends, and from some stocks his father had given him, Kriyananda had $16,000 by the summer of 1968, enough, he felt, to hire professional help, since he clearly was not a carpenter. As it turned out, he seriously underestimated his costs. Two professional carpenters walked out on him, the banks refused to loan him more money because they saw no way "the yoga fad" could last, and Kriyananda found himself strapped with $12,000 in debts and a lien on his land. It took his every effort, and according to him some miracles, to settle with his creditors at $2,500 a month for five months. But by the end of the year the retreat was built and nearly paid off. Over the winter several people lived there as hermits, and in February 1969 Kriyananda called a second meeting in San Francisco to discuss forming a community. This time the response was more enthusiastic. By the spring Ananda's first family settlers began arriving on the land.

But Kriyananda had agreed with his land partners that a community at the retreat site would be only temporary. As he soon discovered himself, families with children and pets were a noisy distraction to meditation, the retreat's central purpose. In June he got a letter from one of his partners expressing concern that the community might not be moved at all and asking him to suspend further construction until they could talk things over. Later that same afternoon, Kriyananda was visiting a friend in Sacramento and had another chance encounter, this time with a real estate agent who stopped in and began talking about "the hottest land buy I've ever seen." When Kriyananda looked into it, he discovered that the site was only a few minutes' drive from the retreat. The owner was a terminal cancer patient who wanted to sell quickly. The land was not even on the market yet, and Kriyananda could only get it if he acted fast.

That night Kriyananda got on the telephone and called everyone he knew. Within twenty-four hours he had promises of loans and gifts totaling $13,500, the down payment required for acreage he wanted. According to the realtor, he had acted just in time. "What you've done is snatch that land right out from everyone else's noses." Even though many of the promises later fell through, the other members reportedly agreed that carrying through with the purchase was the right step. "And so it was that we acquired well over two hundred acres of additional land for our families, farming, and heavier industries."[13] The new land became known as Ananda Farm, as distinct from the Ananda Meditation Retreat some six miles away. Not long after some of the members moved over to take possession of the farm, Kriyananda reports, the terminal cancer patient who had previously owned it became "quite marvellously cured."

But despite this auspicious beginning, it was not long before things began to get out of hand. "One of our first struggles," wrote Kriyananda, "was over the question of drugs, which every newcomer to the community had promised not to take, but which soon began to exercise an attraction again for certain people, especially when things became outwardly difficult. There were a couple of times when I had to be firm, even to asking one person to leave."[14]

Another problem was an "invasion" of new members who had heard a new commune was getting started, and their desire, particularly among the dozen or so who came from a disbanded commune called Ben Lomand, to form a close-knit communal "tribe." "But where people are expected to do everything in common," Kriyananda had written a year earlier, ". . . frictions can quickly mount. A community that strives for such constant, intense 'togetherness' will require miracles of leadership to survive. Consider, however, another type of community: the normal village, where 'togetherness' is not driven down people's throats. There, administration is easily kept to a minimum. Villages have endured, where close-knit communities, lacking a strong leadership, have disintegrated."[15]

At first Kriyananda went along with this deviation from his principles because, he confesses, "we had to admit enough members to make the farm economically possible," by which he meant paying the mortgage on it, which came to the staggering sum (for a commune) of $1,750 a month. "Many of these newcomers were people who had no knowledge of the background of Ananda, nor any special desire to help me, as its founder, to fulfill my dreams for it. Their attitude was perfectly understandable. . . . I didn't want Ananda to turn into a dictatorship."[16] In essence they were not very willing to accept his direction. As an American who called himself only a teacher, he was not given the ready submission so often granted more "official" gurus of Indian birth. "Gradually, however, our people came to experience for themselves the truth . . . that a fair measure of privacy is spiritually desirable, as well as conducive to communal harmony. Thus . . . the community decided on its own that it wanted to become . . . an intentional village, rather than a typical 'commune.' "[17]

The biggest problem, however, was meeting the mortgage payments. For the remainder of 1969 they were deferred by the sellers because of some unfulfilled provisions in the purchase contract, giving Ananda a kind of grace period to get settled:

> But at first people simply did not work together. In fact, some of them didn't even work. And those who did work, and hard, could not generate any real income at the very outset; it takes time to establish a profitable business. [By the time the payments were to be resumed, at the end of 1969,] everything came close to disintegrating completely. The winter was coming, and most of our people didn't know how they would face it. . . . Suddenly we received notices of intent to foreclose. Few of our members could even think in terms of such large sums of money. Drugs became an escape for some of them. People retreated into a kind of fantasy world with regard to the mortgage: If God wanted it paid, *He* would take care of it. This was certainly the bleakest moment in our history.[18]

Many of the members simply left rather than face the burden; others went to the city to seek jobs.

"Nothing within me responded to the idea of *managing* a cooperative community," Kriyananda wrote later. "I wanted to educate them to the thought of accepting real responsibility for managing their own affairs. For I had determined from the start to stick to my original notion of not becoming the community's manager."[19] Nevertheless, Kriyananda was stuck with the job. Reluctantly, he agreed to be responsible for the mortgage payments until the end of May 1970, whereupon he went back to the city to give lessons again. After meeting the payments for four months, he received notice that he would have to pay the additional $4,500 in deferred payments by June 1. Once again he got on the telephone for a series of urgent calls to his supporters. "With God's grace, I paid it, along with the regular mortgage payment for that month, on May 31. I then moved back to Ananda, and turned the responsibility for further mortgage payments over to the entire community."[20] A month later came another disaster: the temple burned down. But by then Kriyananda had screened out a group of dedicated people mostly able to pay their own way, among them carpenters and other craftsmen. The temple was soon rebuilt even better than before and Ananda was finally established on a relatively firm footing:

> Partly by working personally with those members who showed a willingness to assume definite responsibility, partly by offering sound enough reasons for my proposals, and partly by laying constant stress on our spiritual directions, I was able in time to accomplish my objectives.[21]

II

In *Cooperative Communities: How to Start Them, and Why,* the blueprint for Ananda, one of the early chapters critiques the communal settlements of the past. Some of the major criticisms and solutions include the following:

> Linked to too idealistic a view of human nature was the failure of communities—devastating to any but the best established—to screen their applicants. . . . It would be wise, especially in a new community, to take care that only harmonious persons be admitted. . . .
>
> A common failure of new communities has been the tendency to demand too radical a change of their members. In biology there is an axiom that nature never proceeds by sudden leaps. . . .
>
> . . . Let us not expect people to embrace a way of life too radically different from that to which they are now accustomed. . . .
>
> A safe beginning, it seems to me, would be to heed well the fact that most successful colonies have been religiously oriented. . . . In the sense of emphasizing this inner awareness, no community can afford to be lax. . . .
>
> The consensus of persons who have made a study of community life is that some definite communal structure is needed. Coupled to this advice, one always finds mentioned the need for strong leadership. . . .[22]

Philosophically, then, Kriyananda was willing to accept things as they were. People were divided into those of goodwill and those of bad, people and systems were presumed to take great amounts of time and energy to change and therefore shouldn't be rushed, and new communities should be pragmatic and learn something from history. Altogether his was a conservative view of human nature. In the area of economics, Kriyananda was likewise pragmatic in his outlook. In his chapter on this subject, he dismisses communism as "too restrictive, too much out of keeping with the consciousness of our age, and quite possibly tyrannical. It is also a real obstacle to the development of the community's economy."[23]

Economically, his conclusion was that "most people need to feel that they are working for themselves. . . . The soundest course, it seems to me, would be to follow the pattern to which people are in any case accustomed: Let them work for wages, and in turn pay for what they receive. . . . The simplest management is simply to give people the incentive to manage themselves. When they must look out for their own needs, they will bestir themselves well enough to produce." In a later edition of the book, Kriyananda added that "here at Ananda we have, so far at least, accepted as the simplest method the one for which our Western upbringing has best prepared us: Enterprising members have formed their own industries, and employ other members at whatever wages they can afford to pay. . . . So far, the persons most responsible for the community's finances have resisted . . . centralization as unwieldy, and quite possibly as detrimental to individual initiative."[24]

In the first edition of the book, published before Ananda actually began, Kriyananda made several suggestions that Ananda itself did not follow, notably that a new community not get itself into heavy mortgage debt but instead save and pay cash. In the early book, Kriyananda also advocated various *Walden Two*-type devices like the use of labor credits, that the community be the sole employer, and that shares be sold in the community and "dividends" be distributed on that basis. In the later edition, published in 1971 after the fact, Kriyananda dropped these suggestions as unfeasible and no longer recommended them (except avoiding debt) for others. But he had said all along that systems must be practical and open to change. The economic features which stayed the same were the requirement of a membership fee ($1,000 for single persons, $1,500 for married couples), monthly payments toward the mortgage fund (about $35 per person in 1970), and cooperative financial structure to take care of community business. In the new edition, two additional stipulations were suggested, reflecting Ananda's actual experience: that a new member "be able in addition to pay for the construction of his own residence," and "that there be gainful employment for him in the community."[25]

The chapter on government was perhaps the most thoroughly rewritten before the new 1971 edition, reflecting the many differences between Kriyananda's earlier theorizing and the way things at Ananda actually worked out over the intervening years. "Our Board of Directors, which . . . we prefer to call the Planning Board, is elected annually by resident members who have lived here for more than one year. This Planning Board is answerable to the general membership, in which the overall governing power actually resides. The officers, elected by the Planning Board from among its own members, consist of a Spiritual Director (a position comparable to that of president), a General Manager (whose position corresponds to that of vice president), a Secretary, and a Treasurer." Other directors may be appointed "to be responsible, as the need arises, for other specific areas of community activity," but "in order that Planning Board members be elected primarily on the basis of their spiritual dedication and *general* executive ability . . . directors shall not be elected to any of these posts as such."[26]

Thus Ananda differed from an ordinary business corporation mainly in that "idealism, not expediency, should be the final arbiter in all cooperative community affairs." But politically, the line between idealism and expediency was not always clear. A four-member board was clearly easier for Kriyananda to control, for example, than one of six or nine members as he had originally proposed. And in creating the role of Spiritual Director, he found a way to continue exercising supervisory power without being obligated to attend to secular details. "At Ananda, this [presiding] officer's primary concern is the community's spiritual welfare. His duty is to coordinate the secular with the spiritual activities of the community, and, by not becoming too involved in secular matters, to preserve an overall view which might otherwise be lost in the pressures of the moment." Finally, once a trusted lieutenant emerged who was competent in secular matters, Kriyananda simply created a role for him:

> The actual management of day-to-day matters at Ananda is the duty of the General Manager. His function is similar in most respects to that of the manager of a business corporation, with the main exception that spiritual principles are the supreme arbiter of his activities, and that in such matters he confers with the Spiritual Director, as well as, of course, being subject to the supervisory control of the Planning Board.[27]

By the time of my first visit in September 1970, all these institutions—with changes—were more or less established and in place, even though at that point Ananda was not yet a legal corporation (and did not hold elections). The plan was for the Yoga Fellowship that Kriyananda had incorporated in 1968 to become the nonprofit umbrella organization encompassing Ananda's affairs in general. The farm (now known as Ananda Village), on the other hand, was to be incorporated as a profit-making corporation to govern those aspects of community life which did not legally qualify for nonprofit status. In several ways, Kriyananda actually preferred the profit-making form because there would be no restrictions of what businesses members could engage in and thus fewer problems with officialdom and because such a form would help build in concrete incentives to individual initiative and self-support.

Among the private businesses then established at Ananda were a small incense factory, a print shop (both of which paid rent), and the individual production of various arts and crafts items. A luggage factory was to open soon and employ six or seven members. Wages paid by the businesses employing other members, who worked mostly as their needs required instead of routinely, ranged from $1 to $2 an hour, depending on the employer's financial condition. It was not much, but not much was needed. Working for lower wages inside the community was preferred by many to working outside, if money needs were not too pressing. About six of the community's men (with families to support) worked outside now and then as carpenters and subcontractors. Only one of the twenty-seven members of the farm (thirteen men, fourteen women) worked at a regular job outside; one other worked half-time outside.

At the retreat, with twelve members (seven men, five women), no one held outside jobs, though a few worked outside occasionally. Most drew their support from work on behalf of the retreat, which solicited and hosted guests during a season running from May to September. Rates were then $8 a day, $18 for a weekend, $60 for a week, and $200 for a month, discounted about 25 percent for couples and another 25 percent for "karma yogis," meaning committed students of Yogananda with less ability to pay. Retreat members also administered Kriyananda's correspondence courses on hatha yoga and other spiritual topics, coordinated the sale of Kriyananda's books and recordings, worked on construction and meal preparation, and handled donations, accounting, and other business matters. In turn some were paid nominal wages or given a small allowance, plus housing, meals, and other community services. Others worked part-time at their own enterprises, usually arts and crafts.

Physically, the seventy-two-acre retreat consisted of a temple dome, a communal kitchen, a dining and meeting dome, a small dome for receiving guests and visitors, another dome for Kriyananda's dwelling, two small dormitories for single men and women, and a number of scattered cabins, A-frames, and wall tents for guest facilities. The terrain was rolling hills of pine, oak, and shrubby scotch broom and manzanita bushes. Retreat facilities were carefully dispersed over the property to maximize an atmosphere of peace and quiet.

Six miles away, at the farm, the land was divided about equally between an open valley with several old farm buildings, used mostly for gardening and the businesses, and forested hills where individual dwellings were built or tents erected at scattered locations. The two resident branches of Ananda were considered closely related but separate communities: the retreat for monks and unmarried people, the farm for families with children, of which there were then eighteen. In general, the rules of behavior at the retreat were stricter and more programmatic than those of the farm. Due to the seasonal characteristics of the retreat, the discussion of commitment mechanisms that follows below refers to the farm unless otherwise noted.

Sacrifice At both of Ananda's communities, alcohol and drug use were strictly forbidden, especially so since the issue of drug use had split the farm so severely in the summer of 1969. At the retreat there were also abstinence rules against tobacco and eating meat, and sexual continence was strongly preferred as well. At the farm these particular rules were more relaxed but still preferred as community norms. At the retreat the expectations of abstinence were similar to those of Maharaj Ashram or similar monkish communities. At the farm they were like the Lama Foundation: strict on the most potentially divisive points and tolerant on most other matters of individual deportment.

On the dimension of austerity, Ananda was below average for the study but still rather primitive in most respects. The old farmhouse and barn were wired for electricity, allowing the use of community coolers and power tools among other things, but the cabins and tents of the membership did without. There was also a central water source, but it too was far removed from the dwellings, to which water had to be carried. Bottled propane gas was used for heating many dwellings, but a few others made do with wood or no heat at all. There were sewage facilities at the farmhouse, but only privies in the hills. For California the winters were substantial with snows in the wet season, but the climate was seldom really severe. The difficulty of dealing with winter, though, increased with the requirement that each family build its own shelter. Food stamps were available to ease the way but only under the strictest of terms, and Ananda did without them partly as a matter of principle and partly for their impracticality. On the whole the degree of sacrifice at Ananda was average for communes in general. At the retreat the score would have been higher because of stricter rules. Since the farm members mostly had families with children, life there was understandably allowed to be less taxing.

Investment Ananda was the only community in this study to make use of a required entrance fee. In general, it had the second highest level of investment requirements in the study. In addition to the fee, which was not returnable if the member left, there was also a required monthly payment. Physical participation was also expected.

Membership would lapse for those who left the community except for temporary work. Those who stayed were expected to build their own dwellings and help out on community projects at large. But there were no requirements for signing over any other property or income, and any investments in the community beyond the fee were recorded and returned to defectors. The fee requirement made Ananda very unusual among its contemporaries. Otherwise it was a typical exercise in low-rent, cooperative living, distinguished mainly by the regularity and equality of its members' contributions.

Renunciation   Ananda was also very unusual in the degree of its renunciation of the outside world, which was by far the highest in the study. From the farm to the nearest neighbor was a half mile, to the nearest town sixteen miles, and to the nearest city seventy-eight miles—all above-average distances. The farm's insulation was complete in terms of "straight" media, and only the retreat had a telephone. Ananda was also the most isolated group in the study socially. Trips outside were only biweekly on the average. Even more significant was the strictness of Ananda's visitation and membership policies. Overnight crashers were most often turned away unless they came late at night. More polite visitors were usually given a limited tour of the farm, not including residences, and politely sent on their way.

To stay at Ananda as a guest generally required a genuine interest in yoga or some "valid purpose" otherwise. Most such requests were deflected to the retreat, which had facilities for guests and where the number of visitors at any one time could be controlled so as not to exceed the available facilities. The biggest deterrent to the kind of visitors Ananda liked least was this system of polite referral to the retreat, which required strict adherence to the rules and the payment of motel-rate fees. Many drop-in hippies were miffed at these barriers, but the gate keepers of the community could logically defuse their complaints by informing them that many camping areas could be found elsewhere in the vicinity. As the community evolved, in fact, the role of gate keeper became so important that it became institutionalized, with specific persons assuming this responsibility.

The policies regarding new members were likewise unusually strict. As Kriyananda listed them:

> Requirements for membership are that one be a disciple, or at least a sincere devotee, of our Guru, Paramahansa Yogananda, and of his line of gurus; that one have studied, or be in the process of studying, our Guru's correspondence course lessons from Self-Realization Fellowship in Los Angeles, and also our own yoga correspondence course from

Ananda; that one be definitely and completely off hallucinogenic drugs
and alcoholic beverages; that one be able to pay his membership fee
($1,000 for single persons, $1,500 for married couples) upon acceptance, and be able in addition to pay for the construction of his own
residence; that there be gainful employment for him in the community;
and above all, that the community members feel an attunement with
him and accept him.[28]

Ananda's score in this regard was increased by the fact that it
had ejected existing members and blackballed prospective members
several times before. Later in its history, Ananda evolved a committee specifically charged with screening new members. The final decision was made by the planners after consulting community opinion.

Communion   Where Ananda had the highest score on renunciation and several other factors, it had the lowest score in the study on
group communion, sharing this distinction with Libre. In communistic
sharing, Ananda was different from most by requiring equal and universal payments from all members. But these payments were quite
small, and members otherwise were expected to fend for themselves.
Although the community as a whole presumably owned the land, its
buildings, and some tools and equipment, the deed was in Kriyananda's name alone. The original plan to return dividends from communal profits had never been put into practice, nor had the plan for
communal ownership of business. And while all dwellings were communally owned in principle, in practice each home builder was free to
sell or rent his home as long as the new tenant met all the usual
qualifications. Or he could "sell" it back to the community and be
reimbursed for his investment. Most communes in 1970 had no such
provision. Ananda did have a large and well-tended communal garden, but even that was the province of one person, who could have
charged for his efforts had he wanted to, instead of letting others
share in the work or produce as they wished.

Communistic labor at Ananda was a legitimate expectation, and
collective work efforts were common, but unpaid labor for others or
the community was not required of permanent members who made
their payments and were otherwise in good standing. Although many
members worked on a cooperative or voluntary basis for nothing, a
member who worked for another member's business or on a community project like improving the road at the retreat would normally be
paid in wages, however nominal. Informally, members were expected
to devote about twenty to thirty hours a week to working for the sake
of the entire community in one capacity or another, sometimes paid
and sometimes not, depending on the circumstances, the needs of the

community, and the wishes of the worker. Members of the retreat, especially newer ones, were usually happy to give much of their energy to the community and generally spent less of their time on private pursuits. Those who needed less money also gave more time, as did those who assumed positions of leadership and responsibility, and enjoyed considerable status in return. Those who had families at the farm generally found that they had to devote more attention to their own income.

Jobs at Ananda were not rotated deliberately, and no labor sign-up sheets were used except to regulate scheduling among the two or three women who assumed responsibility for the retreat kitchen. The allocation of tasks inside the community took place by the anarchist mode of self-initiation by skills and preference ("attractive labor"), in which members would assume some area of responsibility as their own special province with others occasionally helping out, and by the capitalist mode of being paid wages or selling goods and services for profit. Morally this system was attuned to communal labor, but structurally it was capitalist, with "surplus labor" voluntarily donated as a moral tithe or civic responsibility. The building of Ananda's school, for instance, took much longer than planned because of conflicts with individual income needs.

There was also little that was communal about the patterns of group contact among the members. At the farm individual dwellings were scattered over a wide area and were considered private. There was communal dining only once a week or less (a potluck supper), and there was no fixed daily routine, except norms of rising early and doing private meditation and yoga exercises. While I was there, the community began holding weekly meetings at the request of some of the newer members, but meetings had been tried earlier and abandoned as fruitless. Not long after I left they became irregular again. Even the ritual content of Ananda's life was surprisingly low, given the group's religious orientation, with the entire group gathering ceremonially only once a week for services not unlike Sunday school and church. The emphasis instead was on private practice. At the retreat things were much more regularized in these respects, since some dwellings were communal (the dormitories), communal dining took place three times a day, more group activities were offered, and the daily routine was more programmatic.

The final reason why Ananda's communion score was so low was the absence of any significant hostility or persecution experiences from their neighbors or from local officials. Although some members suspected that the fire at the temple in 1969 may have been the result of arson, it was never proven. The one incident that might have been trouble in the early years had been peacefully turned away at the gate

(a carful of drunk but uncommitted vigilantes). Ananda got along well
with the business community of its area by paying its bills and with
the building inspectors by making sure in advance that all construction was up to code. Even though they were considered "bad news"
when they first moved into Nevada County, they eventually came to
enjoy more respect for their accomplishments and beliefs. There was
a standing joke at Ananda about distinctions the local people made
between Anandans and other longhairs. "Are those hippies?" "Naw,
they're yogis!" Altogether, Ananda's low score on communion was in
full accord with Kriyananda's injunction against "enforced togetherness." As the commune movement later evolved to a communities movement, Kriyananda was proven a fast starter again.

Mortification As at Maharaj Ashram and Lama, the yogic pre-
cepts of Ananda tended to place the source of social problems in the
self. It was considered somewhat illegitimate to make the problems of
one's own karma into problems for someone else. The solutions were
to be found inwardly and in learning to see the God in others, not in
outer systems. Hence, there was little mutual criticism in Ananda's
life even at meetings. It was both socially impolite and philosophically
shaky. If problems like recalcitrant nudity in the garden had to be
addressed, for example, they would usually be addressed in the abstract without naming individuals. Informally, there was apparently
little backbiting.

But the good of the community loomed over all, and although
there was little mortification of the ego by criticism, there was much
more of it by the good examples of others. There were clear patterns of
spiritual differentiation among members on the basis of their selfless
service to the community. The most highly regarded resident, of
course, was Kriyananda, whose status was continually validated by
regular ceremonies (above even him was the example of Yogananda
and other saintly teachers). Next were those members who had the
skills and initiative to do their own work well and still spend much time
on community affairs. These people usually assumed official roles on
the planning board or were validated in their chosen areas of responsibility by Kriyananda and/or the board. The most prominent, in fact, are
mentioned and praised by name in Kriyananda's book. In addition to
structured deference patterns, there were also the humility imposed by
all the formal doctrinal instruction and the probation period required of
new members (one month). Thus Ananda's level of mortification mechanisms was surpassed only by the Lama Foundation's.

Transcendence Ananda was also surpassed only by Lama in its
use of transcendence mechanisms. The power of its ideology was

apparent in its specific relation to one great teacher of historical importance, in its descent through the line to Kriyananda (among others), its intimate explanations of human nature, its detailed elaborations in Kriyananda's books, recordings, correspondence courses, and lessons, and in the common practice among members of assuming Sanskrit names. In addition Ananda's grounds had been blessed by holy men with many prayers, and magical events were reputed to happen frequently. The institutional awesomeness of Ananda's ideology was the highest possible on the measures used here, sharing that distinction with Maharaj Ashram. Swami Kriyananda did not, however, experience nearly the degree of reverence and submission from his followers that was accorded immigrant gurus like Yogi Bhajan by theirs.

In terms of concrete power and authority, Ananda again gained the highest score possible. It was clear that Kriyananda virtually embodied the community and that the authority hierarchy descended directly from him. As Spiritual Director on the corporate blueprint and in actual fact as well, he was the presiding officer in the community. It would be difficult to imagine anyone else filling the role tailor-made to fit himself, at least for many years to come. Only technically was he impeachable, especially since he legally controlled the land, and any efforts in that direction would provoke an unthinkable crisis. As the leader he had a special residence and of course special prerogatives.

The junior officers directly beneath him were chosen for their skills, initiative, responsibility, and naturally their personal loyalty to Kriyananda, cemented through years of working together on behalf of his dream. The second-in-command was Jyotish, the General Manager in the revised lexicon, the person who oversaw the community's everyday managerial affairs. Jyotish was the owner of Ananda's incense factory, a growing and successful enterprise employing many members off and on, and the person who usually stood in for Kriyananda at Sunday services and other such occasions when Kriyananda was not available. He was also Kriyananda's ear and voice in all meetings not attended by Kriyananda himself. Jyotish was the obvious successor. Somewhat below him were the two other trusted members of the board, loyal and competent students of Kriyananda's for years, chosen by the membership on paper but by the deference accorded Kriyananda's wishes in fact.

In sum, Ananda had the third most elaborate commitment structure in the study, behind the Lama Foundation and Maharaj Ashram. Like them Ananda had unusually high scores on renunciation of the outside world, transcendence through ideology and authority, and the mortification of marked spiritual differences between members.

Ananda went even farther by requiring a substantial entrance fee in addition to strict monthly payments.

In all of these respects Ananda differed considerably from the anarchical groups which made up the majority of those in this study. But Ananda's uniqueness is most apparent in its similarity to anarchical groups rather than religious groups in its low degree of communion. One of the findings of this study is that modern intentional communities seem to survive best with a level of communalization that is either very high or very low. Ananda chose the low road in this respect, incorporating within its mode of spirituality and elaborate structure a distinctly American accommodation to individualism and personal accountability.

III

When I returned to Ananda in 1973, the community showed many signs of prosperity. Like Lama and Libre, of which Ananda was a kind of fusion, many new buildings had been completed or begun since 1970, primarily residences. Ananda had also grown in many other respects. Property holdings had been increased with new sites for a monastery and a high school adjacent to the farm. Unlike many communities which had wistfully planned to have a school someday, Ananda's was actually in operation. The population at the farm had grown slightly to thirty (from twenty-seven), while at the retreat it had grown much more to thirty (from twelve). Several new babies had been born at the farm, a sure sign of success. Similarly, there were many new community industries, including the manufacture of toys, flower jewelry, novelties, foodstuffs, and candy (the luggage factory had not worked out). There was also an accounting and shipping service (privately owned) for the distribution of Ananda products nationally.

In 1972 the facilities at the retreat had been substantially renovated, and new construction was being planned for a publications building at the farm, new monastery facilities, and the long-postponed high school building. Expenditures for the village as a whole were divided into four areas—the farm, the retreat, the school, and the monastery—and the estimated budget for 1973 was $75,000. Individual payments had been doubled to $65 a month ($110 for couples), roughly half for the mortgage payment and half for general upkeep. But this sum was still quite small, and Ananda was able to meet approximately 75 percent of its income needs from its internal industries. Only eight members worked outside the community with any regularity, and no mortgage payments had been missed. Except for covering temporary deficits, Kriyananda had not had to support the village for three years. The only evidence of community decline was the garden, which was then (July) in poor shape. Characteristically, it had been Ananda's most communal enterprise and thus perhaps the most likely to suffer neglect.

In general, there had been a mild softening of rules at most levels of village affairs. The families at the farm more or less did their own thing, and attendance at retreat services had become less important and obligatory. Someday soon the farm hoped to have its own temple. Even at the retreat, life had become more voluntaristic and individualized, as evidenced by lower attendance at group services and by the fact that most retreat members had come to cook their own food in their own houses even though communal meals continued to be available three times a day. Celibacy was less emphasized, and there was even a time-payment plan for new members facing the $1,000 entrance fee on a limited budget. Politically things were basically unchanged, with a village-council, village-elder system at the farm serving in an advisory capacity to the overall planning board, which controlled all key decisions. Ananda was still not incorporated. Legal control still technically resided with Kriyananda, who now spent most of his time traveling or in seclusion at the monastery.

It is important to note, though, that for all this evidence of stability Ananda still had a high turnover rate: only 50 percent of the 1973 membership had been there in 1970. Still, this rate was second only to Libre's as the most stable in the sample, and the great majority of Ananda's 1973 members had been in residence for two years or more. Many who left had remained in Nevada County as individual householders nearby, keeping good relations and contact with the mother group. In essence those who left were just more like Ananda than Ananda itself: private and individualistic. Even so it is remarkable that a single community offered as much diversity and choice of life-styles as Ananda did. As *Communities* magazine put it:

> Since the beginning, the focus of Ananda has expanded, evolving to a village life style similar to the ancient Indian ashram, embracing all four stages of life: the stage of the student-disciple, the parcel for the high school; the stage of the devotee-householder, the parcel for the farm; the stage of partial withdrawal from ego-identity with the outer world, the retreat area; and the stage of complete withdrawal, the parcel for the monastery.[29]

Of course, another way of describing this curious synthesis of East and of West is as a free market with something offered for everybody within its institutional embrace. It is ironic that a new intentional community could go so far away from modern city life and so far into the cultural beliefs of a foreign land, only to recapitulate within itself the economic and social values of American capitalism. If we look at Ananda Village not as an exotic retreat but as a traditional frontier settlement, several features of its life jump out which are startling not for their strangeness but for their familiarity. Kriyananda thus becomes the town banker, presiding over a town council of the community's most prominent and civic-minded businessmen, who in turn employ the town's less ambitious working class in their private firms. One might even imagine that Ananda may someday have a chamber of commerce, labor strikes over low wages, or populist political movements among the disenfranchised majority.

In any case, Ananda is evolving a business-based and church-validated aristocracy which may someday bring it internal troubles it does not now foresee. Possibly the mechanics of the system may eventually undermine the spiritual values which gave the community birth; it has happened this way before. But perhaps capitalism is not an inexorable road to conflict after all. Perhaps the inner life of yoga is a sustaining ameliorative or even the antidote. As Kriyananda says, "It is not his systems that bless man, but man who blesses his systems by having the goodwill to make them work."[30]

Notes

1. Swami Kriyananda, *Cooperative Communities: How to Start Them, and Why* (Nevada City, Calif.: Ananda Publications, 1971), pp. 85–86. Described in the frontispiece as the "Sixth Edition," the 1971 publication is actually the second edition and the sixth printing since the first edition's original appearance in 1968.
2. Ibid., p. 3.
3. Ibid., p. xiv.
4. Ibid., pp. xii–xiii.
5. Ibid., p. xiii.
6. Ibid., p. xv.
7. Ibid., p. 57.
8. Ibid., p. 92.
9. Ibid., p. 57.
10. Ibid., p. 70.
11. Ibid., p. 74.
12. Ibid., pp. 74–75.
13. Ibid., p. 81.
14. Ibid., p. 84.
15. Ibid., p. 21.
16. Ibid., p. 83.
17. Ibid., p. 84.
18. Ibid., p. 88.
19. Ibid., pp. 71, 83.
20. Ibid., p. 89.

21. Ibid., p. 20.
22. Ibid., pp. 17–22.
23. Ibid., p. 30.
24. Ibid., pp. 31–33.
25. Ibid., p. 102.
26. Ibid., pp. 45–47.
27. Ibid., pp. 45–46.
28. Ibid., p. 102.
29. "Ananda Cooperative Village," *Communities*, 3 (1973), 6.
30. Swami Kriyananda, *Cooperative Communities*, p. 30.

11

A Question of Trust:
Talsalsan

I

In September 1966 a young seminary student in Boston named Richard Fairfield published the first issue of a new journal about contemporary communal living called *The Modern Utopian*. The following year he moved his operations to California for a variety of reasons, not the least of which was the great intensity of interest and experimentation in communal living around the Bay Area at the time. In early 1968, in addition to his publishing and theological activities, Fairfield started a discussion group on these topics in Berkeley which came to be known as the "Wednesday Night Group."

These discussions, which lasted about a year, were the genesis of at least three subgroups which eventually set out to put theory into practice and become actual communes themselves. One, which stayed on in the Berkeley hotbed, so to speak, was a group marriage called Harrad West, based on Robert Rimmer's book *The Harrad Experiment*. The other two groups were more alienated from city life and moved to southern Oregon. One became Saddle Ridge Farm, discussed in Chapter 13. The first of the three, which became Talsalsan Farm, was founded after only a few weeks of discussion in April 1968. For them it did not take long to decide what they wanted to do, at least theoretically.

The founders of Talsalsan were all in their mid-thirties, professional men and their wives and children, all relatively new to the "counterculture," and all quite a bit older than most of their communal contemporaries. Talsalsan's setting, selected by the two couples who put up the bulk of the down payment, was an old, eighty-acre farm just over the California border in an isolated valley. It was beautiful, economical, and a bargain with all the farming equipment that came with it. The clear waters of the Illinois River flowed right alongside. None of the members, of course, had ever been farmers before; nor, indeed, were they even very well acquainted. Nevertheless they were going to become an agriculturally based group marriage, attempting to break down the barriers of the two-person relationships they had known all their adult lives, in which they felt trapped or dissatisfied. As Fairfield described the group's formation in a brief digression in his book *Communes U.S.A.:*

> Against the better judgment of those closely connected with them in the group, three couples, one single guy, and seven children left the San Francisco Bay Area for Oregon. Others promised to follow, but never did, except to visit. The people in the group had very little exposure to each other but nonetheless decided to live communally, sharing everything in common, including each other's spouse. One couple never really got into the sexual sharing and each of the two other marriages was on extremely shaky grounds.
>
> Previously, they had carried on a brutal suburban existence—pharmacist and housewife; college professor and housewife. The men frustrated and the women unfulfilled. The country, the land, intimate friendships—all these spelled liberation, freedom from the old unhappy pattern; they were desperate to start a newer and more fulfilling life style. That desperation led them to move too quickly. Too many years of wrong habits could not be resolved so easily. Instead, seven desperate adults clung together, each shaking from the weight of his own lack of clarity. It was inevitable that that tiny group would be blown to bits.[1]

As a group marriage, Talsalsan (which means "the river") lasted only about a year. During that time the two shaky marriages switched partners and the third couple left. According to the lone member who remained in residence eighteen months after the founding summer, the failure of the early attempt was attributable to not being honest with each other, not having meetings for mutual feedback, unclear and ulterior motives on the part of some individuals which only later became apparent, and hang-ups about jobs and jealousy which were all the more deeply ingrained because of the ages of the founders.

In August 1969 those who still had a financial interest in Talsalsan retained a lawyer to draw up a trust agreement which would specify the rights and obligations of the farm's owners and the conditions under which they could continue their membership or lose it. The trust agreement had nine conditions, all of them pertaining to financial matters like accounting, mortgage payment sharing, equity

ownership, and liquidation of individual holdings. With the exception
of a few uninteresting legal definitions, these terms and conditions are
reproduced here in their entirety.

I have included this agreement because it represents an uncommon attempt among communes to objectify members' financial obligations and because it is unwittingly revealing of the social and psychological climate at Talsalsan. On the one hand it is a model agreement that might still be useful for many interesting purposes today. On the other hand it was unusual for its time, reflecting the professional, over-thirty backgrounds of its authors, and in the context of Talsalsan history it shows all too clearly that a legalistic contract does not a commune make. On the contrary, it may instead just clarify the route to communal dissolution.

Trust Agreement

WHEREAS, the parties hereto have jointly purchased a parcel of real property known as Talsalsan Farm, and more particularly described in Exhibit "A," which is attached hereto and by this reference incorporated herein, and

WHEREAS, at the time of purchase, the title to said real property was vested in the name of William _____ and Carol _____, husband and wife, subject to an oral trust between the parties hereto, and

WHEREAS the parties have deemed it advisable to reduce the terms of said oral trust and understanding to writing for the purpose of recording same in the Deed Records of Josephine County, Oregon,

NOW, THEREFORE, to provide a permanent memorial of said trust agreement, it is hereby agreed as follows:

(1) That the parties jointly keep . . . a set of books and records showing the various contributions of the parties and necessary expenditures in relation to the purchase and operation of Talsalsan Farm.

(2) The parties shall keep a joint checking account in the name of Talsalsan Farm at the Illinois Valley Branch, Western Bank, Cave Junction, Oregon, and that as much as possible, all income and expenditures of the parties for the operation of said farm shall be by check drawn on said account, with said canceled checks and account to be kept as a permanent part of the books and records of Talsalsan Farm. Said account may be drawn by either Jonathan _____, William _____, or Marion _____.

(3) An accounting shall be made by a person skilled in such operation at least once a year, on or before February 15, for the joint tax purposes of the parties.

(4) In determining the ownership interest that each of the parties has in the whole, there shall first be an accounting of the total capital expenditure of the parties as per the books and records of Talsalsan Farm; the percentage of the total capital expenditure that each of the

parties has contributed as determined from the capital account for each party from said books and records shall be each party's ownership percentage in Talsalsan Farm.

(5) Capital expenditure shall be defined for the purpose of the books and records of Talsalsan Farm as (*a*) capital improvement to a unit or building which had a total cost of One Hundred and 00/100 Dollars ($100.00), or more, (*b*) any part of the original down payment, (*c*) principal portion of any mortgage payment.

(6) The obligation of the parties to contribute to the monthly mortgage payments, fire insurance and property taxes shall be apportioned as follows: A full share to those of the parties hereto that have resided on the farm during the month preceding the due date for said payment, and a one-half (1/2) share for those not residing on said farm. In the event any of the parties refuse to pay their share under the above formula, then their share shall be paid by the other parties and deducted from the capital account of the nonpaying party. If the capital account of any of the parties is reduced to less than Five Hundred and 00/100 Dollars ($500.00), then that party's right to reside at the farm shall cease.

(7) None of the parties hereto may sell their ownership percentage in Talsalsan Farm to someone other than a party to this agreement without the written consent of all the parties hereto, except that if the party that desires to sell presents the other parties with an offer to sell for book value his or her ownership interest, and that offer is refused by the remaining parties, then the withdrawing party may sell his or her interest without the consent of the remaining parties. The terms of sale shall be as in Paragraph 8 below.

(8) In the event of the death of any of the parties, the remaining parties agree to buy the ownership percentage of the deceased party from said party's heirs at law for the book value thereof. Ten percent (10%) of the purchase price shall be due within sixty (60) days from the date of said death with the balance of ninety percent (90%) due within one (1) year.

(9) In the event any of the parties has as a guest any adult person for more than sixty (60) days, then that party's contribution to the insurance, taxes, and mortgage payments shall increase as though the guest had been a party hereto, and the inviting party shall be responsible for the guest's share of the taxes, insurance and mortgage payments for the year following the 60th day.

As it happened, this document did indeed pave the way for Talsalsan's dissolution, at least of the original group. Of the five signatories, only one, a physics Ph.D. named Jonny, was still in residence over Talsalsan's second winter. The others, able to maintain their interest in Talsalsan with only half the payments of residents and with protection for their capital investments, had little to lose by moving out to mull things over. Talsalsan was to continue as a commune, but its owners would now mostly live outside it, taking up the threads of their previous lives. For a resident membership, Talsalsan would have to start all over again.

II

By the spring of 1970, the river valley around Talsalsan had acquired something of a reputation in the underground as a groovy, isolated place where the land was cheap and the freaks outnumbered everybody else. Over the course of the year, many hundreds of long-haired nomads visited the valley. Some of them decided to stay; for those with few resources, a commune was often the most accessible means. There were now at least four communes in the immediate area, and at least three others in close proximity. Having no members, Talsalsan was obviously one of the most accessible, except for the fact that regular financial obligations were required. For that reason, among others, Talsalsan never attracted as many visitors and prospective members as some other nearby communes. Still, over the spring the population living at Talsalsan rose to as many as nineteen. The trust agreement made both entry and exit into and from Talsalsan relatively clear and simple, and the owners held off filing it legally to make rearrangements even simpler. Two or three dozen people spent varying lengths of time at Talsalsan that spring. Over the summer some of Talsalsan's absentee owners came back to stay for awhile. One of them, Dan, was reportedly very intrusive with his insistence on how things should be done.

By September the resident population was back to six; three men and three women, plus one child. Only one member had been there longer than six months or was presently an owner: Jonny Klein, a mild-mannered ceramic physics consultant who found himself in the somewhat unlikely role of community patriarch. The others were a single woman "sort of" with Jonny, a married couple in their late thirties, and another married couple still in their teens. The absentee owners had gone back home. On the day that I arrived, a former resident named Richard was just leaving the community to take an advertising job. He thought that Talsalsan's members were "kidding themselves about having a family here." He was "more honest," he said, about wanting to make money for himself. At least he seemed more industrious. At Talsalsan there was no economic activity during my visit other than the maintenance of a flock of chickens, a goat, and about an acre of marginal gardens and pasture. Financially, Talsalsan relied mostly on savings, plus individual help from welfare, child support payments, and food stamps. Overall, Talsalsan had the lowest degree of commitment mechanisms of any group in the study except Drop City.

Sacrifice   To begin with, the degree of sacrifice required to live at Talsalsan was lower than any other group studied. No forms of oral or sexual abstinence were practiced. Alcohol, tobacco, meat, and drugs were all permitted, though due to the farm's minimal budget and its members' predilections, were used only in moderation. The austerity of farm life was also moderate—indeed lower than any other group I visited—what with full electrical hookups to the main farm buildings, plumbing for water and sewage, the mild climate of the region (warmed year round by offshore breezes from the Japanese Current), and the group-wide use of supplemental social services like food stamps. The most austere feature of farm life was the partial need—for members who could not move into an existing structure or who were not so inclined—to build new dwellings. In the bedroom cabins built at some remove up the hillside from the main buildings, life was somewhat more primitive. Under Talsalsan's equity arrangements, though, building a cabin was a rescindable investment.

Investment   The only significant investment mechanism at Talsalsan, in fact, was the requirement of regular contributions to the insurance, tax, and mortgage payments and contributions to communal food expenses. Commitment through investment was weakened, however, by the maintenance of records and the reversibility of all mortgage payments or any capital improvements in excess of $100. No special fee or contribution was required for admission. No personal property had to be signed over to group use, although there were normative expectations that tools and vehicles would be shared. Several members in the past had undertaken to build their own shelters, but there was no requirement that they do so. Finally, and importantly, nonresident members were not prohibited. Physical investment in group life was not required, and membership could be retained at half price by those living outside the group even if they participated only on their vacations. Taken together, the investment requirements at Talsalsan were as low as any group in the study. It should be noted, though, that regular monthly cash needs, even if only $100 or less, were a substantial barrier to many prospective members who had no income, savings, or anything to invest but themselves. While the reversibility of investment in Talsalsan weakened commitment, at places like Wheeler Ranch or Drop City no cash investments were expected in the first place.

Renunciation   At Talsalsan the degree of renunciation of the outside world was also weak—not quite so weak as at Drop City or

Morning Star East, but for different reasons still rather low. The most unusual thing about Talsalsan in this respect was its lack of insulation from modern media. Geographically it was one of the more isolated groups, at a distance of a quarter mile from its nearest neighbor, 12 miles from the nearest town, and 175 miles from the nearest city over 50,000. But electronically Talsalsan was plugged in. Unlike any other rural group in this study, Talsalsan kept in daily touch with the outside world through a radio, a television, a telephone, and a variety of newspapers and magazines. Again this reflected the backgrounds of the older members, who seemed to find a wholesale withdrawal from modern society less imperative or desirable. One even followed the stock market on a daily basis.

On its cross-boundary control over visitors, new members, and outside trips (about one a week), Talsalsan was more average for communes in general. There was no group policy about visitors, other than their approval by the group at large in the next twice-weekly meeting if they stayed that long. According to the trust agreement, "guests" did not acquire financial obligations to the community until they had been in residence for sixty days. For new members the requirements were stricter. There was an informal probation period of a few weeks, unanimous acceptance was required, and in the past Talsalsan had both blackballed and ejected unpopular members. Eventually a new member was also expected to enter into the trust agreement, though few did so unless their investment expenditures reached a level where they became interested in protecting their equity. There were no particular requirements in terms of beliefs, skills, family situation, or attitude.

Communion Talsalsan was also about average among the groups in its level of communalization, although the components of this score were rather atypical in pattern. Talsalsan had an unusual diversity of age and backgrounds among its membership, and an odd pattern of mutual acquaintance in which the five owners (including one resident) had known each other for over two years, but the resident members had not known each other any longer than two and a half months. Altogether the level of social homogeneity was low. Another pattern of weak communion was the total absence of any ritual content to Talsalsan's life. They had tried holding hands before dinner at an earlier point in farm history, for example, but gave it up "because it seemed to be fake." Seldom if ever was there group singing and dancing, ceremonies, or other special community events. Similarly, there was a relatively low degree of regularized contact among group members. Several, of course, did not live at the farm. Those who did lived in dispersed and private dwellings. With no fixed daily routine to regulate their activities, the resident members typically spent less than 50 percent of their day in group settings. On the other hand, social life at Talsalsan was more regularized than certain other groups with respect to communal dining (once daily) and its scheduled meetings twice weekly.

But where Talsalsan was generally less communal than most groups in terms of homogeneity, ritual, and togetherness, it departed from the norm in the other, more structured direction of communistic sharing and communistic labor. Although (as usual) no turnover of personal property was required, Talsalsan did have regular payment requirements, joint title to the land, and common ownership (under the rules of equity) of all buildings plus the garden, livestock, and a considerable array of tools, furniture, vehicles, and farm equipment. Talsalsan also practiced universalistic job rotation for kitchen-related duties, and required unpaid labor, although no specific number of hours, of all members. Communal work efforts, on farm and kitchen chores especially, were common.

Finally, Talsalsan's persecution experiences at the hands of the outside community were about average for the sample as a whole. Although the valley in general had experienced plenty of trouble, the members of Talsalsan kept up comparatively straight appearances and made a point of doing favors for the local people and consequently had little trouble themselves. On the one occasion when they, too, had vigilante troubles—a carload of drunks taking potshots from the road across the river—they called the police and got results. In a nearby town, a number of local citizens described as "retired Orange County types" had formed the "Illinois Valley Betterment Association" and induced a number of local merchants to put up "hippie patronage not solicited" signs in their windows, but the members of Talsalsan did not rate this discrimination as very serious.

Mortification On ego-mortification Talsalsan also had an average score but, again, acquired it somewhat unusually. Unlike most communes, which had at least limited forms of spiritual differentiation among the members, Talsalsan practiced equality very studiously. Jonny Klein, for example, may have had grounds to claim a kind of higher moral status because of his long tenure and his initiative in matters of group responsibility, but he was an unassertive man without charisma and not so regarded. On the other hand, Talsalsan was even more unusual for the frequency of its group meetings (two a week), often devoted to problems of encounter and mutual criticism. These meetings were taken to be necessary because of the need to handle financial matters and a feeling that the original settlement had failed for lack of them. Privately, however (that is, in response to questionnaires), every member of the community disliked these meetings and felt that the group as a whole was not really open and honest enough with each other.

Transcendence The most conspicuously absent of the factors making for group commitment at Talsalsan were those relating to ideology, power, and authority. Once again Talsalsan was second only to Drop City in the sample for the lowest degree of transcendence before the greater, all-embracing structure of the group. Talsalsan was without any ideology beyond a certain guarded sharing. Unlike many other communes, there was no imputation of magical or other-worldly phenomena to specific group members, great teachers of the past or present, or the community as a whole. Life at Talsalsan, it might be said, lacked even the usual communal mystique about "flowing," serendipity, and other paranormal events. In terms of leadership it was entirely without structure. Jonny Klein manifested more initiative than any other member, but there was no noticeable form of authority hierarchy, special leadership prerogatives, or other rewards for his doing so, and all decisions were reached by unanimity. Similarly, there was no fixed routine or other programing of behavior beyond the scheduled meetings. In short, Talsalsan was an almost perfect political anarchy. The only awesome quality of group life in this regard was the original founders, who represented a negative example, if anything, and whose absentee ownership undermined resident loyalty.

III

When I returned to Talsalsan in August 1973, nobody seemed to be at home. As I was standing around wondering what to do next, Jonny Klein came sleepily out the door and invited me in. The main house, now occupied by him alone, was packed wall to wall with boxes of trash, bottles, and a stunning variety of junk and debris distributed around the furniture. In his bedroom, the only place in the house where there was room enough to sit down without moving something, the television was tuned in to the ABC Evening News. Turning down the television to a low drone he told me the following story.

In the fall of 1970, the teen-age couple left to go to college, with the understanding that they would be coming back the next summer. Jonny and the older couple stayed on through the winter as the core members, with others trickling in and out, growing in number with the spring. Over the summer of 1971, a wave of pentecostal Christianity swept through the valley and Talsalsan was transfigured. The teen-age couple came back from college and became "Jesus freaks." The older couple did too, as in fact did everybody at Talsalsan but Jonny. The second of the two main houses, down near the gate and more open to the paved road, became known as "Hallelujah House," offering a crash pad, free meals, and Christian services to those who wandered down the road. Klein, not so inclined to transfiguration himself, could do little but watch it all go by.

Later that year and in 1972, Talsalsan's other owner (there were now apparently just two) came back from the city and tried to start a school of ecological living at the farm. Despite recruitment through the Free U in Berkeley and the general cooperation of Talsalsan's residents, it never got off the ground. By the spring both the teen-age couple and the older couple had left for good. New people drifted in over the summer of 1972, but Klein found they had little interest in communalism, even though expenses and to some extent income were shared equally at his urging. By the winter of 1972–1973, he gave up. He simply started renting Talsalsan's cabins out at fixed (though lenient) rates to an assortment of ten individuals, some coupled and some not but none interested in making it any more of a commune than that. For the most part, welfare paid the rent.

According to Klein, this was a pattern repeated throughout the valley, and he called it an iron law: "People will live with each other only as close as their feelings." That is why, he said, so many communes had become atomized into communities or dispersed altogether by 1973. At Talsalsan people just didn't really care for each other very much. Most people who went into the commune scene, he said, did so for the wrong reasons—just out of college with nothing to do, without much money to support themselves, just passing time and looking around. For many, communes were the laziest and cheapest way to get by. Klein also explained the Jesus movement at Talsalsan in the same way—as a general state of confusion and indecision and the need for spiritual purpose and leadership. By the summer of 1973, what had resulted was a kind of rent cooperative, which is perhaps what it always was. Klein lived alone, cutting hay for sale, working as a volunteer for the new free clinic in the valley, doing some survey drafting for a friend's subdivision, and dabbling with plans for his dream home up the hillside.

In retrospect, the basic truth of Jonny Klein's "iron law" is easy to see. Without feelings of closeness and mutual destiny, a group such as Talsalsan often turns into what Ken Kesey has called "the communal lie." From the first, Talsalsan was apparently without these feelings. Yet how are these feelings generated? In some communal groups they were preexisting, the product of long acquaintances.

But in most groups they probably did not exist any more strongly than at Talsalsan. Many groups like Drop City or Wheeler Ranch implicitly recognized this state of affairs and did not strain to countermand it, while others like Libre actually incorporated individualism into their structure, with deep and binding feelings left to emerge organically over time. Other groups like Lama and Maharaj implicitly recognized it, too, and buttressed feelings for others with a higher love for God and various disciplinary structures to reinforce it. Almost all of the more successful groups developed some form of ritual content in their lives, again in implicit recognition that words and discussion alone lacked something.

For Talsalsan, though, there was only rationality after the romance had passed the first year. The trust agreement, the meetings—that these were not enough was evidenced by the revival that swept through the community. Even when Talsalsan reacted to the void at its center by becoming religious, caution was reasserted by the owners of the community who did not want their investments moved in that direction. In the end the confrontation between rationality and salvation was the impasse that led to the community's final expiration; it could succeed as neither a contractual commune nor a religious sect, so it became nothing. In a sense the group was done in by the very generation gap and culture clash that gave so many other communes birth.

The valley, though, continued to grow and even prosper a bit as a new frontier for the young and disaffected. By 1973 the more or less permanent "freak" population had grown to about five hundred, and a valley-wide sense of identity was growing that was perhaps more significant than its communes had ever been. Local dropout residents had begun to have village-wide meetings, and there were even efforts in motion to incorporate as a town. The big event of the summer was the establishment of a free clinic in the valley. A young doctor agreed to come in and set up his practice there if the people of the valley would help pay for the mortgage on the clinic and agree to be responsible for it themselves. The need for the clinic fused the valley residents together as they had never been before. For the valley it was a newly exhilarating time. From another point of view it was like an echo of frontier history come full circle, for the straight world had once done the same things itself.

Indeed, the valley became like nothing so much as a wild frontier settlement struggling all over again for prosperity, organization, and respectability, complete with six-gun–toting sheriff and shootouts up in the hills, as well as town meetings and the other rudiments of community building.[2] Some good money was beginning to come into the valley, too. Many local men worked on fire crews for the forest service, and even more had found good pay if somewhat ambivalent work in logging (which had devastated the area a generation or two previously). As Klein put it, "The valley's becoming straighter all the time." Its residents also became more aggressive in defending their right to exist. In 1972, for instance, a bunch of "rednecks" came out to the valley intending to shoot up the place, but somehow leaked their plans in advance. A select group of men was waiting for them when they arrived and not only took their guns away from them but beat them up. The valley was now theirs, to do with for better or worse what their forefathers had done.

Notes

1. Richard Fairfield, *Communes U.S.A.: A Personal Tour* (Baltimore: Penguin Books, 1972), p. 225. Fairfield writes of Talsalsan obliquely as "Talsen."

2. The shoot-out was one of several bizarre episodes connected with a group called "The White Muslims." They came to the valley in 1972 and camped up in the hills, mainly on someone else's patented mining claim. All but one member was white. I was unable to learn exactly how they became followers of Allah, only that several of them were apparently Vietnam veterans. Some of them wore Muslim robes, but the most remarkable thing about them (since strange costumes were no big news) was that they all carried guns—often 30-30 rifles—wherever they went. This caused a great deal of consternation and fear in the valley, and the White Muslims were not generally liked. The shoot-out took place between a valley resident named Black Mike, who had originally befriended them, and Abdullah, the White Muslims' only black. It happened because Abdullah, in a fury of Islamic puritanism, got after Black Mike's girlfriend and beat her up for watering the garden without enough clothes on. One thing led to another, and about four days later Black Mike cut Abdullah in half with a shotgun. In the pretrial grand jury, his action was ruled justifiable homicide. In the early summer of 1973, the White Muslims decided to travel to Canada over the high-altitude Pacific Ridge Trail with mules and donkeys. Sending their women ahead by other means, they got only as far as Ashland, twenty-five miles away. There is no forage at high altitude that early in the growing season, and by the time they made it to Ashland, their pack animals were worn out and emaciated. After selling their stock at a considerable loss, the White Muslims disappeared.

12

Son of Sociology:
Crook's Creek

I

The story of the Crook's Creek Family begins rather improbably in 1967, when the sixteen-year-old son of two university sociologists dropped out of high school to join the hippies and explore their new culture. His name was Greg, and 'for a year or two he knocked about aimlessly, thinking that if nothing else came up, he would go to sea. Meanwhile, in New York City, the editors of *Life* magazine were preparing to print the most evocative photo essay about modern rural communes ever published in a national magazine. The group they immortalized was the Family of Mystic Arts near Sunny Valley, Oregon, a spiritualist commune founded in 1968. In *Life*'s July 18, 1969, issue, the story appeared as "The Commune Comes to America." With lush color photography and sympathetic narration, the Family of Mystic Arts was enshrined as the prototype of all that was good and beautiful about the new back-to-the-land commune movement.[1]

To the thousands of disaffected young people who read and were influenced by the article, it was almost a vision of heaven—beautiful people, beautiful setting, and a harmonious new way of sharing and living with others. As Judson Jerome reported in his *Families of Eden*, the commune afterwards experienced some two thousand visitors a year, even though its name and location were not revealed; the word simply got out along the underground grapevine.[2] One of those visitors was Greg, now seventeen or eighteen, who stayed with the group for several months until he determined that he wanted to start a new commune himself. Greg came to the Family of

182

Mystic Arts in advance of the publicity, but the appearance of the *Life* article must have improved his recruiting considerably, for what became the Crook's Creek Family was organized in the weeks just following its publication.

In 1969 Greg returned home, secured the social and financial support of his parents, and began to make contact with old friends and new friends with similar interests in communal living and getting back to the land in Oregon. The decision to go ahead was reached in a two-week period of intense discussions and planning in late July 1969. The group members had known each other an average of one year, with some cases of better acquaintance and several others of much less. That summer, Greg and another young man, Chuck, found 160 acres of unimproved forest land in the general vicinity of the Family of Mystic Arts and bought it for $10,000. With a twenty-year mortgage and payments of $90 a month, the price was incredibly low even given the fact that the land had been logged over in the not-too-distant past. In addition to beauty and economy, another important factor in their choice was the land's isolation—it was surrounded on all sides by national forest. The land was purchased by the group, with the names of seven persons on the deed.

In August six of them moved onto the land, with the seventh person on the deed, Timmy, plus others, to join them the following spring as outside obligations were cleared up and some money saved. That fall the initial settlers, with help from some of the others on weekends and vacations, constructed a large, octagonal lodge out of logs with twelve-foot sides and a thirty-foot diameter. On one side they built an extension for a kitchen, and in the middle they assembled a central fireplace with a hooded exhaust, surrounded by a circular lounge area which was surrounded in turn by tables, beds, and other furnishings around the walls. It was an ingenious and practical structure for the $400 it cost to build it, including the commercial fireplace which alone accounted for half the expense. For the first winter, just like the hexagonal lodge at the Family of Mystic Arts, it was the commune's home.

Over the spring and summer of 1969, the size of the Crook's Creek Family doubled to twelve as those who had agreed to join the group later gradually moved in. Most of them came in the spring. The last of the original planning group to show up was Timmy, who arrived in the late summer (bringing on a crisis that will be discussed later in detail). With the arrival of spring and the new residents, the members of Crook's Creek began to build bedroom cabins by couples at considerable distances from the main lodge, "segmenting" themselves just as the Family of Mystic Arts and so many other communes had done in reaction to the intensity of living under a single roof.[3] Using salvaged doors and windows and lower-grade lumber seconds, the cabins cost an average of $200 apiece. The membership also began construction of what they called a crafts lodge, which was to include a pottery studio, a leather shop, a woodworking shop, and a darkroom for photographic equipment. They also planted a small, quarter-acre garden and acquired two goats and a flock of chickens.

By the time I arrived in September of 1970, Crook's Creek had evolved a clear conception of itself as an intentional "family" based on collectively owned property and arts and crafts industries. It had a sexually balanced population of twelve adults, said by many communal observers to be the optimal size for such groups. All were from middle-class backgrounds and most were college dropouts, averaging a little over twenty-one years of age. There were no children, and they preferred not to have any, a fact which seemed curious to me at the time. In retrospect, it seems almost obvious that the implications of child-rearing responsibilities would not be lost on the son of two sociologists. He had been steeped in it, he told me, and his conversation was liberally dotted with complex analyses of the dangers of the nuclear family and institutionalization. With children, Crook's Creek would be forced to grow up faster than it wanted.

II

Without advance knowledge or a detailed map, Crook's Creek would be very difficult to find. Unlike Talsalsan or Saddle Ridge, it was not located in a cluster of other latter-day homesteaders but instead well off the beaten track down two miles of unmarked gravel and dirt roads from the nearest asphalt pavement. Crook's Creek was also completely unpublicized and as far as I know never mentioned by name or location in any of the books, articles, journals, and newsletters about communal living published since its founding. This high degree of withdrawal was reflected in the fact that Crook's Creek received very few outside visitors, usually an average of only one a week and then mostly just friends. The access road dead-ended at the commune, and scarcely anyone without business there ever wandered in. This was the way Crook's Creek wanted it. The group thus showed a seriousness of intent to escape that is possibly underrepresented in this study, which is made up of groups that were generally better known or more accessible (and sometimes self-advertising). With the exception of the three groups which were based on religious ideologies, Crook's Creek had a stronger commitment structure than any of the others.

Sacrifice This structural commitment was not particularly apparent, though, in the degree of sacrifice to which the members of Crook's Creek were obligated to submit, which was about average. In terms of austerity, it was more primitive than most, since all buildings had to be built from scratch and since there were only wood fires for heat, a seasonal water supply that had to be carried by hand, and an outhouse for sanitation. These inconveniences were offset by the availability of generator-stored electricity at the main lodge for the stereo and other uses, by the mild southwestern Oregon winters, by the groupwide use of food stamps and other emoluments from parents and the state, and by the lack of any norms favoring oral abstinence or sexual continence apart from the typical communal practice of serial monogamy (that is, one partner at a time.)

Investment In its use of investment structures, though, Crook's Creek expected a bit more, indeed as much as any other group in the study except possibly Ananda, which required an entrance fee where Crook's Creek did not. But unlike Ananda, or any other group I studied, Crook's Creek required the turnover to the commune of all income and all property other than personal effects and whatever was left behind outside (which was preferably to be brought in and turned over to the commune, too). All money, tools, vehicles, and goods inside the community were held and shared in common. In addition, no records of contributions or indebtedness were kept except for the money spent on the original down payment, where contributions were unequal. Not even that was considered returnable to defectors from the group "unless there was a clear case of need and the family was able to pay it," as Greg put it. Crook's Creek's investment requirements were also strict in requiring members to be responsible for their own shelters and by the prohibition of nonresident members. Readmitting an absent member required much the same procedures as admitting a new member.

Renunciation Crook's Creek also practiced a high degree of renunciation of the outside world; only Lama and Ananda were more withdrawn. At distances of 2 miles from the nearest neighbor, 10 miles from the nearest incorporated town, and 168 miles from the nearest city (Eugene), Crook's Creek was well above the average level of physical isolation. In communications media, too, Crook's Creek was well insulated, with only "movement" publications to connect it with outside events. The cross-boundary control dimension to renunciation was also higher than average. Trips to town were biweekly, less frequent than in most groups. Restrictions concerning visitors included a time limit of about two days to their stay, a limit to their numbers ("very few"), and an agreeable attitude and purpose for being there. It was my personal experience as a professional commune visitor to be scrutinized more carefully at Crook's Creek than at any other group that comes to mind. At the time I was the only visitor there. One member in particular had a persistent suspicion that I was a narcotics agent, even after I joined in on a giant, cigar-sized joint. He constantly monitored my behavior whenever I was within his sight. Since my visit seemed to have the support of Greg, though, he never suggested throwing me out, at least not in my presence.

In screening new members, Crook's Creek used a probation period of about two months, or "until it feels right," at which time the group would meet to discuss the new member and see if unanimous approval was forthcoming. Like most communes with such systems, whether or not acceptance would be unanimous usually became apparent in advance of a formal meeting. A blackball, in effect, could be issued informally without a group declaration. Using this hybrid of individual feelings, informal gossip, and interpersonal encounter, Crook's Creek had blackballed at least three prospective members over the previous year. Crook's Creek had also ejected an existing member, which in fact happened in my presence. Exactly how it happened is worth describing in some detail, and I have included the story as a classic example of a modern commune dealing successfully with its most delicate social issue: rejection.

The ejected member's name was Timmy, and Timmy had a bad case of galloping immaturity. He was moody, touchy, and given to roaring off on his motorcycle at the tiniest slight to his dignity. He behaved with a sort of sulking theatricality around the women, who found him childish, while the men were often annoyed with his flights from confrontation and the fact that he seldom helped with the work. He was bringing everybody down and was an obvious liability to the group's future. But Timmy had put up some money in the beginning and had his name on the community deed. The case of Timmy made the others at Crook's Creek realize that their collective deed was an inconvenience and maybe even a mistake. They were thinking about transferring title to a nonprofit corporation (which would have bylaws and provisions for legally changing the membership). But Timmy refused to take his name off the deed. He could sense that he was disliked, and even though others in the group would take their names off too, Timmy was afraid (with good reason) that if he lost his legal claim to be there, he would be asked to leave. He wanted very much to stay.

Timmy had come into Crook's Creek at the formative stage of its development when the members-to-be were planning to make a land purchase. Even though the other members did not know Timmy very well, they were eager to make their move and were short of cash, so when Timmy offered to buy in, they accepted him. He seemed agreeable enough at the time. Getting to know him better was hindered for a long time by his decision to stay in the city and join them in the spring, which he postponed until later that summer. By the time he arrived, the rest of the group had been working and living together in their new home for up to a year, and Timmy simply did not fit. Perhaps with such a delayed arrival he wouldn't have fit in even if he had been more adult. In any case, the other members had by then become rather close and tightly knit, and most wanted Timmy out. To get what they wanted, they turned to Greg, the social nucleus of the group. His tender age notwithstanding, Greg had a natural gift (perhaps enhanced by his professional parents) for giving the group direction by seeking out, moderating, and channeling the opinions of others into collective agreement. More of a switchboard than a ruler, Greg gave the others a feeling of leading themselves merely by facilitating communications. He was also, along with a couple of other men, the source of most of the group's policy and project ideas.

While Timmy was off on one of his moody motorcycle rides, Greg convened the people of Crook's Creek in the main lodge to decide what to do. Some members could scarcely contain their anger about Timmy. They agreed that Greg, being the most unruffled and diplomatic among them, should carry the bulk of the discussion with Timmy when he returned. While the others should participate a bit, they should avoid appearing to gang up on him. When Timmy returned later, Greg invited him to talk. Timmy was defensive and on edge, but Greg and the others were extremely gentle with him, sprinkling compliments and favorable remarks throughout the encounter.

Slowly and gradually, Timmy was eased away from his bitterness by soft-spoken, positive coaxing and reassurances that the deed change was "just good sense" and that the issue was "unrelated to him personally." Timmy settled down but remained skeptical. He said he wanted to know Greg's feelings in the "unrelated" area of whether or not he would still be welcome to stay. Greg very tactfully said that he didn't think he felt close enough to Timmy yet, that no, he wasn't sure their trips meshed, that he wanted to make very sure they did before something much worse than what was happening now happened again later in the winter, when things got more intense. Timmy thought silently for a while and then said that he was not going to take his name off the deed now, but he might later.

When Timmy made that remark, one of the women in the group could contain herself no longer. "I just can't relate to anyone who won't respond to the good of the group," she said angrily. "Especially over something as simple as this. I've already taken *my* name

off. It just blows me out!'' Livid with rage, she stalked out the door
and slammed it behind her. Timmy was stunned. For several silent
minutes he just sat staring at the floor. Finally, gently, Greg told him,
"You must have known that was there.'' This stirred Timmy from his
stupor, and getting up and mumbling something, he rode off on his
motorcycle again. When he came back that evening, he agreed to
remove his name. In the interim, Greg told me that if their psychological strategy did not work, they would return his original share of
the down payment and forcibly boot him out, leaving him to go to
court if he cared to, though it was very doubtful he would. But this
was not necessary, for after a short term of gradually escalating snubs
and ostracism he left on his own.

It was no accident, perhaps, that he was the group's only mate-
less member. A single male in an isolated community of couples is
often a destabilizing influence. As in so many such communes, it
might have made a difference—for at least a while longer—if he had
been mated, too. As it was, he exemplified the grounds for turning
away tentative members as explained by Greg: "incompatibility, not
being together enough, and not sharing the same trip as the family.''
In the wake of this episode, Greg went further and explained to me
his theory of "complementarity" that should apply to selecting new
people. "Each new person must get the group *higher* than it was
before—not just not bring people down, but not dilute the high that
already exists, and then take it even higher.''

Communion   On the various measures of communion, Crook's
Creek again scored higher than average for the study as a whole, with
only two other groups having higher scores. To begin with, the members had known each other for one to two years and were all less than
five years apart in age, a relatively high degree of social homogeneity.
They also drew the study's highest score on the degree of communistic sharing, with requirements for the turnover of all income and
property to the group and communal ownership of the land, all buildings, tools, autos, livestock, and the garden.

Even so, there were significant loopholes in this system of communal ownership. Money was kept in common, and any nontrivial
expenditures required a collective decision. But a fair portion of it
was set aside in "stashes" for individual projects. And like the land,
which was retained in the name of individuals rather than a collective
charter, actual legal title to personal property was not formally transferred to the group. All goods were expected to be shared (for instance, all car and truck keys were to be left in the ignition, and no
permission was necessary for any member to use them), but there
were no legal grounds for denying a defector his previously private

tangibles if he decided to leave. This was typical of even the most communistic groups of the modern era. There was almost always some way out of collective ownership.

On communistic labor, Crook's Creek was less strict and about average for the sample as a whole. Uncompensated labor for the sake of the entire community was a preferred, legitimate expectation but not elevated to the level of a requirement. Communal work efforts were common but obviously decreasing in importance as the members' attention turned toward the construction of their private cabins and other individual pursuits. There was job rotation in the communal kitchen via a sign-up sheet, but it was equalitarian only in the winter. In the summer, as long as there was building to be done, kitchen tasks were mostly the province of women. Tending the livestock and the garden and working on collective undertakings like the crafts lodge were tasks distributed on a voluntary, self-selected basis, usually by men.

Regularized group contact was also about average. On the one hand, communal dining twice daily, regularly scheduled meetings once a week, and the comforts and entertainments of the main lodge meant that the average member spent a majority of his waking hours in group settings. On the other hand, the bedroom cabins to which the members retired every night were private and widely scattered, each out of the sight of the others. There was no fixed daily schedule beyond a horn to awaken people for breakfast and collecting for supper in the evenings. Similarly, the ritual content to life at Crook's Creek was rather sparse, with periodic group meditations "when the mood occurs," usually about weekly. There were no mealtime prayers, and the only special events celebrated were the usual birthdays, Thanksgiving, and Christmas. Group singing and dancing was infrequent, though I was told it increased in the winter. Music was important to the commune but more in passive than active ways. Finally, there had been no incidents of legal or vigilante harassment or economic discrimination in Crook's Creek's history to add a negative component to its strength of communion; nevertheless, Greg felt that over 75 percent of the people in the local area were hostile to the group's existence.

Mortification Like most modern communes, Crook's Creek did not have very strict mechanisms for subordinating individual egos to the greater moral authority of the group. But as we saw earlier in the case of Timmy, what there was of it could be subtle and effective. Like Saddle Ridge and other such groups with relatively strong communal ambitions, the role of interpersonal confrontations was important. The formal meetings once a week were openly expected to be just as devoted to encounter and mutual criticism as to the business affairs of the day. Crook's Creek did not often go as far as Saddle Ridge, though, in calling general meetings specifically devoted to encounter. But except for stricter probation arrangements for new members, Crook's Creek was just as scrupulous as Saddle Ridge in avoiding distinctions among members on moral or spiritual grounds.

Transcendence The only dimension to commitment in which Crook's Creek dipped well below average was the component of transcendence. Like most familial, nonreligious anarchies, Crook's Creek made little use of these mechanisms. For an ideology it had only the collected "trips" of its existing members and a general interest in communal sharing. Greg's sociological sophistication notwithstanding, it had no integrated and detailed philosophical system, nor was it linked to great teachers, historical traditions, or beliefs imputing paranormal powers to either the group or its members. Evaluation of prospective new members was measured more in terms of whether they "felt right" or "meshed with our trips" than by conversion to any specific ideological imperative. This lack of institutional power over individuals was reflected in the absence of any fixed or detailed daily routine. If there was an ideology, it was only the antiauthoritarian anarchism common to so many other groups, scarcely having the function of inducing personal surrender but instead forestalling it. On the other hand, there were elements of informal patriarchal authority even though the membership was consciously striving for equalitarian relationships throughout group life. As we saw in the Timmy episode, the members of Crook's Creek were in general agreement about who embodied the group best, who had the most reliable judgment in questions of the group's best interests, and who to turn to and trust in difficult situations, even if he was only nineteen years old and enjoyed no special rewards for his service.

To the degree, then, that Crook's Creek represents a type of withdrawn familial anarchy not often detected in the surveys of sociologists and journalists, these are the characteristics of the type: greater degrees of personal investment, more extensive sharing of property, greater isolation, more distrust of strangers, closer similarities in age and background among members, and more intense interpersonal relationships. In general, these things make such groups stronger, but the last factor, the intensity of life in groups this tight and withdrawn, is a two-edged sword. On the one hand, it can lead to the warmth and wonders of intimacy; on the other, it can be as volatile as a powder keg, requiring special kinds of personalities to survive the times it goes off.

III

When I visited Crook's Creek again in July 1973, it looked just as I left it, with the same buildings and the same number of people, but only Greg and another male member, Don, were still there from the original group I had visited in 1970. Since Greg was temporarily absent, Don brought me up to date on Crook's Creek history. It was a hot day, and he and the eight or nine other people lolling about the main lodge were all nude, mostly resting or reading. Except for one woman who got up to put on a brassiere, the others ignored me as I sat fully dressed and talked with Don. All but one other woman were apparently visitors, the other members being off on a trip with Greg.

According to Don, the new group was much more open and honest than the old one had been. There were real failures of communication among the original people, he said, hidden reservations about sharing, secret plans, suppressed resentments, and sexual conflicts. The other members had gone back to the lure of city trips, left to find new jobs or mates, or, as Don put it, "went off expecting to come back but just never did." If they came now, he said, they would not be especially welcome, certainly not if they made any legalistic claims to be there because their names were still on the deed. The hassles over ownership of the land that had been involved in the Timmy problem, then, had never been resolved. No corporate charter had ever been created, and the deed was still in many old members' names, but Don did not seem to think this was very important or care very much about changing it. He did not expect to see most of the old members again.

On all tangible measures, there had been almost no physical changes at Crook's Creek over the course of the three years. The buildings still unfinished in 1970 had been completed; otherwise there had been no new construction or improvements in utilities and no growth in community property, industry, or population. The crafts lodge had been completed but seldom used as it was intended. There was little craft activity apparent in the lodge, and it was mostly used as a storeroom and crash pad for guests. For income the membership made the money they needed by doing occasional hay bucking, ditch digging, construction, or other temporary jobs. Over the years they had cultivated good relations with their neighbors and got work, help, and free milk from them. At one point the commune had planned to manufacture and sell antler hash pipes but ended up making only a couple and giving those away. The main focus of collective activity had now turned to a suit against the Bureau of Land Management, reportedly with the support of the Sierra Club and an environmental activist lawyer, to prevent clear-cutting in the adjacent national forest.

Internally, Crook's Creek proceeded now as then without explicit leaders or schedules. In general, life there had become even more informal than it had been before. There were no longer posted sign-up sheets for kitchen chores, for instance, and the members now ate separately more often. The regular meetings had now become irregular, membership and visitation policies had been relaxed, and cooperative work efforts were now obviously minimal. Communal sharing, it seemed, worked best at Crook's Creek when there remained little at stake. Personally I felt that Crook's Creek was in a rut. Still, it remained intact as an organization, the members were reasonably comfortable, and the group was still making its $90 payments without worrying about structure, deeds, or equal shares. There was still a genuinely communal spirit at Crook's Creek, too. Like Saddle Ridge, it was still capable of surviving and hanging loose at the same time. And in sharing of property and income they still went farther than any other group in the study. These were not trivial accomplishments, even if achievable only by high turnover and subsistence living.

Perhaps the strangest and most telling episode that happened over the interval between my visits was the death of Greg's girlfriend Holly in 1971. According to Don, she began to feel as if everybody else was on a higher and more meaningful plane of existence than she was and suffered increasingly from the conviction that she was worthless and left out. In the end, Don said, she went completely crazy and hung herself. But the strangest thing about this incident was the reported reaction of Greg and the rest of the group. Apparently Greg was puzzled about it but not shaken up, nor did it cause any trauma to the group as a whole. "I mean it's a flash, man, when somebody does themself in," Don said, "but that's the way things go. Their head gets in a certain place and there's nothing anybody can do about it." I could never decide whether this attitude displayed an especially courageous view of human destiny or just an especially impersonal lack of compassion and human responsibility. Whichever, it said something very significant about the nature of the group and the indolence that had settled in there by 1973, as perhaps it had in the commune movement as a whole.

Notes

1. John Stickney and John Olson, "The Commune Comes to America," *Life*, July 18, 1969, pp. 16B–23.
2. Judson Jerome, *Families of Eden: Communes and the New Anarchism* (New

York: Seabury Press, 1974), p. 185. Jerome did not visit the Family of Mystic Arts or mention it by name, but his reference to the *Life* article left no doubt about who he was writing about. Robert Houriet did visit the Family of Mystic Arts in January 1970 and reported on it in *Getting Back Together* (New York: Avon Books, 1972), pp. 114–120.

3. The term "segmentation" for this phenomenon was coined by Benjamin Zablocki. "Unwilling to undergo a complete transformation of self," he writes, "most commune members, nevertheless, eventually conclude that some modification of absolute anarchism is necessary if the commune is not to dissolve in chaos. . . . One [modification] is segmentation either of the commune itself into a number of smaller 'families' or subcommunes, or of the life into communal, cooperative, and individualistic areas." See *The Joyful Community* (Baltimore: Penguin Books, 1971), pp. 311–318. Wheeler Ranch (by the name of "Freedom Ranch") is given as an example of both types of segmentation. His example of "privacy of domicile" segmentation, which he calls "Dry Creek," could very well be Crook's Creek.

13

Forever Choice,
Forever Changes:
Saddle Ridge Farm*

I

Like Talsalsan Farm, Saddle Ridge Farm was one of several communes which evolved from the Wednesday Night Group organized in Berkeley by *The Modern Utopian*'s editor Richard Fairfield in early 1968. The Wednesday Night Group began as most academic discussion groups do, by reading books. Among them were Heinlein's *Stranger in a Strange Land*, Skinner's *Walden Two*, Rimmer's *The Harrad Experiment*, and Huxley's *Island*, all fictional accounts of imaginary communal societies. But soon these discussions came to seem too abstract and impersonal, and the group divided itself into several subgroups of about ten people each to talk about feelings as well as ideas and to do things together instead of spending all the time talking. In April 1968 the Talsalsan subgroup left the city to live on their newly acquired farm in southwestern Oregon. In September of that year, proceeding much more slowly but much less deliberately

*The name "Saddle Ridge Farm" is a pseudonym, regrettably the one exception to the goal of explicit historical accuracy stated earlier in this book. "Saddle Ridge" member Elaine Sundancer, whose book about the group is cited extensively in this chapter, requested that the actual names of her commune and the nearby village be removed. To her, the commune and the unincorporated township where it is located are still fragile experiments vulnerable to invasions of unwanted visitors or media attention; moreover, she feels responsible to her community to observe its wish for privacy. Given the irreplaceable value of Sundancer's thoughtful insider's account, however dated the fear of invasion seems now, her request has been carried out.

even so, the founders of Saddle Ridge found a choice seventeen-acre site of their own just down the road.

During the spring of 1968, the participants in the Wednesday night meetings eventually made their gatherings more into parties than discussions and began to see a lot of each other outside of the meetings as well. Among the subgroup that later became Saddle Ridge, the resolve to leave the city and buy some land apparently dates from a four-day camping trip to the Sierras the original six members of Saddle Ridge took in June. It was an exhilarating trip, and soon after it several members of the group decided they could not stand the city anymore and spent the remainder of the summer looking for land. In September one of the couples in the group found the seventeen-acre parcel and wrote the others to come look at it, which they did, but with mixed feelings. They cast the *I Ching* to decide whether or not to buy it. The *I Ching* told them to wait, and so they waited.

One night later that month, with half the group in Oregon and the other half in Berkeley, they talked it over long-distance, still without resolution. In the aftermath of the phone call, two men on the Berkeley end, Peter and Roland, the group's two oldest members and both experienced gardeners, decided that it was good land and that they just couldn't spend another winter in the city. Between them they had enough money to make the down payment, and that very evening they set off hitchhiking to Oregon to make the deal. The land was purchased in the names of Roland, his wife (who stayed behind), and Peter. The couple who found the land moved in immediately, Roland and Peter a bit later, and the two other original members followed the next spring.

The seventeen-acre site they named Saddle Ridge Farm was heavily forested, mostly second-growth timber making a comeback in the hills and along the valley after logging and mining activities some two decades earlier. Also included on the property were three acres of meadow with deep topsoil, a small but year-round stream, a tiny old house, and two ramshackle outbuildings. A mile of dirt road separated the farm from the nearest paved road, giving Saddle Ridge a fair measure of seclusion from straight neighbors. Most of their neighbors were by then longhairs anyway, coming in large numbers in 1968 to camp or build cabins along the nearby river, a development which the founders of Saddle Ridge took as a good omen. Altogether it was almost ideal for their needs: enough size for a small group, an increasing number of hip neighbors, good land and water, plenty of space to garden, and the seclusion to swim in the buff.

Despite a gestation period of about eight months prior to buying the land, the founding members of Saddle Ridge knew surprisingly little about each other and in many respects were scarcely acquainted. "In some ways we knew each other well," wrote Elaine Sundancer in her early history of the group called *Celery Wine,* "and in other ways not at all."

> It was as if we'd skipped all the ordinary getting-acquainted questions: where are you from, what do you do, and so forth. I knew Jonathan [Roland] had been raised in England, because there was still a trace of cockney in his voice, but I had no idea when he'd come to this country or why. Most of us had had some sort of contact with college [Sundancer herself was an honors graduate in political science from Swarthmore], but I didn't know—still don't—who had studied what or where or who had graduated. . . . It was just "Anyone who needs a ride to the demonstration can ride with us." . . . Questions about the past, or speculations about the future, were unnecessary.[1]

In the midst of this tentative, familiar, but distant friendship clique without bonds or roots, it was perhaps necessary that one or more among them pushed out of the uncertain confusion. "We often say," wrote Sundancer, " 'We never would have chosen each other.' In the city, most of us probably wouldn't be friends."[2] More than anyone else, the person who pushed out of the confusion was Peter. "Gordon [Peter]," says Sundancer, "was the one who was really into it, I think. I myself didn't believe for a minute that we were really going to buy land and go live together in the country. It was a pleasant excuse for being together, that's all, for driving around the country and camping overnight."[3]

Peter, according to journalist Robert Houriet (who did care about personal backgrounds and used real first names), was a Goddard graduate who had once been field secretary for a communal peace group near Voluntown, Connecticut, and later helped found the War Resisters League on the West Coast. But as a protester he eventually ran out of steam, he told Houriet in the litany that was common to virtually all communes of the era: "How many times do you need to run your head against the wall to learn that society isn't going to change because of political demonstrations? You begin first by changing yourself, then your friends, and working outward. Creating a new life-style that speaks more strongly than political slogans."[4]

According to Wednesday night organizer Fairfield, Peter's enthusiasm and leadership qualities were apparent from the beginning:

> Paul [Peter], a free-lance gardener, was . . . the aggressive force behind the group, although he had attended the Berkeley meetings only intermittently and had not been an early member. Back in those days, his broad smile and his enthusiasm had made him well liked and sought

after in the group. He had developed both farming and manual skills, which gave him confidence about living on the land.[5]

But as we shall see, Peter's leadership did not extend beyond the founding phase of Saddle Ridge life. Peter always insisted on giving Saddle Ridge a clearer structure by imposing a membership procedure and limiting its size. "From my anthropology course at Goddard," he told Houriet, "I learned that the maximum size for most small groups to function is about twelve people."[6] Peter was never to gain agreement from the others on this point, until, ironically, he himself had left. For the first three years of its existence, Saddle Ridge was in constant flux. The original members themselves had wandered into involvement under such casual circumstances that it took them a long time, and many members come and gone, to agree eventually on closing the gate to newcomers.

Over its first winter, Saddle Ridge had only four resident members until the other two original members arrived in the spring. It was a long rainy winter for four people sharing the one tiny house. According to Sundancer, "Their unity was a matter of appearance only. They had agreed on the desire to leave the city and garden together in the country. That had carried them through the winter, but now they were faced with new questions. There was a feeling of uncertainty, rather than a united momentum."[7] The arrival of the newcomers did not much affect the general feeling of uncertainty, but it did boost the group's momentum. It was their first spring together on the land, and everyone set to putting in fruit trees, planting a big garden, and attending to dozens of other projects. The couple who had originally found the land built a large A-frame cabin for themselves up the hillside. They were Saddle Ridge's first serious home builders.

Shortly after finishing their dwelling, however, they also became Saddle Ridge's first defectors, much to the surprise of everyone else. More buildings would be needed to get the group through the next winter, they said, but they didn't see that happening. Later, they told Sundancer that the new baby they had had just weeks before their departure led them to "freak out" with the responsibilities of parenthood. But even before they left, new members started arriving, and the revolving door had begun.

Throughout Saddle Ridge's early history, there was chronic ambivalence about new members and visitors, usually resolved by the vacuum of indecision and lack of clear collective purpose in favor of an open-door policy allowing the "flow" to pulse in and out the driveway as it would. What kind of reception a visitor received depended on the particular members encountered and what kind of mood they were in: from one day to the next, newcomers could be told to go away or could be welcomed with warm hugs. "To a person who walks up the driveway," wrote Sundancer, "it looks as if we're a unit. But we're not, we're a collection of individuals."[8]

It is quite clear from Sundancer's work that the priority at Saddle Ridge in the early years was personal freedom rather than group commitment:

> We've all said that we were just here for as long as the spirit moved us, that we might leave at any time. . . . We call ourselves a family, and our life provides many of the satisfactions people once used to find in their families, but the key thing about a family is that you're born into it, you have no choice; and the key thing about this place is that you have a choice all the time.[9]

Over the summer of 1969, several new buildings were erected. But in an atmosphere pervaded by tentativeness and choice, all of them were quite small ("Every one of those buildings was built by one or two individuals, usually with almost no communal discussion involved"[10]), and only one of them, a small A-frame built by Roland and his girlfriend, was a dwelling. The other projects were a sauna cabin by the stream, a goat shed, a storeroom, and a geodesic outhouse. In Oregon's dry summer climate, most members slept out of doors when they could. For the most part, it was a time for enjoying themselves, enjoying the flow coming in and out of the driveway, and working on small-scale, group-spirited but privately initiated projects.

Attempts to get larger-scale building projects under way, like a communal house and a studio, were not as successful. Tentative plans for starting a school also came to nothing. By the summer of 1969, Saddle Ridge had a shifting population of fifteen or twenty adults and nine children ranging in age from three to eight. The school project slumped for several reasons: practical difficulties, lack of pressure from truancy authorities, and the absence of sustained initiative. "There was plenty of contributing energy, but no one to be cardinal energy. . . . If there had been one person here who was really into it, one person for the rest to home in on, we would have had our school."[11] On the other hand, the garden, the central focal point of the commune's consciousness, was a great success. Several hundred pounds of canned and frozen vegetables were packed away that fall to supplement the group's diet of government surplus commodities and store-bought bulk grains.

In the meantime, the great communal exodus of 1969 flowed through Saddle Ridge and the surrounding area by the long-haired hundreds:

All summer there were people passing through; hitchhikers who needed a place to spend the night, newly formed communal groups who needed a place to stay while they looked for land, people who were curious about communes, friends of friends. They would stay for a day or two or three. At any one time it wasn't very clear who lived here, who was visiting, who was in between. We had gotten together so recently; none of us making any long-range promises. . . . When we were living down in Berkeley, daydreaming about living in the community, we assumed that we could choose the people we wanted to live with. When we said "commune" we imagined a small group of people, formally accepting or rejecting new members. . . . This isn't how things have worked out here at all. As we began to live in the country, as our minds relaxed, . . . we found ourselves living in a way that we hadn't imagined six months earlier.[12]

Another change over that summer was a collective (but not universally welcomed) adaptation to the tentativeness of the membership and the flow of visitors by abandoning Saddle Ridge's original housing plan. Back in Berkeley, Sundancer says, "we expected that each person or couple would probably build a private shelter in addition to the communal main house. We didn't explicitly say, this is what we're going to do, but as I recall fragments of casual conversation I think that's what we all had in mind."[13] But instead, Saddle Ridge's free-for-all summer evolved with the onset of the cold and rainy winter into a simpler arrangement. The children slept in the little farmhouse attended by one adult. Most of the remaining membership communally shared the large A-frame built that spring. It was not that the Saddle Ridgers were sexual omnivores seeking a group marriage (if anything the reverse was more the case), but rather that they were single or loosely attached people for whom this arrangement was the least taxing and most convenient. For privacy they substituted politeness. When a couple did what couples ordinarily do alone, the better part of discretion for the others was simply to pretend that they were, in fact, alone.

This arrangement was not, however, without its casualties among the membership. In general, it favored the younger single men and women (especially those with children) and put a certain level of stress on older and more permanently bonded members. The first of 1969's new couples, for example, soon decided that they needed more privacy, more arts and crafts space, and more quiet and orderliness, and consequently they left and rented a vacant cabin at nearby Talsalsan. "At the farm," the woman of the couple later told Sundancer, "everything is so crowded and noisy. Why were we living like that . . . ? We came out here [from New York City] to make our lives better, not to live in a rural slum."[14]

Another development that came with winter was the need for

more cash to pay the community's bills. Over the first year a combination of savings, temporary earnings, subsidies, and the "flow" had been enough to meet the farm's very modest income needs of some $400 a month: mortgage payments of $100, another $200 for food (the one-acre garden and commodities being far from making them self-sufficient), and an additional $100 for gas, car repairs, taxes, electricity, and other expenses. Over the winter, however, what there were of temporary local jobs (like cutting firewood and fenceposts, freelance gardening, harvesting lily bulbs for a local farmer, planting and thinning trees in the national forest) mostly dried up as the weather got wet and cold:

> Almost everybody went down to the city for a month or so, at some point during the winter. We had all left the city recently, and we had friends we could visit. Down in the city it was easier to get a job and earn a little money. We enjoyed the taste of city food, and we enjoyed hot baths. Life at the farm was so intense that it was a pleasure to get away for a while. . . . It was a pleasure to be able to look back at the farm from a distance of several hundred miles and say, why the hell am I living there? And after breathing city air and hassling city hassles for a couple of weeks, you clearly remembered why.[15]

For the most part they did remember, and they did come back. But the next spring another casualty of Saddle Ridge's crowded free-form style was Peter, the person singly most responsible for the commune's existence in the first place. Peter had always been unhappy with the commune's open-door policy and much preferred that the group take a united front and close the door. On this point he got little agreement, and few members were willing to back him up. In general, his communal vision was more serious and intimate than that of the others but also more academic and remote from the here-and-now. It was his formality, aloofness, and critical intellectual arrogance that alienated him from several of the others. In *Getting Back Together,* Robert Houriet records an excoriating incident involving Peter as he talked to the group about organizing a hip church and school in the nearby village, speaking with phrases like "anticipating the objections of the straight community" and "appointing a committee that would embrace a spectrum of society." In reliving the drama of Jesus and the twelve disciples, Peter sometimes forgot to talk his family's language:

> Peter made sense to me, but his choice of words angered both Claudia and Elaine.
> Claudia screamed, "It's not what you say, it's *how* you say it that makes me so mad."

Then Elaine took over. It was as if she were peeling an onion. "All the time I've known you [they had once been lovers] I've had the notion you were trying to keep things from us . . . as if we were children and you were trying to spare us the pain of knowing all the cares that weighed on your shoulders. . . . It's a kind of insidious paternalism, and you're the leader. You had the foresight to press on and buy the land when everyone else was holding back. But now you try to influence us just by the tone of your voice. . . ." Elaine halted. Silence.

"Go on," said Peter.

Claudia: "Why don't you come out and tell us how you feel? Instead of using all this formal shit. I've very, very rarely seen you express the real *you*. The other night with the record player was one time. You were passionate, angry, frustrated, but it was you."

Peter (meekly): "This has been a very helpful conversation."

Claudia: "Fuck! There you go again. By the very *tone* of the words I can tell it hasn't sunk in."[16]

This particular encounter ended with a kiss and a hug, but this was not enough to keep Peter from drifting away from the group. That winter he retired to a small cabin where he wrote, meditated, and practiced yoga. The rest of the community saw very little of him. He then left for the city, returning in early spring of 1970 to plant some fruit trees, but after a while he moved (temporarily) to Talsalsan. The last point of real contact he had with the group was a dispute over admitting a new member calling himself Reuben (actually Irving), who had previously been kicked out of three other communes and was not well liked at Saddle Ridge either. At least two members, including Peter, told Reuben he had to leave, but Reuben refused. "I *know* you don't like him," Peter told the others, "I *know* he turns you off; I feel like it's not fair of you, not to tell him to go away." But the thoughts that Sundancer remembered having of the incident turned out to be the majority opinion: "Okay, so I don't like the guy, but I'm under no obligation to tell him so. . . . Maybe there is some reason why he's meant to be here."[17]

Reuben stayed, and from that point on Peter was estranged from the group. "The living bond that had made Gordon [Peter] an intimate part of the family had eroded. I don't know at what moment that became clear—maybe it was when someone asked him if he would clear his shelf so someone else could use it."[18] Later that spring (1970), Dick Fairfield talked with Peter at Talsalsan and recorded his parting thoughts of Saddle Ridge:

"Yes, [Saddle Ridge] Farm has become too open for me. I'm still interested in an intimate family-style commune. [Saddle Ridge] Farm is too loosely structured, too open ended. With new people coming in all the time, it's too difficult to really get to know them. People need to spend more time with each other to become an intimate family. It can't happen here. It's too open, not enough structure."

"This place is OK as a sort of halfway house. But if you're interested in a more intense communal life experience, you've got to get together with a fewer number of people and work through problems together to understand where each other is at. That's where we went wrong here. We *thought* we wanted the same things but we didn't have any experience living together and working problems out with each other."

Despite these negative comments, Paul [Peter] expressed some sadness at leaving [Saddle Ridge] Farm. He had not wanted to leave. "I've invested a lot of myself in this place," he noted. "I would have preferred to have remained."

"But—" I repeated several times, as he dug his hands back and forth in the soil, over and over again.

"But the people who are here like it the way it is," he said.[19]

What might be called Saddle Ridge's "Peter Principle," then, was that planning, structure, membership restrictions, and leadership—at least of the sort displayed by Peter—were better done without. "You were wrong," a member of another commune once scolded Sundancer about the Peter experience. "How could you not be sensitive to your brother . . . ? What he wanted should count more with you than any outsider."[20] But the fact of the matter was that, for Elaine and most of the others, "the farm is a place where I can work on myself, a place where it's okay for me to go through changes."[21] Peter's ideas of structure and intimacy clashed with the central value of Saddle Ridge life, which was to explore the self and whatever else came along without restrictions, boundaries, rules, or coercion "because I really want to do it," as Sundancer put it, "not because some nagging voice outside myself told me so."[22]

In a way, this was the rallying cry of prosperity's children in communes everywhere, save those who joined authoritarian religious orders for need of a more concrete rudder than this to guide their lives. For Saddle Ridge, freedom to experience unbridled change was of the essence, and choosing Peter over newcomers, even one as disliked as Reuben, simply was not what they felt. "We couldn't make that be true by wishing it were true; we didn't want to pretend. We haven't ever made that kind of commitment to each other. None of us has ever promised to stay here, and yet some of us, making our choices day by day, are still here. There has been a continuity, a coherence about this place—not very much, but enough."[23] For Saddle Ridge—and the counterculture in general—freedom was more important than intimacy.

Another anecdote related by Sundancer, concerning a transient who lectured to the members about the need for organization and leadership, rather neatly sums up Saddle Ridge's basic philosophical point of view. It might just as well have been Saddle Ridge's rebuttal to Peter or their former professors at Berkeley. "We explained to him that, 'That's right, you can't tell anyone here to do anything, you can only ask them.' 'But that's not efficient,' he said. 'That's right, it's not. WE ARE NOT INTERESTED IN EFFICIENCY.' "[24]

II

In at least one respect, Peter's complaint about Saddle Ridge's being too open-ended was exaggerated. Of Saddle Ridge's 1970 population of fifteen adults (nine men, six women), plus five children, 73 percent had been there six months before and 60 percent had been there twelve months before. By these measures of turnover, Saddle Ridge was the second or third most internally stable commune in this study. In other respects, however, Peter's complaints were more accurate. Members of the commune estimated in the summer of 1970 that about thirty different people, not counting visitors, had lived in but left Saddle Ridge in the previous twelve months. Visitors, in turn, were estimated in the hundreds. Thus while Saddle Ridge did have a certain continuity or coherence as claimed by Sundancer, it also had one of the highest rates in my study of temporary and transient residents. Peter was also correct in his assessment of Saddle Ridge's lack of structure. Saddle Ridge's total of commitment-inducing structural features was the third lowest in the study, its level of organization surpassing only Talsalsan and Drop City, and then not by much.

Sacrifice   Predictably, Saddle Ridge practiced no forms of abstinence. Although alcohol, sugar, and meat were generally not preferred, all were used from time to time both by individuals and by the group at large as money and circumstances varied. Food and nutrition were central preoccupations of Saddle Ridge life, but despite a great deal of discussion and argument about it (or perhaps because so many divergent feelings were thereby revealed), there was never any consistent group policy regarding the oral pleasures of the membership except a general interest in good health and eating lots of garden vegetables. Sexually, Saddle Ridge was likewise without a group policy. Some members were rather abstemious by nature while others had more of a taste for promiscuity. Like most communes, Saddle Ridge tended to pair off in flexible, serially monogamous relationships. As a group it was neither continent, exclusively bonded, nor profligate.

In terms of austerity, the second dimension of sacrifice used here, life at Saddle Ridge was somewhat more severe. "By traditional economic measurements," wrote Sundancer in a paean to the logic of voluntary primitivism, "we have a very low standard of living. We are crowded, we heat all our water by hand, we have an outhouse instead of a flush toilet, we live on rice and vegetables and powdered milk. We're willing to accept this lack of comfort, because with it comes the freedom to run our own lives, to work when and how and because we want to."[25] In addition, Saddle Ridge was obliged to build at least some of its own buildings and, in the absence of gas, to cut firewood for its wood stoves.

But compared to the other communes in the study, Saddle Ridge's level of austerity was less impressive. The farmhouse and outbuildings, for instance, were wired for electricity (by the previous owner, but put to good use by the Saddle Ridgers for lighting, freezing, music, tools, and later a washer and dryer). With the addition of a well and taps to the kitchen, Saddle Ridge's water supply was more reliable than most. Similarly, Saddle Ridge's winters were almost as mild as those at Wheeler's Ranch in northern California. Finally, Saddle Ridge's burdens were eased by surplus commodities at first and, at the time of my visit, by food stamps and other forms of welfare.

Investment   The use of investment mechanisms at Saddle Ridge was almost as low as any other group in the study, on a level with open-land groups like Morning Star East and Drop City. Only the Guild of Colorado and Saddle Ridge's neighbor Talsalsan made less use of investment, with both keeping books and returning investments to defectors, which Saddle Ridge did not do. Nor did Saddle Ridge require a fee or contribution for admission, the signover of property, or the turnover of income. Although income sharing was a legitimate norm, "there isn't any *rule*, 'everyone throws in what they have.' " Most members kept private stashes for personal needs or, as in the case of Sundancer, for "get-away" money if the time for leaving came.

Loose though this arrangement was, Saddle Ridge's budget was so extraordinarily low that there were seldom crises that the "flow" or a month's work in the city couldn't fix. Only once did they miss their land payment (meeting their obligations instead with five cords of firewood). "If you live in a place," Sundancer explained, "and the mortgage payment comes due and you have some money in your pocket, you feel like throwing it in. Or if someone doesn't, he doesn't stay. No one says, 'You have to leave, because you don't want to help make the payment.' He just goes away after a while, that's all."[26]

Financially, Saddle Ridge got by without structure, but only at a minimal, month-to-month level. Saddle Ridge likewise did without other forms of investment like required physical participation. There was no requirement that anyone had to build a shelter, and few members did. Clearly, however, the crowded conditions and seniority rights of members already there meant that shelter building would be necessary for most newcomers if they planned to stay over the rainy winter, and this obviously served as a kind of informal population control. Finally, there was no formal requirement of physical residence or presence for membership, although informally membership status tended to lapse or be challenged with sustained absences.

Renunciation   Saddle Ridge's degree of insulation from the outside world was slightly above average, both in terms of location, with above-average distances to the nearest incorporated town and the nearest city, and in terms of media, with the absence of newspapers and magazines, television, and telephone. Saddle Ridge's insulation was offset, however, by a near-total lack of cross-boundary controls over visitors and new members. There were no visitation rules, and only the fact that 5 or 10 percent of visitors were sent away by annoyed individual members distinguished Saddle Ridge on this count from Drop City or Morning Star East. Saddle Ridge was never considered open land by its members, but as in the open-land groups, the flow of new people was deeply related to its vitality.

One function of "letting it flow" was, of course, an implicit exchange of hospitality for potential contributions of money or energy from outsiders. Mentioning the group's partial dependence on donations, even if mystified as "money manifests," often stimulated visitors' giving. Another function of the visitor flow was communication. Travel from commune to commune, in fact, was probably the single most important communications medium for groups like Saddle Ridge. "Gossip about mutual acquaintances is always traveling through the grapevine and a complete stranger often turns out to be a friend of a friend of a friend."[27] Still another function of the flow was recruitment of new members. It was, in fact, Saddle Ridge's primary method:

> People arrive here in all sorts of ways. They are hitchhiking and one of us picks them up. They are looking for their friends who are living someplace around here. They are driving around . . . just for the fun of visiting places. They are old friends of ours from back in the city. Some people arrive saying, "I'd like to find out about joining the commune." They don't stay. Some people arrive saying, "I'd like to stay here overnight." Sometimes they wind up living here.[28]

Theoretically the unanimous acceptance of new members was required, and usually a prospective member who wanted to stay would call a meeting or ask at least some of the others, but as the Peter-Reuben episode demonstrated, this was far from a coherent or consistent membership screening policy in actual fact. Individual members sometimes took it upon themselves to tell prospectives to go away, but as a collectivity Saddle Ridge had never formally black-balled anybody or developed any principles, rules, or requirements distinguishing desirable members from undesirable ones. Saddle Ridge's degree of renunciation of the outside world, then, was comparable to that of the open-land anarchies.

Communion In terms of structural mechanisms fostering the experience of communion, Saddle Ridge was closer to the average for the sample as a whole, though still slightly below it. The homogeneity of its membership was rather high, with prior acquaintances averaging one to two years and an age distribution averaging in the middle twenties and not varying markedly (transient and temporary residents were generally younger).

In communistic sharing, its structure was again similar to open-land groups. The community as a whole owned the property (although legal title remained in the names of three individuals); it owned all the buildings (though builders retained priority in using dwellings); and it owned some, but not all, tools, furniture, and autos (with ambiguity and occasional conflict over priority rights and permission). No formal signover of property was expected, although communal use was generally standard. Each person had a shelf for things like personal items and good clothing, but old clothes were shared. The produce of the garden was shared equally, though usually tended unequally by those most interested. Sharing of income was equalitarian in principle but unregulated and unequal in fact. An implicit norm of equal contributions was tempered by each individual's ability to pay, a lack of interest in formal bookkeeping, and the level of individual commitment and motivation but was reinforced by informal social scrutiny and a tendency for the level of personal contributions to hover around a minimal common denominator.

In its degree of communistic labor, however, Saddle Ridge was more structured than open-land groups, even though the communal work ethic was basically the same. "Each person does what he chooses to do, and somehow all the necessary things get done. (Corollary: 'If it didn't get done, it wasn't necessary.')"[29] Sign-up sheets for cooking and housework were tried, then abandoned, and then tried again, catching on after about a year of confusion and complaints of unequal effort. Uncompensated communal work efforts apart from housework were common and undertaken daily by most members without formal planning or assignments. For the most part, each member had his or her own special province for group-spirited labor, such as the garden, the goats, auto repairs, canning and cooking, and so on.

These tasks were generally assumed along traditional lines of sexual differentiation. But more than most communes, perhaps because of the highly politicized Berkeley backgrounds of many members, Saddle Ridge displayed a healthy degree of cross-sexual work sharing. It also went one step beyond open-land groups in viewing community labor as a preferred, legitimate expectation rather than strictly voluntary, but it stopped short of elevating these expectations to the level of requirements, save for the kitchen sign-up sheet. Saddle Ridge also went beyond most open-land groups by creating an effective (though informal) system of sharing child-care tasks among the membership, notably arrangements whereby a different person (usually but not necessarily a mother) would stay in the main house with the children at night or tend to their needs during the day.

In regularized group contact, another dimension of communion, Saddle Ridge was slightly above average. In the winter, at least, most housing was communal. Throughout the year communal dining usually took place at least twice daily in the old farmhouse that served as the kitchen, living room, library, and children's dormitory. Group meetings were called spontaneously by individual members and never scheduled more than one day in advance. On the average they took place weekly, more often than in most communes. Another factor promoting regular contact among members was the relatively high population-to-acreage density. On the average, members spent about two-thirds of their waking hours in group settings of some sort. The old farmhouse at Saddle Ridge served as the community's social center and was the hub of everyday affairs.

On the other hand, Saddle Ridge's communion score was lowered by the comparative absence of group rituals beyond occasional group sauna baths and the celebration of traditional events like birthdays and holidays. Unlike many communes, Saddle Ridge did not make a practice of mealtime prayers or group singing and dancing. Over time several members became involved in such gatherings with neighbors and with a local fundamentalist church, but it was usually necessary to go outside the community for these experiences. Group meditation at Saddle Ridge had been tried, abandoned, revived with more general interest, and then discontinued again by the time of my visit in September 1970. While there was a vague general recognition at Saddle Ridge of the importance of group ceremonies, putting that understanding into practice was not something the membership seemed able to agree on for very long. Although Sundancer writes that group meditation and chanting were institutionalized at Saddle Ridge by 1970, this was anything but apparent to me in September. More typical of my perceptions was this exchange recorded by Robert Houriet:

> "Hip life changes too fast . . . that's what we need, a few rituals. Like at Morningstar, after they planted their garden, they held a fertility dance and a fuck-in."
> "Groovy, maybe that's what our tomatoes needed this year. Last year they were puny."[30]

The practice of collective ritual at Saddle Ridge seemed something that the inhabitants found compelling but not convenient over sustained periods.

The final dimension of Saddle Ridge's communion score, persecution experiences, was likewise low. At the time there was an antihippie vigilante committee operating openly in a nearby town, but Saddle Ridge itself had never been assaulted. Nor had it ever experienced any serious discriminatory reactions from building and health officials or other local bureaucrats like food-stamp agents. Indeed, a few local professional service workers went out of their way to help.

Public relations across the cultural barriers of the county were not exactly rosy, but in general face-to-face relations between Saddle Ridge and its neighbors were good. Saddle Ridge residents did not rate the economic discrimination practiced against them by some merchants as even "somewhat serious," and the negative feelings about them locally were ascribed to a minority of the local citizenry. The local judge had thrown out one deputy sheriff's trumped-up charges against hippies so often that the deputy resigned. The same judge was also instrumental in getting another deputy fired for dereliction of duty in a rough encounter with a hippie. The members of Saddle Ridge had good reason to feel that the local courts were fair and honest. A local chapter of the American Civil Liberties Union had also helped out the first year, when harassment of hippies along the nearby river had been high. According to the Saddle Ridgers, the vigilante actions were usually perpetrated by the teen-age sons of angry middle-class retirees and small businessmen. But Saddle Ridge was just inaccessible enough not to be bothered.

Mortification In its structures of ego-subordination or mortification, Saddle Ridge had a pattern very similar to Talsalsan's, which perhaps relates to the fact that both communes were born of the same

Berkeley background, indeed the same discussion group. In neither case were there overt or formal distinctions made among members on moral or spiritual grounds, nor were there any formal structures or deference, probation, or instruction in community doctrines. Like Talsalsan, Saddle Ridge assiduously avoided status distinctions. Most likely this was partly responsible for the fact that Saddle Ridge remained persistently secular despite its best efforts to be more spiritual. The one area of community life which might have given rise to invidious status distinctions was selfless work, but the obvious inequalities in this respect did not seem to create very strong ranking tendencies. "Some are more skilled than others. Some are just harder workers than others. It doesn't seem to matter very much. It's as if we've all just decided not to worry about that stuff. As if it's more important to not have people working out of anxiety; to have them working, when they work, with real energy going into what they're doing."[31] This is not to say, of course, that social distinctions did not occur at more informal levels. As this anecdote recorded by Sundancer shows, Saddle Ridge had its lower-status members just as any other social group does:

> Yusef spoke, his voice gruff, his Rumanian-accented voice that reminds me of my grandfather. "I wasn't here at the meeting," he said. "But I've felt the same thing that Will has—that people won't listen to me. If I say I want to do something, it has no effect. If Will and I had called a meeting and told people how we felt, they would have just argued with us or ignored us. No one ever does what I want them to. Maybe it's because I don't always know the right words, I don't know. So . . . I feel as if no one listens to me because I'm not as good a worker as Jim or Jonathan.[32]

The difference at Saddle Ridge was that these questions were addressed openly in encounter-group type meetings, which provided a secular equivalent to the confessional ceremonies of religious societies. A reading of Sundancer's *Celery Wine* suggests that the holiest moments in Saddle Ridge's life were the embraces and hand holding that often followed in the wake of these confrontations. In the beginning, Sundancer relates, most meetings were budgetary or otherwise pragmatic in their topical content and not very often occasions of mutual criticism. But as time went on, they increased both in frequency and in their emotional and confrontational content. They could be brutally honest and confuse almost as often as clarify, but they were also Saddle Ridge's most vital social institution and the closest it knew how to come to ceremonial tribal affirmation.[33] Saddle Ridge and Talsalsan, both with highly verbal, educated memberships, were the two groups in the study scoring highest on mutual criticism.

Transcendence Of all the many variables falling under the heading of transcendence commitment mechanisms, only one could be said to apply to Saddle Ridge: a sense of tradition going back before the community's founding to the prior organized group in Berkeley. In other respects, Saddle Ridge made virtually no use of this class of mechanisms, reflecting the utter primacy of equalitarianism and individual choice at Saddle Ridge over the organizational values of institutional structure and programing. Ideologically, Saddle Ridge had something in common with the themes of the human-potential/self-actualization movement, with its emphases on interpersonal encounter, the open expression of feelings, and working through changes, but this added up to very little that could be described as an awe-inspiring philosophical system deriving from any particular teachers of historical importance. Nor was group commitment reinforced by attributions of special powers either to the community or to certain of its members. For magical underpinnings Saddle Ridge had only the hippie axiom that "things happen because they were meant to happen," or as Hunter Thompson once put it, the assumption that "Somebody—or at least some *force*—is tending that light at the end of the tunnel."[34]

Saddle Ridge did have perceptible values, but in almost every respect they were the opposite of the canonical, visionary, and assertive qualities of ideology, reflecting instead the day-to-day concerns of a "haphazard collection of individuals who may leave at any moment."[35] Scanning through the pages of *Celery Wine* reveals some of these values as follows:

1. Deliberate ambiguity in collective self-definition. ("We are tempted to artificially define ourselves, quickly, just for the comfort of knowing who we are. But that doesn't work. A living organism defines itself by its actions; it doesn't need a label; and its boundaries change over time.")[36]
2. A general disinterest in planning for future uncertainties. ("We've never tried to make decisions about what we'll do in the future. It's always, at most, here-and-now we feel that we'll probably do so-and-so, and it's always open to change.")[37]
3. A kind of situational ethics adapted to deal with rapid and subtle changes in circumstances. ("It was odd that we should be saying 'yes' [or 'maybe'] to strangers we'd met by chance, and 'no' to an old friend who politely wrote a letter asking for an invitation, and then again it wasn't so odd . . .")[38]
4. A high degree of tolerance for individual moods and inconsistencies.

("The person who played Uptight last month plays Easy this month. We don't take the scene of the moment too seriously.")[39]
5. A patient trust that conflict and confusions would be resolved as time and destiny benignly unfold. ("We haven't ever voted on an issue. We just talk. . . . Sometimes our minds are not clear, and we try to wait until clearness comes. . . . We wait, and if we wait long enough what we need to do becomes clear.")[40]

Instead of relying on higher-order principles, then, Saddle Ridge was oriented to the pragmatics of the libertarian moment: "At the farm, we're living so closely together that any bad vibes you put out get bounced right back at you. . . . And one person who's in a good mood can bring the whole house up. It's a closed system: what you put in, you get back. Under these circumstances, 'love your neighbor' isn't a moralistic preachment, it's simple self-interest."[41]

Saddle Ridge was likewise devoid of institutionalized structures of power and authority. No single individuals embodied the community or assumed any overt distinction in terms of leadership or its prerogatives; not Sundancer, not Roland, and certainly not Peter, whose status had slumped from prime mover to social isolate as Saddle Ridge relaxed into anarchy. Institutionalized hierarchical relationships were anathema at Saddle Ridge, though in fact, as we have seen, there were informal variations in prestige and influence recognized among the membership. Likewise, there was no programmatic daily routine to order the members' behavior beyond the kitchen sign-up sheet. Otherwise members worked and played as they pleased. Finally, there were no mechanisms of "ideological conversion" to induce the internalization of commitment among the membership: no vows, no consistent procedures affecting new members, and nothing but the vaguest forms of scrutiny to determine the seriousness of their intent.

Other forms of decision making at Saddle Ridge were just as vague. "Most of the decisions around here are made by individuals. 'Do what you think best; if it bothers me, I'll let you know.' Let the people who are most interested in something, who are willing to do the work, make the decisions about it." Sundancer continued:

. . . [Sometimes] things are so important, so interesting to everyone, that we decide them as a group. Anyone can call a meeting—they just say to people, "Let's have a meeting tonight," or put a sign on the kitchen door. Everyone comes. . . . Usually there is some here-and-now question that we have to deal with as a group, and the talk stays focused on that. Often after a while we go around the circle, listening to each voice, trying to listen instead of arguing. We're trying to get our energies running together; the talk is just an aid, not the point of the whole thing. Sometimes a clear group decision will emerge. Sometimes most of the emotional weight is on one side, and a few people will say, "Well, I'm not really happy about this, but I see it's what we are going to do." . . . Sometimes one person thinks we've decided to do one thing, and someone else remembers it quite differently! So lately people have been saying, "Hey, I think we've decided thus and so, *is* that what we've decided?" as the meeting breaks up in confusion.[42]

At Saddle Ridge, then, the process of decision making was much like its organization of work. "When there's empty space you move into it; when you see a job that needs to be done, you do it."[43] In a way it was not unlike the laissez-faire economics of Adam Smith. "You control your own emotions, and that's all you control. The whole thing takes its shape from thousands of individual decisions, and no one controls what the whole thing is like."[44]

III

When I returned to Saddle Ridge in July 1973, I found that it was the only communal group among the several in the area in 1970 which was still in existence. While it could not exactly be described as prosperous, for the most part Saddle Ridge had held its own. The population had declined from fifteen to ten, but the big communal lodge that had been only a dream in 1970 was now about half-completed. Constructed in three tiers, it had washing, bathing, and storage facilities planned for the first story; a living room, kitchen, and fireplace on the second level; and adult bedrooms plus a children's room on the third level. Even though only half-completed, it was a huge and impressive structure for something built only with hand tools. People at Saddle Ridge were generally "into" being more alone, Elaine told me ("I myself am really hurting for some private space"), but their energy was, nevertheless, going into the group house.

The biggest change at Saddle Ridge over the three-year interval had been, predictably, the departure of 73 percent of the 1970 membership. Only four members remained from that period, and only two had hung on from the founding year of 1968–1969. But the most significant change was that the ghost of Peter had come home, and Saddle Ridge was now more or less closed to newcomers. "In a way," Elaine had written in 1970, "it would be easier on everyone concerned if we flatly said, 'We're closed.' We could relax and enjoy our time together, without constantly thinking 'suppose he stays.' "[45] Over the winter of 1970–1971, less than a year after Peter had left behind the argument that it *should* be closed and remain a small, intimate group, Saddle Ridge had belatedly followed his advice as the residents finally began to congeal as a unit. "We all sort of came to agree," Elaine told me, "that we really didn't want anybody living here unless we all loved them." Characteristically, this decision had been reached intuitively, by accretion and roundabout consensus, rather than by a formal vote.

With this implicit decision, apparently Saddle Ridge had found stability despite itself, for all the members present in 1973 had lived there for at least two years. "Now," Elaine said, "there are so many established patterns that new people would find it very hard to fit in." But on the periphery of Saddle Ridge's life, a great deal of coming and going had obviously continued. The entire network of people who had lived at the farm and become a part of it, she said, now numbered over sixty, over a five-year period, giving them an enormous extended family as well as stability.

Saddle Ridge had survived despite a commitment score that was the third lowest in the sample and by far the lowest among those groups which did survive. In terms of Rosabeth Kanter's theory of structure and commitment, Saddle Ridge could not have been predicted to be a success. In retrospect, there seem to be four major reasons why it was.

First, it was not truly so difficult, in practical terms, for Saddle Ridge to sustain itself as a corporate entity regardless of its modest income and internal changes. Like many another commune, it had a very minimal overhead. A collective budget of $400 a month, even doubled for inflation, still came to only a piddling monthly share per member. "Maybe we're cheating," Sundancer had written, echoing the bottom-line, but seldom admitted, embarrassment of the children of prosperity in communes everywhere. "It's easy for us. No matter what we say or do, the hospital in Norton goes right on existing."[46] It was also easy in the sense that personal investment was so low and that an exit to other options was always open if the going got too intense:

> We were living very close together, and yet everyone was free to leave. Free, because we hadn't made any commitment to each other, any long-term promise to stay, and also free in a practical sense: we were all mobile, had all left the city recently, had friends and jobs to which we could return. No one was trapped.[47]

The same things could be said, of course, for most communes. Under similar circumstances, several of the groups in this study which failed might have survived too. But unlike Drop City, Reality, or Morning Star East, Saddle Ridge depended on no outside benefactor who could pull the rug out from under them. Unlike Talsalsan, the power to influence group affairs was denied to members choosing to spend their time outside the community. And unlike Wheeler Ranch, relations with local citizens and officials posed no threat to Saddle Ridge's continued existence. An important aspect of the easy living, then, was the absence of outsiders who might be motivated and capable of engineering its demise.

Secondly, Saddle Ridge found a solution to the problems of turnover and change. For the first two years of its existence, the majority of members subscribed to an open-land philosophy of natural selection and variety, even at the cost of its most instrumental founder. "People should be able to select themselves," a member named Jack told reporter Houriet, "tell themselves that they don't belong here . . . stay for a week or two and decide that this isn't the spot or that they haven't any more to learn from the people here. Also, being closed would shut us off from change."[48] Although the Saddle Ridgers did in fact close themselves off, they did not have to repress their obvious appetite for change and new stimulation. Instead, Saddle Ridge gradually came to a hardening of the definitions between member and visitor in such a way that the two could no longer be so readily confused.

For three years the group saw fit to keep these definitions ambiguous until a core group had selected itself out of the uncommitted flow and finally crystallized as a mutually recognized unit. At the same time, however, Saddle Ridge kept the gate sufficiently open to let a limited number of newcomers—and many old friends—come in and stay for a while, leaving it to the strength of their deepening and solidifying internal relationships to maintain group integrity. Without really trying, and perhaps without fully realizing it, Saddle Ridge evolved a system optimizing change and continuity simultaneously.

A third major reason why Saddle Ridge worked was its realistic recognition of interpersonal diversity, conflict, and ambiguity. Perhaps it was the inheritance of Berkeley, but more likely it evolved through practical experience, especially the experience of chronic ambivalence and change. Mature in all respects the Saddle Ridgers were not, but sophisticated and honest in human relations they were:

> At the very lowest level, the level that has to be there before you can build anything else, what we say to each other is, "I'm willing to put up with you—with all the little irritating things you do, that may not ever change. I accept you as you are, I'm thankful that you're willing to put up with me." We don't say it in words. Our lives intertwine in

a thousand ways. If someone chooses to stay here, that says it for him.[49]

Coupled with this was a willingness to compromise and boost each other. "Everybody has their turn to get depressed," Sundancer told me in 1973, "and when it happens the rest of us just sort of lean in their direction."

But even with all this unspoken intertwining and leaning, words were still crucially important at Saddle Ridge. Like Sundancer herself, the members of Saddle Ridge were well educated and usually verbal. A fourth major reason why Saddle Ridge survived, then, was the solidarity gained through its constant verbal confrontations. In many communes of the era—particularly on open land—there seemed to be a tendency for such meetings to decline and fade away as a conflict-ridden nuisance, but at Saddle Ridge they increased both in frequency and importance over time. Similar meetings at Talsalsan and LILA were not enough; indeed, they seemed to hurt as much as they helped. The difference was that at Saddle Ridge meetings were not scheduled but spontaneous, called because "we want to" rather than "we have to." In the absence of any other collective focus, intense interpersonal encounters became the essence of Saddle Ridge life. The Saddle Ridge family went to these meetings with a zestful anticipation that was readily apparent even to an outside observer. It was as if the verbal groping together was more important than the content of the words themselves. As Marshall McLuhan might have put it, "the meeting was the message."

> Some meetings are trivial. . . . Some meetings feel bad—we want to decide about something but we just can't get it together. . . . But . . . there are some meetings, when someone says something that lets me know that he loves this place, or that he sees something the same way I do, that makes me feel close and warm. And then sometimes as we're talking together I have the feeling that we're making a jump together— that one energy is flowing through all of us. Sometimes one senses that a deep level of unity has been reached, and what we've decided tonight isn't true just for tonight—that a little more of our communal shape has been manifested to us.[50]

Vague and groping though it was, never knowing one day where it would be going the next, Saddle Ridge had survived the cynicism of the early 1970s surprisingly intact. Of all the groups in the study, Saddle Ridge came the closest to preserving the hip communal ideal that had been born in an altogether different social and economic atmosphere in the 1960s. They still believed in the light at the end of the tunnel, even if Hunter Thompson had called it "the essential old-mystic fallacy of the Acid Culture."[51] It did not matter, at least for the ten who remained of the seventy passing through, that the light came slowly, or had yet to take them beyond the poverty they had voluntarily embraced. For them the magic of the tribe was still alive:

> We don't want to organize things. We don't want one person to tell other people how to behave; we don't want to control things. No RSVP's, no parties where you invite a select group of friends, no Book of Common Prayer, no minister. But we need some way to come together. We speak of a gathering of the tribes, but the Indians were supported by traditions from since the world began, and we're out here on our own. Perhaps we yearn for something out of a fairy tale: for the whole valley to find itself gathered around a campfire as if by chance, or by following some signal in the forests, or some sudden sign in the stars.[52]

Notes

1. Elaine Sundancer [pseud.], *Celery Wine: Story of a Country Commune* (Yellow Springs, Ohio: Community Publications Cooperative, 1973), pp. 10–11. Sundancer uses pseudonyms for all the members of the group. Real names are bracketed.

2. Ibid., p. 105.

3. Ibid., pp. 11–12.

4. Robert Houriet, *Getting Back Together* (New York: Avon Books, 1972), p. 88. Houriet writes of this commune as "High Ridge Farm" but uses the real first names of members.

5. Richard Fairfield, *Communes U.S.A.: A Personal Tour* (Baltimore: Penguin Books, 1972). Fairfield writes of this commune as "Magic Farm" and, like Sundancer, uses pseudonymous first names for the members. Real names are bracketed.

6. Houriet, *Getting Back Together,* p. 88.

7. Sundancer, *Celery Wine,* p. 30.

8. Ibid., p. 61.

9. Ibid., pp. 156–157.

10. Ibid., p. 75.

11. Ibid., p. 85.

12. Ibid., p. 57.

13. Ibid.

14. Ibid., p. 98.

15. Ibid., p. 80.

16. Houriet, *Getting Back Together,* p. 91.

17. Sundancer, *Celery Wine,* pp. 79–80.

18. Ibid., pp. 97–98.

19. Fairfield, *Communes U.S.A.,* pp. 223–224.

20. Sundancer, *Celery Wine,* p. 64.

21. Ibid., p. 106.

22. Ibid., p. 156.

23. Ibid., p. 64.

24. Ibid., p. 52.

25. Ibid.

26. Ibid., pp. 115–116.

27. Ibid., p. 28.

28. Ibid., p. 61.

29. Ibid., p. 49.

30. Houriet, *Getting Back Together*, p. 103.

31. Sundancer, *Celery Wine*, p. 51.

32. Ibid., p. 121.

33. Psychologist Dan G. Minner has suggested to me that these meetings may have been a reenactment of previously rewarding and reinforcing group discussions experienced in college.

34. Hunter S. Thompson, *Fear and Loathing in Las Vegas* (New York: Popular Library, 1971), p. 179.

35. Sundancer, *Celery Wine*, p. 89.

36. Ibid., p. 89.

37. Ibid., p. 64.

38. Ibid., p. 60.

39. Ibid., p. 107.

40. Ibid., pp. 92, 107.

41. Ibid., p. 83.

42. Ibid., pp. 91–92.

43. Ibid., p. 49.

44. Ibid., p. 163.

45. Ibid., p. 147.

46. Ibid., p. 125.

47. Ibid., p. 82.

48. Houriet, *Getting Back Together*, p. 90.

49. Sundancer, *Celery Wine*, p. 106.

50. Ibid., p. 94.

51. Thompson, *Fear and Loathing in Las Vegas*, p. 179.

52. Sundancer, *Celery Wine*, p. 123.

14

Commitment, Change, and the Two Faces of Subsidy: Analysis and Interpretation

Over the three years from 1970 to 1973, from my first set of observations to my second, seven of the communes in this study ceased to exist, or "failed" as corporate entities. Five of them, on the other hand, "succeeded" and managed to sustain themselves as communal organizations. The one remaining group, the Guild of Colorado, came to an ambiguous fate in which it failed as a genuine communal organization but continued existing as a kind of family farm pretending to be more. This chapter is an examination of how some of these groups managed to hold themselves together over the rocky years of the early 1970s while slightly more than half of them could not.

Rosabeth Kanter's theory of commitment, based on her studies of nineteenth-century communes, predicts that those groups which employed more commitment-inducing structural features in their organization would be more likely to survive than those groups which employed fewer such mechanisms. This is the central hypothesis which guided this study from the beginning, as it did Kanter's own. Looking only at the period 1970–1973, it is possible to say, with several qualifications and reservations, that this hypothesis tended to be true of modern communes as well as those of the nineteenth century.

But looking back from 1973 all the way to the beginning of the modern commune movement in 1965, we find just the opposite. In this study, at least, the groups with the longest total life spans through 1973 tended to be those with the *weakest* commitment structures. Examining different time frames, then, suggests strikingly different results for the theory of commitment and underlines the importance of taking historical context into account even over such a short period. In the prosperous early years of the movement, the most successful communes were the more open and unstructured ones, contrary to the theory of commitment. In the harder times following 1970, however, it became apparent that the more rigorously organized groups were more likely to survive in the long run.

To reach these conclusions, three sets of analyses were made for each of the six categories of commitment mechanisms and for the total use of such mechanisms. First, the use of these mechanisms in the modern commune movement was compared to the use of such mechanisms in the nineteenth-century groups studied by Kanter. In general, this comparison produced the unsurprising result that modern groups used many fewer commitment mechanisms of all types than earlier groups did. Second, groups which survived from 1970 to 1973 were compared with those that did not in terms of their use of the various forms of commitment. This comparison showed that "investment," "renunciation," and "mortification" are as strongly related to communal survival today as they were in the nineteenth century, but that "sacrifice," "communion," and "transcendence" are only weakly or even negatively related to communal survival today. Finally, use of the various types of commitment mechanisms was compared to total group life spans through 1973. Measured this way, only sacrifice and renunciation were widely used in longer-lived groups, while the other four types of commitment were either unrelated to life spans or negatively related.

On balance, these findings may seem to prove Kanter's theory untrue, but as we shall see, this conclusion would be hasty. The formula for communal success changed dramatically from the 1960s to the 1970s, and all but one of these changes moved in the direction that Kanter predicted. All things considered, more conservatively structured communes still seem to have a better chance for long-term survival today.

The logic of this analysis requires at least two different definitions of organizational "success": one stated in terms of total communal life span through 1973, and the other in terms of survival over the period from my first observation (1970) to my second (1973). Since the communes founded at earlier dates would obviously have longer average life spans by 1970 than those founded later, it is important to examine the possibility that systematic differences between groups founded in different periods may confuse the analysis as a true test of the theory of commitment. It is also possible that there is a natural life cycle in the evolution of communal groups, and that groups founded earlier may have been at more advanced levels of development by my visits in 1970 than those groups founded more recently.

Information related to these two questions is summarized below in tables 1 and 2, which compare the structural and life-cycle characteristics of those groups founded in 1968 or earlier (table 1) with the

Table 1 Structural and Life-Cycle Characteristics of Modern Communes Founded in 1968 or Earlier

Group	Sac	Inv	Ren	Com	Mor	Tran	Total	Life Span*
(X) Drop City (O)	5	3	6	19	1	0	34	7.9
Lama (C)	11	4	18	32	6	15	86	5.7
Libre (C)	8	4	17	16	2	6	53	6.6
Saddle Ridge (F)	5	3	8	21	3	1	41	5.3
(X) Talsalsan (F)	4	1	10	20	3	2	40	4.8
(X) Wheeler's (O)	9	4	10	19	1	9	51	5.1
Mean	7.0	3.2	11.5	21.2	2.3	5.5	50.8	5.9

(X)=Group did not survive through 1973. (O)=Open (F)=In Flux (C)=Closed circa 1970
*From founding date through 1973.

Table 2 Structural and Life-Cycle Characteristics of Modern Communes Founded in 1969 or Later

Group	Sac	Inv	Ren	Com	Mor	Tran	Total	Life Span*
Ananda (C)	9	5	22	16	4	17	73	4.9
Crook's Creek (C)	8	7	17	25	3	3	63	4.5
(X) LILA (F)	9	4	14	24	2	6	59	.8
(X) Maharaj (F)	15	4	14	22	5	20	80	2.4
(X) Morning Star (O)	12	3	7	24	1	3	50	3.8
(X) Reality (F)	11	4	16	19	1	6	57	3.5
Mean	10.7	4.5	15.0	21.7	2.7	9.2	63.7	3.3

(X)=Group did not survive through 1973 (omitting the Guild of Colorado). (O) = Open (F)=In Flux (C)=Closed circa 1970
*From founding date through 1973.

characteristics of groups founded in 1969 or 1970 (table 2); 1968/1969 is an especially useful demarcation for at least three reasons, two being basically matters of analytical convenience. This date divides the sample equally, and given the difficulty of establishing a new community in the winter, it also separates the two halves cleanly. The most important advantage of this demarcation, though, is that it marks the passage of the commune phenomenon from a marginal social curiosity to a major social movement.

Comparing the commitment scores of groups founded earlier with those founded later shows clearly that earlier groups were less structured and less rigorously organized than the later ones. On all six commitment variables, the groups founded after 1968 had consistently higher scores. This would imply that the groups founded after 1968 had a better chance of surviving through 1973 than those groups founded earlier on more optimistic assumptions. If so, the evidence would be biased in favor of Kanter's theory. But this was not the case. A slight majority of the failures in this study were founded after 1968, not before. On this point there appears to be no problem in comparing success measured by total life span through 1973 and success measured by survival from 1970 to 1973.

Nor does it seem to matter what life-cycle phase the groups were in by my first visits in 1970. A very plausible scenario for such a cycle would begin with a period in which the group is very fluid and open, then change to a period of flux with openings for some new members but only under certain conditions, and then climax with a reasonably stable population and closure from newcomers (except, possibly, under the strictest of conditions). For simplicity, these stages might be called "open," "in flux," and "closed." But as tables 1 and 2 show, these stages were well distributed on both sides of the 1968 demarcation, with a slight tendency for completely open groups to have earlier founding dates. Apparently, then, life-cycle phase is largely irrelevant to the issue of comparing longevity with survival as alternative measures of success.

Anticipating a later discussion of the role of subsidies in the modern commune movement, it might also be noted that they too were liberally sprinkled on both sides of the 1968/1969 demarcation. In general, though, patronage became somewhat less generous in the later period, when the commune movement was already beginning to lose some of its mystique in advanced zones of the counterculture. The rich, it seems, are always well informed about developing trends, especially when giving away their inherited wealth.

Since considerations of communal life cycles, alternative measures of communal success, and subsidies do not seem to bias the discussion, the way is now clear to look in more detail at how

Kanter's six types of commitment were related to communal success or failure and how these relationships apparently changed over time.

Sacrifice In Kanter's theory of communal commitment, the concept of membership sacrifices for joining means that membership would be more costly. Therefore it would not be lightly regarded or given up easily, thus increasing the stability and longevity of the commune. For indicators of sacrifice, Kanter used variables like oral abstinence, celibacy, and physical austerity. For nineteenth-century communes, she found that groups requiring higher degrees of sacrifice from the membership lasted longer on the average, with the differences she observed between successes and failures likely to happen only one time in ten by chance. For modern communes, the relationship between sacrifice and survival is more complicated.

To begin with, modern communes used fewer and milder sacrifice mechanisms than their nineteenth-century counterparts. In Kanter's study, 62 percent of the communes of a century ago practiced one or more forms of oral abstinence; that is, they had rules against consuming substances like meat, stimulants, and intoxicants. In modern communes, only 31 percent, or half as many, had any taboos of this sort. Similarly, 33 percent of the nineteenth-century groups Kanter analyzed practiced celibacy, while only 15 percent of the modern groups practiced or preferred continence, a mild form of celibacy. Although table 3 shows scores on sacrifice that are larger than those found by Kanter, this is only because the concept of sacrifice was expanded for the contemporary setting to include the presence or absence of such things as psychoactive drugs (abstinence) and modern utilities (austerity). Using only the indicators developed by Kanter, the sacrifice scores of modern groups would have been lower than those of nineteenth-century groups, indicating a tendency toward greater self-indulgence among the communes of today.

Table 3 Use of Sacrifice Mechanisms, 1970–1973*

Mean of successful groups (N=5)	8.2	Standard Deviation = 3.15
Mean of unsuccessful groups (N=7)	9.3	Mean = 9.09 (N=12)
	$r_{rho} = -.26$	

*The Guild of Colorado was omitted from this analysis due to ambiguities in the status of its success or failure.

As table 1 shows, the differences between the sacrifice scores of the groups which survived from 1970 to 1973 and those which did not are not very great. By the criteria of either the U-test or the r_{rho} test, these differences are not even close to statistical significance. Of more interest is the fact that the groups which required more sacrifice were slightly *less* likely to survive this three-year period rather than *more* likely to survive as predicted by Kanter's theory. When sacrifice scores are related to total group life spans, however, this relationship goes from negative to positive, or from an r_{rho} of $-.26$ to an r_{rho} of $+.63$, which is statistically significant at a high level of probability (.025). In other words, those groups requiring more sacrifice of their members had significantly longer life spans over the entire period 1965–1973, but by 1973 they were more likely to have failed.

Assuming that this relationship is not simply an error resulting from chance, we might speculate that the functional social value of sacrifice somehow changed from survival-enhancing to survival-inhibiting as the economy moved from prosperity to recession in the early 1970s, especially in terms of physical austerity. In the prosperous late 1960s, when open-land and anarchic groups were dominant on the communal scene and a greater sense of optimism about the movement generally prevailed, higher levels of sacrifice may have been functional on several levels. For one, the commune movement was still very young, and modest beginnings could easily be rationalized as inevitable for the first few years. For another, high levels of austerity served to distinguish the early communes from the middle-class culture of affluence they were rejecting. For still another, austere conditions provided an opportunity-by-necessity to learn many new (that is, premodern) skills. In the atmosphere of bucolic romance that pervaded the early days of the commune movement, these self-sufficiency and craft-related experiences were exhilarating and highly valued. And finally, but certainly not least, in the 1960s these austerity experiences were tempered by the option to return to the mainstream economy, where part-time, temporary, or full-time work was readily available if needed. In other words, the members of the early communes had little reason to expect—then—that austerity might be a permanent condition of their communal lives. The expectation that with time and experience they would improve their lot would be only natural.

With time and experience, however, the survival-enhancing virtues of sacrifice became muted at each of these levels. First, by the early 1970s the commune movement was no longer young, particularly given the rapid pace of change surrounding it. Perhaps it became less easy to rationalize poverty, especially for anarchic groups whose economic horizons were limited in any case. Second, their austerity still distinguished them from their rejected middle-class backgrounds, but events like the Manson murders, the Altamont murder, the collapse of the student protest movement, and the rise of radical feminism demonstrated that the hip underground was not without its mor-

224 The Children of Prosperity

al contradictions too. Third, the newfound skills and self-sufficiency experiences impelled by austerity inevitably lost some of their romance and excitement as the years went by and they became a bit more like ordinary chores and work. Finally, the option to return to the mainstream economy more or less at will was dampened severely by the onset of recession. For the groups with the highest levels of austerity, then, the condition of poverty may have begun to appear permanent by the early 1970s and hence reduced commitment rather than enhanced it.

It is worth noting that the four most austere communes—all failures by 1973—were all owned and ultimately controlled by either one member or by outsiders. Without legal land tenure or true popular control in these communities, it is easy to see how their economic prospects were limited. Given the children of prosperity's comfortable backgrounds, it seems unlikely that they would indefinitely endure harsh and unpromising living conditions. By this line of reasoning, those groups with better living conditions and more realistic hopes for improvements in these conditions were better equipped for inducing commitment over the long haul, through bad times as well as good. If so, the meaning of communal sacrifice would have to be revised to take account of such factors as class background, the business cycle, expectations about future living conditions, and psychological phenomena like relative deprivation.

Investment A second aspect of Kanter's theory suggested that communes requiring higher investments of their members would thereby give their members more stake in the fate of the group and hence be more likely to survive as organizations. Among the communal investment mechanisms investigated were requirements for physical participation of all members, financial contributions and property signovers at admission or while a member, and making commitments of money, property, and labor irreversible. Table 4 shows that communes with higher investment requirements did indeed survive the period 1970–1973 more successfully than those requiring less investment. Although this association falls short of significance at an r_{rho} of +.40, by the criteria of the U-test it is only a hair's-breadth away at the .05 level.

Table 4 Use of Investment Mechanisms, 1970–1973*

Mean of successful groups (N=5)	4.6	Standard Deviation = 1.44
Mean of unsuccessful groups (N=7)	2.7	Mean = 3.83 (N=12)
	$r_{rho} = +.40$	

*The Guild of Colorado was omitted from this analysis due to ambiguities in the status of its success or failure.

Compared to the results Kanter obtained for nineteenth-century communes, modern communes in general used far fewer investment mechanisms than their predecessors. The most conspicuous difference between the centuries is the relative lack of requirements for financial contributions and property turnover among the modern groups. In part this reflects the fact that so many modern communes, particularly those in this study, were subsidized in their land tenure by nonmembers. But an even more important factor was the air of tentativeness that pervaded most modern communes. By and large the members of the new communes did not have much by way of personal resources, were not very sure that their individual futures were synonymous with the groups they joined, and were not very inclined to sink what resources they did command, except time, into collective enterprises with highly problematic destinies. There were many other horizons, after all, for the children of privilege. The one dimension of investment in modern communes that did roughly parallel the nineteenth-century ones was the frequent use of the concept of irreversibility, mainly because of a general distaste for bookkeeping and the lack of surplus resources to reimburse defectors.

When the relationship between investment and survival is recalculated in terms of total group longevity over the entire period 1965–1973, however, we find a slight tendency for those communes with the longest life spans to use *fewer* investment mechanisms (r_{rho} = −.16). This change over time suggests that investment became more important to communal survival in the harder times of the 1970s. Moreover, key elements of the "flow" began to dry up. With the collapse of the radical underground movement as a united front around 1970–1971, communes began to be seen as naive and improbable in the eyes of the press and many of the young as well. The "flow," then, brought fewer visitors and sympathizers who were in a position to contribute surplus resources. Similarly, the patrons who had been so important in subsidizing the early communal ventures began to back out, both from disillusionment and from effects of the recession. Likewise, the onset of a recession economy meant that there was less surplus and salvageable material around for the asking than there had been in the 1960s, when creative scavenging was so effective that many early communes scarcely needed money at all. Finally, the mood among those still committed to the commune movement in the early 1970s changed from open-ended optimism to a more realistic appraisal of the difficulties of creating and sustaining new communities. For all of these reasons, it is not surprising that a more sober attitude toward investment prevailed among those groups which survived the decline of the prosperity of the 1960s.

Renunciation   A third aspect of Kanter's theory of commitment predicts that communes whose members give up emotional attachments outside the group will be more successful than communes practicing lesser degrees of renunciation. Indicators of renunciation were taken to be such factors as geographical isolation, a lack of contact with outside media, strict cross-boundary controls regulating the passage of members and visitors in and out of the groups, and disavowal of the traditional marital dyad or conventional family-child unit. In Kanter's study, all of these factors save ecological separation (geographical isolation) clearly distinguished the more successful from the less successful nineteenth-century communes as her theory predicted. As table 5 shows, the same distinction holds true for modern communes as well. Measured by an r_{rho} of $+.42$, the association between renunciation and communal survival from 1970 to 1973 is the strongest such relationship over this period. This relationship falls short of significance by r_{rho} standards, though it is close; by the criteria of the U-test, it is significant at the .05 level (one-tailed test).

Table 5   Use of Renunciation Mechanisms, 1970–1973*

Mean of successful groups (N=5)	16.4	Standard Deviation = 5.10
Mean of unsuccessful groups (N=7)	8.3	Mean = 13.25 (N=12)
	$r_{rho} = +.42$	

*The Guild of Colorado was omitted from this analysis due to ambiguities in the status of its success or failure.

These results are almost identical to those obtained by Kanter for nineteenth-century communes. In general, though, modern communes differed from nineteenth-century communes by being less standardized in their dress, less ethnically based, less institutionally complete or self-sufficient, and less inclined to regulate the sexual or familial lives of their members. It may be that modern communes were also more attentive than their nineteenth-century counterparts to screening visitors and new members. Kanter records only 12 percent of her groups as having rules for interaction with visitors, whereas 67 percent of modern groups had at least one such rule. More likely this only reflects the fact that the present study examined these processes in more detail. It seems very unlikely that modern communes could have been much more casual about visitors and new members than most of them actually were. For those which were stricter, however, the rules made a difference to their survival.

When renunciation is examined in the longer time frame—total longevity through 1973 in years—the same pattern holds up, with an r_{rho} of $+.35$. Next to the relationship between sacrifice and longevity, this is the second strongest association between commitment and communal life span found in this study. More important still, it is the *only* such relationship which remained consistently strong and positive in both of the time frames examined. We can thus say with some confidence, then, that isolation from the outside world and strict controls over visitors and new members are two of the key factors in communal success. Regardless of the century examined and regardless of the historical and economic differences between time frames in the modern setting, the degree of renunciation appears to be the single most reliable, consistent, and unambiguous predictor of communal survival from the standpoint of commitment. To paraphrase Peter Rabbit of Drop City and Libre, one of the most important things a commune can do to protect its integrity and boost its chances for success is to learn to say no.

Communion   Another dimension of Kanter's commitment theory is the predicted effect of communion mechanisms in fostering group participation, "with members as homogeneous, equal parts of a whole, rather than as differentiated individuals."[1] Those communes using more of these mechanisms in their stronger forms, Kanter found for nineteenth-century groups, were more likely to last longer. A wide variety of structural arrangements, she found, support this apparent communal need for equality, fellowship, group consciousness, and group dependence. Among these were homogeneous personal backgrounds and prior acquaintance among members; group ownership and control of property and other forms of communistic sharing; various forms of communistic labor; high levels of regularized group interaction resulting from communal dwellings and dining halls, limited individual privacy, and frequent group meetings; various forms of group ceremonies and rituals; and mutual experiences of persecution at the hands of outsiders. For Kanter's nineteenth-century groups, communion was related to communal success more strongly than any other type of commitment. But when modern communes are examined in the same terms, this relationship fails to emerge even weakly. As table 6 shows, there was no apparent association between the use of communion mechanisms and communal survival from 1970 to 1973.

Breaking communion down into its component parts produces

Table 6   Use of Communion Mechanisms, 1970–1973*

Mean of successful groups (N=5)	22.0	Standard Deviation = 4.44
Mean of unsuccessful groups (N=7)	21.0	Mean = 21.42 (N=12)
	$r_{rho} = -.08$	

*The Guild of Colorado was omitted from this analysis due to ambiguities in the status of its success or failure.

little added clarification. For the components labeled communistic sharing, communistic labor, and ritual, there is virtually no difference between the groups which survived through 1973 and those which did not. For the other three components, the differences are slight. Under the heading of homogeneity, there was a tendency for members of surviving groups to be slightly more similar in age and to have been previously acquainted with each other slightly longer. Conversely (and contrary to Kanter's theory), there were also tendencies for surviving groups to have slightly less regularized interpersonal contact internally and to have undergone somewhat fewer persecution experiences.

Comparing these results with those obtained by Kanter for nineteenth-century groups sheds a bit more light on the situation. The average score on communion for all modern groups, for instance, is just about the same as the average score for unsuccessful or short-lived groups from the nineteenth century. Similarly, the scores Kanter obtained for successful nineteenth-century groups are much higher than those of successful groups today. Quite possibly these differences merely reflect the fact that all of Kanter's nineteenth-century successes were dogmatic religious sects, many of which took the biblical injunction to "share all things in common" seriously and practiced communism as a central aspect of their Christian beliefs. The groups in the present study, however, were less likely to be religious, and none practiced Christianity as a group. Taken as a whole, modern communes were more secular, more individualistic, and less ritualistic than their nineteenth-century counterparts and were considerably less interested in communion.

In the modern setting, this was true even of successful religious groups like Ananda, which made a point of emphasizing private property, the profit motive, and self-reliance rather than group responsibility. Ananda shared with Libre, a deliberate anarchy that also succeeded, the distinction of having the lowest communion score in the sample. Even the Lama Foundation, which made by far the highest score on this variable, was less communal than the average successful commune of the nineteenth century. It would seem, then, that the practice of very little communion appears no less related to success in the modern setting than the practice of a great deal of it. Groups like Libre and Ananda may not truly be very communal, but they may be stronger communities for the fact that they make little effort to contravene the basic cultural assumptions of the mainstream society which gave them birth. The experience of the Lama Foundation, on the other hand, suggests that communalism must be taken comparatively far to the other extreme to be noticeably effective in influencing commitment. Under the rubric of communion, then, there may be two paths to success rather than just one. The first more or less accepts the individualistic, noncommunist social philosophy of the host culture rather than defying it; while the other develops a communism that departs radically from the host culture rather than just marginally.

On the other hand, there is evidence that the relationship between communion and survival predicted by Kanter might still prove true in the long run, or at least truer than indicated above; the stretch of time she examined, after all, was twenty-five years. When communion scores for modern groups are related to total group life spans, the association is considerably more negative than for the shorter and more recent period 1970–1973 (r_{rho} = −.30 compared to −.08). In the 1960s the longer-lived communes were actually the more anticommunal ones. By 1973, however, many of these groups had ceased to exist, and the association between communion and group survival changed from a fairly strong negative relationship to the lack of any clear-cut relationship at all, a net change in a positive direction. Quite conceivably, this trend will continue into the future, and by the time twenty-five years have passed, this aspect of Kanter's theory will be vindicated.

In the meantime, intense communalism quite clearly was not exactly the children of prosperity's *métier*. In most modern communes the degree of communistic ownership, for instance, was usually just collective ownership of land, and in some cases, the land's buildings (with domestic tenure reserved for builders). Property and income were shared in sometimes generous ways but seldom on any systematically equalitarian basis, and every commune has its stories about hidden reserves of private cash, conflicts over permission to use privately owned property, or communal dinners abruptly interrupted by an ex-member coming to claim "his" table and chairs. Communistic labor usually fell within the same sort of limitations. Most often it could be more accurately described as voluntaristic "cooperative" labor, with little organized effort to distribute labor programmatically or fairly. These forms of communalism inevitably require a certain measure of social coercion and ordered regularity, and to this the children of prosperity were not very favorably disposed.

Nor were they very strongly inclined—or at least not for very long in most cases—to other forms of orderly sharing like scheduled communal dining, communal dwellings, frequent group meetings, or the sustained absence of individual privacy. The modern communal landscape is replete with groups which began with one big building for everybody to live in, but soon afterward began developing satellite dwellings, eating communally less often, and holding fewer regular meetings. Finally, the ritual component of modern communal life was seldom very substantial beyond holding hands prayerfully at dinners. This happened not so much because the need for it was not recognized, but mostly because the educated and secularized children of prosperity were so often unable to invest it with the necessary legitimacy.

In assessing the limits of communalism for the children of prosperity, Kriyananda perhaps said it best: "Where people are expected to do everything in common, . . . friction can quickly mount. A community that strives for such constant, intense 'togetherness' will require miracles of leadership to survive."[2] The one successful exception to his principle in this study, the Lama Foundation, did indeed enjoy miracles of leadership, or at minimum an ingenious organizational strategy. In another culture, with its back to the wall and a nation to build like the Israelis, with strong religious and ethnic ties like many of the successful communal sects of the nineteenth century, or with deep and unquestioned tribal rites and traditions like the pre-Columbian American Indians, this might not be valid. But in the competitive, privatized, highly mobile culture that produced and conditioned the children of prosperity, Kriyananda's statement has a strong ring of truth. This is one of the reasons why communards seeking intense communalism gravitated toward religious communities of discipline by 1973. In a devoutly religious atmosphere, it is much easier to create rites and traditions where none existed before and to mute the anarchic influence of private egos and desires. Those not seeking such intense communalism generally gravitated toward more individualistic arrangements or drifted back to the cities to meet a more conventional destiny.

Mortification A fifth dimension to Kanter's theory of commitment holds that those communal groups employing more mortification mechanisms will be more likely to succeed than those using less. The functional effect of commitment through mortification is to require that a commune member sees himself as humble and ineffectual without the group and that he thereby reshapes his identity to meet the conditions for ideal membership set by the group. Mortification, wrote Kanter, "can be a sign of trust in the group, a willingness to share weaknesses, failings, doubts, problems, and one's innermost secrets with others. At the same time, its use is also a sign that the group cares about the individual, about his thoughts and feelings, about the content of his inner world," thus facilitating commitment and generating loyalty through the systematic "invasion of phenomenological privacy."[3] Moreover, the function of mortification processes is to remove personal pride as a source of interference with the group's moral and normative integrity.

The indicators used by Kanter to test for mortification strategies included the presence or absence of confession and mutual criticism and surveillance of members by leaders or each other; various forms of spiritual differentiation among the membership based on moral or spiritual grounds, on the basis of intelligence or skill, or in terms of probationary versus tenured membership; mortifying sanctions against deviants such as public denouncement, denial of a membership privilege, or prohibition from participation in a community function; and deindividuating mechanisms such as wearing uniforms. As table 7 shows, the use of this class of commitment mechanisms in modern communes was very low. Even the successful modern communes had mortification scores that averaged only half those of the unsuccessful communes of the nineteenth century. This indicates quite clearly, I think, that individualism and the sanctity of individual autonomy are much more deeply cherished values among today's communards than they were a century ago. Modern communes were so devoid of the mortifying sanctions and deindividuating mechanisms outlined by Kanter, in fact, that these aspects of mortification were dropped from the analysis.

Table 7 Use of Mortification Mechanisms, 1970–1973*

Mean of successful groups (N=5)	3.6	Standard Deviation = 1.61
Mean of unsuccessful groups (N=7)	2.0	Mean = 2.67 (N=12)
	$r_{rho} = +.30$	

*The Guild of Colorado was omitted from this analysis due to ambiguities in the status of its success or failure.

Table 7 also shows, however, that even the scanty levels of mortification mechanisms that were used made a difference for communal survival from 1970 through 1973 ($r_{rho} = +.30$). Those groups practicing more spiritual differentiation among members and/or higher levels of mutual criticism were indeed more likely to succeed over this period. This relationship falls just barely short of significance by the criteria of the U-test (.05 level, one-tailed test); it is somewhat further away by the standards of r_{rho}. Relating mortification scores to total communal life spans, however, indicates that there is no relationship between these variables over the longer time frame ($r_{rho} = -.01$). Once again it seems that the hard times of the early 1970s tended to favor those communes making more use of mortification mechanisms, just as they favored communes making more use of four out of the five other kinds of commitment.

It is worth noting that the two main kinds of mortification mechanisms explored in the modern setting, mutual criticism and spiritual differentiation, seldom seem to be used simultaneously or to the same degree in any given group. In religious groups like Ananda, Lama, and Maharaj Ashram, spiritual differentiation was quite common and evident, but much less use was made of mutual criticism. Religious groups appear to favor mortification by superior virtue and to avoid direct interpersonal encounters. Nonreligious groups like Saddle Ridge, Talsalsan, the Guild of Colorado, and Crook's Creek, on the other hand, were much more inclined to use mutual criticism than spiritual differentiation. Possibly one approach is the functional equivalent of the other. Groups that use neither, however, appear to be more vulnerable to failure.

Transcendence   The final component of Kanter's theory of commitment predicts that those communes using more surrender or transcendence mechanisms will have a higher survival potential than those using fewer such mechanisms. Transcendence here means subordinating individual decision-making power to the greater power of the group, becoming so involved with this larger system of authority that it gives both meaning and direction to the individual's life, fusing personal identity and group identity in such a manner that carrying out the group's demands becomes morally necessary for the maintenance of the self. "For surrender [transcendence] to occur," wrote Kanter, "the individual must first experience great power and meaning residing in the organization."[4]

As indicators of transcendence, Kanter explored institutionalized awe first in terms of transcendental ideologies and philosophies investing the group with special distance and mystery to its members and then in terms of hierarchical relationships of power and authority which presumably accomplish similar results. She then examined programing by rules of personal conduct and detailed daily routines; ideological conversion through tests of faith, vows, and other procedures for choosing new members; and, finally, prior traditions which imbue members with a sense that their group is something greater than its immediate or recent experiences. For nineteenth-century groups, Kanter found that transcendence mechanisms were second only to communion mechanisms in distinguishing successful from unsuccessful utopian communities. In the modern setting, however, the effect of transcendence on communal survival appears to be either negative or nonexistent.

As table 8 shows, modern communes varied tremendously in their use of transcendence, more so by far than in their use of any other class of commitment mechanisms. Group scores on these characteristics range all the way from 0 (Drop City) to 20 (Maharaj Ashram). Not surprisingly, the three religious communities (Lama, Maharaj, and Ananda) made much more intense use of this dimension of

Table 8   Use of Transcendence Mechanisms, 1970–1973*

Mean of successful groups (N=5)	8.4	Standard Deviation = 6.61
Mean of unsuccessful groups (N=7)	6.8	Mean = 7.33 (N=12)
	$r_{rho} = 0.0$	

*The Guild of Colorado was omitted from this analysis due to ambiguities in the status of its success or failure.

commitment than anarchistic and open-land groups. Nevertheless, there was apparently no overall relation between gradations in the use of transcendence and communal survival from 1970 to 1973 (r_{rho} = 0.0). In terms of total communal longevity between 1965 and 1973, in fact, this relationship was decidedly negative ($r_{rho} = -.26$).

This pattern and its change over time exactly parallel the association between communion and survival. When anarchistic and open-land groups were in their heyday in the early years of the modern commune movement, most of the transcendence mechanisms were completely antithetical to the feelings and intentions behind the formation of these groups. Ideology was generally vague, eclectic, and difficult to agree on even negatively. Power and authority and any form of hierarchical relationships were anathema—in good part the very things that modern communards were reacting against. Tight daily routines and other forms of behavioral programing were generally thought to deaden spontaneity and freedom, two of the hip world's most highly cherished values. Vows, screening, and other mechanisms of insuring the committed conversion of new members were often considered authoritarian, prejudicial, or unnecessary. Most such groups were still too new and loosely assembled for tradition to count for much. In open-land groups particularly, these mechanisms were the least likely of all the varieties of commitment to be countenanced. Comparing the transcendence scores of modern communes with the scores of their antecedents in the nineteenth century, we find once again that modern groups made far less use of these mechanisms in their social organization, with today's successes scoring lower, on the average, than yesterday's failures.

But as with communion, the passage of time and the demise of open-land groups in the early 1970s changed the association between transcendence and survival in a more positive direction, from a negative relationship to a zero relationship. The end result was to reveal two markedly distinct paths between transcendence and survival. One of them, a path of steadfast antiauthoritarianism (paralleling the mortification path of interpersonal encounter), was followed by Crook's Creek, Libre, and Saddle Ridge Farm (average transcendence score, 3.3). The other, a path of programmatic and hierarchical religious ideologies (paralleling the mortification path of moral and spiritual status systems), was followed by Lama and Ananda (average transcendence score, 16.0). Either path seems workable, other things equal. Apparently those groups in the middle (average scores for communal failures, 6.8) had the lowest survival potential. Once again, libertarian anarchism and authoritarian mysticism seem oddly equivalent.

Total Commitment Just as Kanter predicted that each of the six types of commitment-inducing mechanisms would be related to communal success, she argued that summing them all together into scores describing overall commitment would also predict communal success or failure. As we have seen, however, the theory of commitment does not work very well in predicting success as defined by longevity in years through 1973. Only two of the six variables, sacrifice and renunciation, were positively related to communal longevity at all. The other four were negatively related, with effects opposite of those predicted, at least in the early years of the modern commune movement. It is to be expected, therefore, that the net overall effect on communal life spans through 1973 of all commitment variables combined would also be negative, and in fact it is, with an r_{rho} of $-.36$. If this were our only evidence, we would have to conclude that modern communes with *less* structure were more likely to be long-lived than those with more, that elaborate commitment structures hurt more than they helped, and that the theory of commitment is mostly false or of limited usefulness in diverse historical circumstances.

In a way this makes a great deal of sense, given the children of prosperity's preoccupation with freedom, choice, and self-fulfillment. We must remember that social organization in general, and the theory of commitment in particular, involves things like hierarchical relationships, relatively permanent attachments and sunken costs, constraints on the liberty to enter or leave these attachments casually, and numerous other limits on individual choice and personal autonomy. None of these things sat well with the hip culture of the 1960s. Indeed, they were the gist of its rebellion. To a great extent communal organization and individual freedom are contradictory opposites. Small wonder, then, that the longest-lived communal groups during the period when the counterculture was flourishing were those which provided the easiest entry and exit. It was completely in character.

But we must bear in mind that the time period covered by this study is relatively short. However fast the pace of change may be accelerating today, the period covered is still just a fraction of the entire human generation studied by Kanter. People take on more sober responsibilities as they get older. They become more conservative and realistic as it becomes steadily more apparent that their choices are not unlimited and that the world will probably not be made over in their lifetimes. Even if the modern commune movement cannot exactly be dismissed as a modern version of the medieval children's crusade, there is no question that it was a movement made up of people scarcely initiated into adulthood with many changes in their futures. By 1973, with the erosion of the self-righteous zeal of the 1960s and the onset of a serious economic slump, things were changing. The relationship between commitment and communal survival was changing, too.

Table 9 Overall Use of Commitment Mechanisms, 1970–1973*

Mean of successful groups (N=5)	63.2	Standard Deviation = 16.07
Mean of unsuccessful groups (N=7)	53.0	Mean = 57.25 (N=12)
	$r_{rho} = +.15$	

*The Guild of Colorado was omitted from this analysis due to ambiguities in the status of its success or failure.

Table 9 shows that with the passage of time, the expected relationship between commitment and survival reversed yet again, this time as Kanter had originally predicted. Communes which survived the critical period 1970–1973 did indeed have more rigorous commitment structures. In statistical terms this relationship was slight ($r_{rho} = +.15$), but at almost every level the *direction* of change was uniform and the *degree* of change was quite pronounced. All trends over this period (except sacrifice) were toward greater commitment-reinforcing structures as groups with less structure began to fail. The communes which survived were those which had been built on more conservative organizational assumptions. It is not at all unreasonable to expect that by 1990, when the surviving communes of the modern period will be about twenty-five years old and span an entire generation, this trend will have continued to develop and the relationships predicted by Kanter will be more evident. The fact will always remain, however, that in the beginning, for at least a little while, modern communes successfully defied most of the proven principles of communal organization.

In understanding why some communes succeeded and others failed, there is at least one more important factor to be considered: the role that gifts and subsidies played in the destiny of the modern commune movement. I credit my own suspicions about their importance to a conversation with a man named John Allen, leader of a New Mexico commune variously called Biotechnica, Synergia, and the Theatre of All Possibilities, which I discovered too late to include in my original study.[5] Allen told me in 1973, when it was becoming clear that the New Mexico commune scene had all but completely collapsed, that the single most dangerous threat to the commune movement—or "former commune movement" as he put it—was not authoritarian repression, immaturity, or bad social design but subsidies taken from outsiders. Subsidized groups, he argued, are always subject to controls or expropriation at the whims of the subsidizers. "Sooner or later you can be sure that they'll figure out a way to get what they paid for, or else take it back."

As we have seen over the course of the thirteen ethnographies, many modern communes were established with assistance from some kind of benefactor. This study probably exaggerates the role of large subsidies, since most of the communes examined here were founded when the movement was still pregnant with promise and hence attracted such benefactors. But even the more obscure and remote communes like Crook's Creek were partially subsidized by parents and the government. It was a rare commune, indeed, that did not have one or more sources of outside support. The important point to remember is that many of the most novel communal experiments on the landscape, such as Lama or Wheeler's Ranch, would probably never have happened without help. This was the positive face of subsidy in the early days of the movement.

The negative face was revealed only later, around 1973, when many of the early benefactors indeed "took it back" just as John Allen had observed. The specific historical cause behind five of the seven communal failures in this study was the withdrawal by benefactors of their support. This is not to say that commitment factors were unimportant, because the benefactors' disillusionment was intimately bound up with what they saw happening with their resources—or failing to happen. The responsibility for what they saw belongs mainly to the groups themselves. Groups like Lama and Libre, which demonstrated higher levels of both commitment and responsibility, have not had such troubles with their patrons (being clever enough to make donations irrevocable in the first place). Nevertheless, the peculiar good-bad nature of subsidy deserves our attention for one last bit of analysis to pair with the rest.

Table 10 examines the relationship between the single most important type of subsidy to rural communal groups, gifts of land, and whether or not these gifts seemed to make a difference to their success or failure by 1973. Each group was placed in one of two categories. In the first, a commune's land was donated essentially free, either as an outright gift or for use without rent. It was assumed that a subsidizer in this category could be a single person inside the commune as well as an outside benefactor, so long as that single person was solely responsible for land-related debts and payments. The sec-

Table 10 Communal Land Tenure and Survival, 1970–1973*

Survival	Free Land, Fully Subsidized	Partially Subsidized or Not Subsidized
Successful (N=5)	1	4
Unsuccessful (N=7)	5	2

$$X^2 = 3.09 \ (.10 \text{ at } 1 \text{ d.f.})$$
$$C = .42$$

*The Guild of Colorado was omitted from this analysis due to ambiguities in the status of its success or failure.

ond category included all other groups whose land was only partially subsidized or not subsidized at all. As it turned out, each category contained six communes. Fully half of the groups in this study lived on land requiring no payment at all (not counting, in some cases, taxes). As table 10 indicates, only one of the six communes with fully subsidized land tenure survived through 1973, whereas four of the six groups which were not fully subsidized proved to be successful. This relationship is sufficiently strong (probable only one time in ten by chance) to conclude that the role of subsidy in the modern commune movement was very important both positively and negatively.

Exactly why the chances of communal failure seem to increase with subsidy—or more precisely, with free land—depends to some extent on one's sympathies and assumptions about human nature. On the one hand, there was probably little real incentive for communards to develop or commit themselves to land they did not actually own or completely control. How could they value something highly that they did not work to get? On the other hand, there is little evidence that most of these groups would not still exist today had they not been evicted, even if the settlers changed faces every year. It could easily be argued that the concept of open land did not die of its own folly, but was instead willfully crushed by authoritarian repression, as in the case of Wheeler's Ranch or the original Morning Star, or by hung-over hip capitalists with other things on their minds as with the rest. In any case the open-land groups are gone now, leaving the communards of the future to ponder the hippie vision that everything should be free and to remember the hazards as well as the blessings of getting something for nothing.

Notes

1. Rosabeth Moss Kanter, "Commitment and Social Organization: A Study of Commitment Mechanisms in Utopian Communities," *American Sociological Review*, 33 (August 1968), 510.

2. Swami Kriyananda, *Cooperative Communities: How to Start Them, and Why,* 2nd ed. (Nevada City, Calif: Ananda Publications, 1971), p. 21.

3. Kanter, "Commitment and Social Organization," p. 512.

4. Ibid., p. 514.

5. Fortunately, Allen's remarkable group *was* studied by historian Lawrence Veysey, who produced, in the process, the most artfully constructed, thorough, and insightful ethnographic account yet written about a modern commune. See *The Communal Experience: Anarchist and Mystical Counter-Cultures in America* (New York: Harper & Row, 1973), pp. 279–406.

15

Children of Prosperity: The Destiny and Legacy of the Modern Commune Movement

Most of us were born between 1940 and 1950. . . . We grew up with the "cold war," the "space race," and the "crisis in education"—all propaganda efforts designed to lure large numbers of young people into becoming teachers, engineers, scientists, media technicians, etc. We were fooled in the same way the Okies were lured to California by the growers. Five jobs were promised when there was only one job available. . . . In 1960 the cold war was flourishing and no Ph.D. ever dreamed that 1970 would see Ph.D.s driving cabs and applying for welfare.

So here we are. We can write dissertations, we can teach school, we can design bridges, program computers. . . . And we're free. Free because we're irrelevant. We're the avant-garde of a tidal wave of surplus talent, training, and glorious expectations.[1]

In the late 1960s, a new and entirely unpredicted phenomenon emerged on the American scene: the modern commune movement. From very modest beginnings in Colorado and on the West Coast around 1965, coinciding with the birth of the hippie, the movement grew geometrically over the next half decade until by 1970–1971, now generally recognized as its zenith, there were thousands of new rural communes sprinkled across the American countryside, wherever the land was cheap, the terrain unsuitable for commercial agriculture, and the scenery beautiful.

In and around the cities and campuses, still more thousands of communes were flourishing by 1970. Altogether informed guesses place the total number of people involved in one form of communal living or another during this period at something like a half million.[2] By contrast, only six hundred communes are known to have been formed over the entire three-hundred-year history of America prior to 1965. Even accounting for obscure and forgotten experiments over this vast stretch of time, there were surely less than a thousand. The scale of the modern movement completely dwarfed everything communal that had gone before, and did so in only five years.

By 1973, however, this massive retreat from the cities and institutions of our society was generally considered—not altogether accurately—to be moribund. By then it was also ignored by the media which had once made it a *cause célèbre* and done so much to stimulate its growth. Stories of communal failures were common and painful enough to destroy the feeling that communes were any longer a live option. The commune movement waned still more when the end of the Vietnam era made this form of retreat seem less urgent and the onset of economic depression made it seem less feasible.

But a social movement of this scale cannot be ignored even if it has become moribund, and the fact is that many communal groups established in the 1960s survive today. It is amazing that there has been so little follow-through to find out what separated the successes from the failures, what these outcomes tell us about the character of the American young, and to what extent these alienated bands of psychedelic pioneers may have been pointing the way to our national future, in spite of their self-righteous claims to be doing exactly that.

Who were these people in the first place? There seems to be universal agreement among social scientists that the vast majority were white, came from middle-class and professional homes, had been to college and often held advanced degrees, were twenty to thirty years old, had used psychedelic drugs, and had been at least peripherally involved in the protest politics of the time.[3] Little is known about the subtleties of their family backgrounds, but apparently they were precocious beginners on the road to rebellion, with a history of "early conflicts with parental authority and equally early teen-age experiments with sex and drugs," to quote the results of one study in California.[4] One prominent scholar (with a Freudian bent) even described them as "father rejectors" driven to flaunt all forms of authority.[5] True or not, this line of reasoning does not explain why the commune movement happened when it did, on the scale it did, or why it even happened at all.

More important were the things that happened to the children of prosperity after leaving home for college and the brightly shining futures they had been led to expect. Although many factors contributed to the rise of interest in communal living, two stand out far above the rest: the spread of psychedelic drugs and the mounting opposition to the Vietnam War. The growth of these trends and the growth of modern communes from 1965 onward were virtually synonymous. The contribution of the antiwar movement was essentially negative, creating widespread feelings that a society capable of producing such a revolting war must therefore be immoral and rotten throughout. The contribution of drugs was essentially positive, producing visions of cosmic unity, personal liberation, and loving groups of like-minded peers, visions which left mainstream America pale by comparison. In other circumstances the critique and the vision might have gone their separate ways, and perhaps for the most part they did. But where they met, an interest in communal retreat was born.

The communards of the late 1960s believed that mainstream America was morally bankrupt and unsalvageable by ordinary means. Campaigns of persuasion brought only Humphrey versus Nixon in 1968. Direct confrontations with authority brought officially sanctioned murders at Kent State, Jackson State, and in Black Panther communities. The only "alternative"—a word which changed in tone from theoretical desirability to personal desperation—became a strategy of retreat. The mood was one of preparing for Armageddon and of ambivalence between no longer giving a damn about anything but personal release and hoping to demonstrate to America that a better answer could be found.

The bitterness ran deepest where it was most personal. Interest in communal retreat was strongest among those who had been jailed for exploring their own consciousness, who had been clubbed for expressing their civil rights, who stood to be drafted to fight a hated war, and who felt impelled to throw away career plans because the society offering them was no longer morally worthy of participation. Like similar social movements throughout history, the modern commune movement was a combined product of social upheaval and personal threat.[6]

But in the background was another factor, prior to all the others and ultimately even more important. Without the prosperity of the 1960s, ironically fueled by a wartime economy, it is doubtful that the very heirs and heiresses of that prosperity would have come to reject it so totally. For the children of the post–World War II baby boom, prosperity brought college for millions, and with it, new ideas, new criticisms, and new experiences with politics, drugs, and group living. In a way such opportunities placed them atop a gigantic pyramid of

striving, suffering, and abundance built under them by their parents
It was planned to better prepare them for the future, but it also gave
them a vantage point to reinterpret the future for themselves.

So they loftily pronounced their parents wrong while simultaneously enjoying a life of leisure, educational stimulation, and the absence of traditional responsibilities. But it would be worse than facile
to dismiss the new communards as spoiled ingrates. As poet Gary
Snyder has observed, they were the first generation in history with
the resources, education, and technology to have the whole world and
all of history as a choice-matrix for answering the question of *how to
live*. From the standpoint of human evolution, theirs was a highly
significant pinnacle. What is the meaning of "progress" in this life,
after all, if not to bring more people this kind of choice?

In any event, the luxury of social criticism is most readily available to those free enough to explore other options. In America in the
late 1960s, finding fault with bourgeois materialism was mainly the
privilege of its second- and third-generation inheritors. They had
grown up with its advantages and thereby had the direct opportunity
to find it lacking for the full and rewarding life they had been conditioned to expect.

In less prosperous times, in fact, it is questionable if the modern commune movement would have gotten under way at all. The
historical record shows that communal experiments are uncommon
and do not fare well in times of economic depression. In a way they
might seem more practical under such circumstances, and they probably are. But depression more often brings retreat of another sort:
back to traditional family ties and conventional economic struggle.
But the prosperity of the wartime economy of the 1960s was a favorable climate for communal experiments in several ways. For one
thing, it meant the option to plug back into the system if such
experiments failed. For another, it made it easy to get part-time or
temporary work to keep them going. For still another, it meant the
availability of subsidies from outside patrons. And finally, it meant
great reservoirs of surplus materials and "waste" available for salvage and recycling, reducing the need for cash. All this would
change in the early 1970s with the onset of recession.

As noted earlier, the great bulk of modern communes, at least
for a while, were urban rather than rural. They were nevertheless
the least important aspect of the phenomenon. As Judson Jerome
says in his *Families of Eden*, "Urban communes tend to be variations on the rooming houses or shared apartments that have always
been part of urban and academic life. In these settings, communalism is largely a convenience."[7] In any event, urban communes were
far less innovative forms of social experimentation than rural ones,

and ultimately much less serious. Except for co-ops and monastic religious centers (about which more will be said later), urban communes had largely disappeared or changed into less communal forms by 1973. The survival rate of rural communes through this period, on the other hand, seems to have been at least 30 percent.[8] This was also the approximate five-year rate of success for the communes of the nineteenth century.

It would be a mistake to infer from these figures that modern communes were failures, since venerable American institutions like small businesses and happy marriages fail at unseemly high rates too. Modern communes have been no less successful than the mundane American dream. We only judge them more harshly because they attempt to be more.

Of all the many ways that modern communes might be divided into categories, there are basically two types that matter most. One might be described as anarchistic, libertarian, individualistic, voluntaristic, free-form, unstructured, or open, based on what Judson Jerome once called a "blissful state of positive paranoia . . . the belief that the universe is a conspiracy for one's benefit." For the children of prosperity, this attitude came easily while they were young and free in a climate of abundance. Throughout the latter half of the 1960s, this was by far the most common type of commune. There were important variations on this theme, of course, but what they all held in common was an antiauthoritarian, leaderless, and anarchistic spirit.

The other primary type could be described as religious, disciplined, structured, authoritarian, hierarchical, transcendental, or as "total institutions." Such communities are usually known as monasteries, spiritual retreats, or ashrams, and are usually led by "inspired" or "evolved" charismatic leaders. Here too there are important subvariations, but once again they all have something in common: a willingness among the membership to submit to authoritarian oversight and behavioral programing in the interest of their "spiritual growth" and "inner development." Historically, groups of this sort have been the most successful, or at any rate the longest-lived. In the 1960s such groups were a distinct minority, but in the depressed times of the mid-1970s they equaled or displaced anarchistic communes as the most common.

These two types represent the polar extremes of the youth movement of the 1960s. On the one hand, it was individualistic, expressive, equalitarian, gregarious, and anarchistic to the core. On the other hand, political cynicism and the drug experience carried the seeds of introverted withdrawal, the breakdown of inherited values like achievement, marriage, and careerism, and other forms of deprograming leading to aimless living and a revival of interest in supernatural powers and internal transcendence. Taken together these two themes embody the classic conflicts between freedom versus authoritarianism, spontaneity versus order, and individualism versus surrender. As historian Lawrence Veysey has pointed out, anarchism and mysticism were "the two most striking intellectual tendencies in the counterculture of the 1960's."[9] They are history's two great highways to the utopian fusion of self-fulfillment with the ideal of community.

In her landmark study of nineteenth-century American communes, Rosabeth Kanter compared about ten communes that survived for twenty-five years or longer with about twenty which lasted only a few years, testing her theory that successful communes would be those which required more sacrifice (abstinence and austerity), investment (financial and physical), renunciation (isolation from outsiders), communion (communistic sharing), mortification (ego-loss), and transcendence (surrender to authoritarian, ideological hierarchies). All these factors, she discovered, clearly distinguished the successes from the failures. All her successes, in fact, were authoritarian religious sects, and most of the failures were secular anarchies.[10] The gist of my own work was to see if this is, in fact, a perennial theme in communal movements, or if instead there was something about the modern movement which could successfully defy these axioms, as it seemed in the late 1960s.

For a while, at least, modern rural communes did succeed in defying most of these axioms. Even as late as 1973, the longest-lived groups were not those with rigid authoritarian structures but instead the free-form anarchies. Drop City, for example, founded in Colorado in 1965 and probably the first true hippie commune, managed to survive for eight full years in a state of total organizational chaos. It only failed when the long-departed founders removed an embarrassing clause in the deed that the land was to be free forever and then evicted the new generation of tenants, leaving Drop City's bizarre, multicolored domes to be stripped and vandalized rather than preserved as the Hip National Monument they deserved to be as the first geodesic community in America.

As long as the prosperity of the 1960s lasted, so too did most of the anarchies, even though their populations often turned over annually and sociological theory gave them a poor prognosis. The only one of Kanter's six variables which had a clear and unambiguous relation to communal survival through 1973 was her concept of renunciation. Longer-lived communes over this period were more isolated than most geographically, more insulated from modern media (telephones, newspapers, and especially television), more likely to have elaborate rules regulating visitors, and more likely to have restrictive policies toward screening and accepting new members. If there was any single key to success over the modern communal decade, it might be summarized as the capacity to say no.

Between 1970 and 1973, though, things in general began to change more in the direction that Kanter had predicted. Groups which survived this period, whether anarchist or religious in philosophy, had two additional characteristics that Kanter had found to be so important a century earlier. For one, they required more investment of their members, both in time and money. With the recession of the early 1970s the magic of the "flow" dried up, and only those groups demanding more personal investment from their members were adequately equipped to meet their resource needs. Groups surviving over this period were also more likely to use ego-reducing mechanisms like frank confrontations or humbling spiritual status systems, which Kanter lumped together under the heading of "mortification." The secular anarchies were more likely to use candid encounter, while the religious groups preferred the more impersonal approach of mortification by superior virtue. These two paths to reducing the sin of personal pride were not often used in combination, but either worked better than the absence of both.

The other organizational characteristics that Kanter investigated, however, were not related to group survival even through the depressed economic and political climate of the early 1970s, at least not as predicted. A high degree of sacrifice, for instance, was tempo rarily associated with communal success in the prosperous times of the 1960s, when abundance was easily accessible and therefore just easily rejected. But the groups which survived the recession years of the early 1970s were those less impoverished and self-denying. When fat times turned to lean, the lure of middle-class comforts was stronger than a willingness to endure sustained hardships.

One of my most peculiar findings was that communal sharing, supposedly the essence of what communes are all about, was not related to survival at all and in fact seemed to shorten group life spans. This was true even of many religious groups, which generally fared better when they accepted conventional American values like private property, the profit motive, and individual self-reliance. Indeed, the only truly communistic feature of most modern communes was owning or sharing land together. Almost every other form of communal sharing was completely voluntary. Not that it was uncommon, but the children of prosperity's needs for privacy and personal autonomy apparently ran deep. The level of sharing typically diminished over time if the group survived. In essence, modern communards were always individualists more than communalists.

A similar pattern held true for Kanter's concept of "transcendence," or surrender to strict ideological and hierarchical demands. As with communal sharing, those groups requiring more deference of their memberships actually had shorter rather than longer life spans through 1973. Over the critical 1970–1973 period, there was no difference between the success rates of the authoritarian and anarchical groups. It was the confused groups in the middle, needing leadership but not trusting it, which had the poorest record of survival. Apparently American young people at the time were better equipped for either total individualism or total obedience than for the ordinary democracy in between, which would seem to say something unfortunate about our culture.

It is important to note, though, that both communal sharing and hierarchical organization were more positively related to success in the 1970s than in the 1960s. This hints that time brings pressures for change in the direction of more structure, as predicted by Kanter, in every sense but enforced hardship and sacrifice. It also suggests that when still more time elapses, Kanter's theory will be vindicated. The more rigid and authoritarian groups will probably triumph in the long run as long as they provide reasonably comfortable living conditions and don't censor too many personal habits. These changes also signal the transition from individualistic anarchies to authoritarian religious communities as the more dominant form on the communal scene after 1973. But it must be remembered that for its first eight years, the modern rural commune movement successfully snubbed at least half of the organizational principles supposedly determining its destiny.

By 1975, if my estimate of a failure rate of 60 to 70 percent is correct, there were over a thousand rural communes still existing in America from the 1970 apex, though often with changed names and character and usually shunning the "commune" label. Given the fact that this number exceeds the number of communes formed throughout our entire previous history as a nation, it would be perilous to conclude that the movement is dead. And many other groups have formed since then, under the new banner of the "communities movement." It even has its own magazine called *Communities*, founded in 1972 as a merger of three competing antecedents and still publishing regularly today. There are a number of signs that a meaningful intercommunal network of communication and exchange has finally taken hold.

However, there are also signs that at best the communities movement is on a plateau, engaged in a holding pattern which may be weakening, even though the back-to-the-land movement as a whole continues to gain momentum. *Communities* is a publishing midget, for example, next to its more sophisticated and popular above-ground colleagues like *The Mother Earth News* and *The Whole Earth Cata-*

log. Both of these counterculture giants grew up with the commune movement, but the key to their success has been servicing the back-to-the-land and do-it-yourself movement in general. Both of them phased out their coverage of communes around 1972. Since then, incidentally, new magazines addressed solely to spiritual issues have arrived: *The East/West Journal* and *The New Age Journal*. Both far surpass *Communities* in circulation, though in many respects their concerns are similar, and together they announce the parity that religious communities had achieved with secular ones by the mid-1970s.

Another successful publication is a periodically revised book called the *Spiritual Community Guide for North America*.[11] According to a count I made in its 1975–1976 edition, there were at least 1,300 spiritual centers and communities in the United States by the mid-1970s. Anyone who's done a little traveling on this circuit knows this is an underestimation by at least 25 percent, and probably more. Less than one hundred of these are permanent rural communities, suggesting that in addition to dominating the present commune movement in absolute numbers, the spiritualists have also shifted its most important locale back to the cities. But this is somewhat misleading, since among all the ashrams, Jesus communes, and Hare Krishna houses listed in the *Guide* are a considerable number of centers that are really just business offices or gathering places. Urban and religious groups on the one hand and secular and rural groups on the other appear to be in approximate balance today, calling to mind Lawrence Veysey's observation that "in twentieth-century America . . . the idea of inner withdrawal from the materialism of the society competes, more or less as an equal, with the idea of a left-wing withdrawal from that same materialism."[12]

On the religious scene, there appear to be two primary types of communal organizations operating today. One type includes gregarious, salvational "religions of conventional enthusiasm," as Veysey describes them. Their appeal lies mainly in the all-embracing social support they offer to homeless and disoriented drifters with no other place to call home, and they are very aggressive in proselytizing likely candidates on the streets, typically offering a free meal, free literature, or a place to sleep as inducements to join the fold. Examples of this type include the International Society for Krishna Consciousness (Hare Krishna), Sun Myung Moon's Unification Church, the Jesus movement, the Divine Light Mission (formerly led by Maharaj Ji, the teen-age "perfect master" discredited by his own mother), and the Children of God (led by a young man called Moses David, who identifies himself with the Pied Piper and Don Quixote).

All these movements are tightly organized on a national scale and altogether have attracted several hundred thousand followers, although only a minority of them live in organized communal housing. Smaller and more localized variants include convicted drug-distributing messiah Alan Noonan's Messiah's World Crusade or the One-World Family (California), frustrated rock star Mel Lyman's Brotherhood of the Spirit or Renaissance Church (Massachusetts), and psychedelic prophet Steve Gaskin's The Farm (Tennessee). In all of them mysticism, authoritarianism, charisma, and communalism are linked hand in hand. Some of these groups (Divine Light Mission and Children of God) are considered so disreputable that the *Spiritual Community Guide for North America* does not even mention them. We can bet that the "Moonies" will not be listed again in the next edition!

The other type of sectarian religious communes are more intellectual, less aggressive in recruitment, more impersonal, more oriented to individual inner development, less authoritarian in organization, and generally seem to attract more competent members. Usually such groups are smaller and more localized, though several have a number of centers and communities around the country. Regional to modestly national groups of this type include Zen Buddhism, A'Nanda Ma'rga, the Naropa Institute, Sufi Brotherhoods, the Self-Realization Fellowship, Seekers After Truth, Sri Chinmoy Centers, Vendanta, and a number of other religious organizations. There are dozens of smaller groups of a similar but ideologically diverse nature scattered about the country. The biggest of all is Yogi Bhajan's Sikhist Healthy-Happy-Holy Organization ("3HO"), which claims one hundred ashrams nationwide and straddles the two types in character.

Both types are generally communal in nature, but what they have most in common is a dedication to what LSD and dolphin researcher Dr. John C. Lilly has called "metaprogramming and reprogramming of the human biocomputer."[13] Leaving the old identity behind and reconstructing a new self are the basic themes uniting all these divergent organizations servicing the needs of the blissed-out and the blitzed-out. One type emphasizes external discipline and organization building through obedient work and aggressive recruitment, which gives life a long-sought purpose. The other type emphasizes a more adult form of internal discipline through meditation. Here the goal is to control the striving and desiring ego, to tap deep inner powers, and to dwell in an enlightened state of cosmic consciousness that one guru calls the "Self of selves," unwittingly suggesting that this is the highest form of egotism of all.

Taken together both types are the inheritors of the commune movement's ideology of "working on yourself" as opposed to the student-radical ideology of "struggle against the system." Given the extremely small number of radical or open-land communes which survive today, it is clear that spiritual beliefs are a much more favorable basis for communal living than revolutionary analysis or free-form anarchy. In this sense the modern spiritual movement has been overwhelmingly triumphant over its radical and libertarian detractors.

If secular anarchies dominated the first half of the modern communal decade, religious communities of discipline dominated the second. Looking at these years in perspective, it is not hard to see why, as the prosperity and psychedelic euphoria of the late 1960s gave way to the depression and existential despair of the early 1970s. Today, with the war ended, the economy regaining normalcy, and a new if still tentative sense of hope abroad in the land, apparently the religious communities have peaked out too. The era of communes as a mass movement has more or less ended. It has clearly stopped growing in its original form, at any rate, and the time has come now to assess its long-term impact.

Chances are, I think, that the most important impacts this movement left on our culture will prove to be neither communalism nor spiritualism, but other things entirely. There is very good evidence, for example, that the back-to-the-land aspect of the movement has changed our society enormously. Recent studies by social demographers and population experts have shown that since 1970, for the first time in this century and most likely for the first time in the history of the nation, the classic flow of Americans from country to city has been reversed. Between 1970 and 1973, the period during which so many rural communes failed, there was a net migration of over 1 million people from the cities *and* the suburbs into sparsely populated rural areas. The very highest rates of population growth in America since the peak of the rural commune movement have been in rural counties where the largest urban centers consist of fewer than 2,500 people.[14]

The implications of this reversal are staggering. An urbanizing trend which has dominated our entire history as a nation is turning around, and the experts agree that noneconomic factors are playing a critical role in the new trend. As demographers Calvin Beale and Glenn Fuguitt have written, "Under conditions of general affluence, low total population increase, easy access to all areas through improved transportation and communication, modernization of rural life, and metropolitan concentrations in which the advantages of urban life are seen to be diminished, a downward shift to smaller communities may be both feasible and desirable."[15]

Intuitively, this is the direction that Americans are moving today. As rural homesteaders, retirees, small businessmen and craftsmen escaping the cities, young immigrants to declining old rural towns, employees of the new decentralized manufacturing, and ex-communards who stayed in rural areas on their own or joined the more individualistic communities movement, our population is spontaneously deurbanizing itself. As many as 500,000 Americans are estimated by *Organic Gardening and Farming* magazine to be serious about building new lives on small farms.

There can be little question that the rural communes of the 1960s played a major *avant-garde* role in these developments. They were the "antennae" (as Ezra Pound once said of artists) of incipient cultural change. As the first major probe back to the countryside in generations, they pioneered the way out of urban pollution and alienation. They did not often succeed as communes, but they did succeed in initiating and inspiring a new interest in rural living that will be with us for a long time to come. Today the vast majority of Americans live in giant cities; yet the polls say that about 75 percent of us would rather live in rural or small-town settings. This imbalance between the way we aspire to live and the way we actually live may ultimately be the most important issue of our age, and the rural communards of the 1960s were the people who set it in motion.

Another wide ripple set in motion by the modern commune movement was its revolt against specialization and careerism in the interests of greater self-sufficiency and personal growth. For the new generation of young people, these still remain momentous decisions. Will their future in an age of chronic change be better assured by a flexible variety of skills and interests or by a concentrated assault on making it in one particular occupation? On what the wise choice would be, our scholars are in disagreement. On the one hand, we have historian Lawrence Veysey, saying "The kind of thing that so many academics long to say—that to try to be universal, to try to fulfill several roles equally well, must inevitably result in mediocrity in an age of specialization."[16] On the other, we have poet Judson Jerome: "From the point of view of the old culture, the new culture's emphasis upon diversity of activity seems to be dilettantism; its de-emphasis upon productivity seems regressive. But these are exactly the characteristics which may create the kind of economic objective toward which all contending factions of the body politic would be willing to strive."[17] Personally, I side with Jerome.

Still another ripple set in motion by the commune movement is the development of a healthy new interest in the politics of decentralization, aimed at bringing the mass institutions of our society under more popular and local control. More by what they represented than by what they actually did, the communes dramatically illustrated the lack of community, personal fate control, and political efficacy in modern society. In shrinking back to small groups and striving for self-sufficiency, they showed by extreme example that the way to win the battle of powerlessness is through self-reliance and control over your immediate community environmenι. The commune movement is usually thought to have been apoliticaι, buᵗ tnere were many cross-overs to this line of thinking during the commune years from the ranks of both traditional liberals and radιcaιs.

Today, a new decentralist politics has emerged, based more on the analysis of institutional scale than the analysis of social class. This is basically the position of the radical or populist movement of our time, with many refreshing ideas coming from both right and left, all directed at the recovery of small-scale Jeffersonian democracy, neighborhood control, personal efficacy, and local self-reliance. Even corporations are starting to see the wisdom of decentralization. "Small is beautiful," the new wave is telling us today, showing many signs of being the future leadership of our country. The politicians would do well to take note. The historians would do well to remember that the communards anticipated these developments by taking the idea of decentralization as far, in modern America, as it can possibly go.

But historians will also remember that the new communards accomplished much more by trying than they did in fact. By refusing to accept their own social conditioning and taking a blind leap of faith into the unknown, they captivated a nation's attention and even changed its direction. But they also showed how deep our social conditioning can be and how fragile the American capacity for community. Community requires giving up a certain measure of individual freedom and letting other people penetrate our lives. But the children of prosperity were trained to think they were special, and their parents' values of achievement, individualism, and privacy were more deeply planted than they knew. In many ways they had trained incapacities for the communal experience. The deepest incapacity of all, perhaps, was the inability to put group success above individual destiny. The main obstacle to utopia today, says sociologist Philip Slater, is that we are still hung up on the competitive motivational patterns we were trained to have by earlier generations which grew up with scarcity. According to Slater, "Nothing stands in our way except our invidious dreams of personal glory."[18]

Most of the children of prosperity today are still plagued by this transient dissatisfaction. At their best, though, they are continuing to explore new directions out of this impasse by becoming ever more flexible in an age of chronic change. The cultivation of multiple alternatives, the attempt to choose the best of several possible worlds, the quest for social justice and personal happiness, the recovery of popular fate control, the determination to explore old frontiers in the countryside and new ones inside the mind—these are the traits that the children of prosperity are carrying into the future and will leave as their legacy.

Notes

1. Flyer issued by a San Francisco commune, quoted in Judson Jerome, *Families of Eden: Communes and the New Anarchism* (New York: Seabury Press, 1974), pp. 107–108.

2. Ibid., p. 16.

3. See James R. Allen and Louis J. West, "Flight from Violence: Hippies and the Green Rebellion," *American Journal of Psychiatry,* 125 (September 1968); and David Whittaker and William A. Watts, "Personality Characteristics of a Nonconformist Youth Subculture: A Study of the Berkeley Nonstudent," *Journal of Social Issues,* 25 (April 1969).

4. Cited in Lawrence Veysey, *The Communal Experience: Anarchist and Mystical Counter-Cultures in America* (New York: Harper & Row, 1973), p. 454n.

5. Gordon Rattray Taylor, *Rethink: A Paraprimitive Solution* (New York: E. P. Dutton, 1973), pp. 44–45.

6. For a detailed examination of such phenomena over a long span of European history, see Norman Cohn, *The Pursuit of the Millennium,* 2nd ed. (New York: Harper Torchbooks, 1961).

7. Jerome, *Families of Eden,* p. 16.

8. See Chapter 1.

9. Veysey, *The Communal Experience,* p. 9.

10. See Rosabeth Moss Kanter, "Commitment and Social Organization: A Study of Commitment Mechanisms in Utopian Communities," *American Sociological Review,* 33 (August 1968), and *Commitment and Community: Communes and Utopias in Sociological Perspective* (Cambridge, Mass.: Harvard University Press, 1972).

11. Eric Perlman and Havertat [pseud.], eds., *Spiritual Community Guide for North America (1975–1976)* (San Rafael, Calif.: Spiritual Community Publications, 1974).

12. Veysey, *The Communal Experience,* p. 69.

13. See John C. Lilly, M.D., *Programming and Metaprogramming in the Human Biocomputer* (New York: Julian Press, 1972).

14. Calvin L. Beale and Glenn V. Fuguitt, "The New Pattern of Nonmetropolitan Population Change," paper presented at the Conference on Social Demography, University of Wisconsin—Madison, July 15–16, 1975. Published by the Center for Demography and Ecology, University of Wisconsin (CDE Working Paper 75-22), August 1975. See also Roy Reed, "Rural Population Gains Now Outstrip Urban Areas," *New York Times,* May 18, 1975.

15. Beale and Fuguitt, "The New Pattern of Nonmetropolitan Population Change," p. 18.

16. Veysey, *The Communal Experience,* p. 321.

17. Jerome, *Families of Eden,* pp. 103–104.

18. Philip Slater, *The Pursuit of Loneliness* (Boston: Beacon Press, 1970), p. 150.

appendix A

Notes on Fieldwork

The sample on which this study is based contains thirteen communitarian groups from four western states: Colorado, New Mexico, California, and Oregon. The composition of this sample was a combined product of planning, chance, and circumstance. One of the first decisions I made in planning my initial fieldwork was that my tour would have to be restricted geographically because of limited personal resources. Since I then lived in Colorado and most modern communes seemed to be located in the West, I limited my work to this area.

Over the winter of 1969–1970, using three published lists of communes then available, I wrote letters to some forty or fifty rural and urban communes asking permission to visit for a while and gather information for a book, enclosing self-addressed postcards for replies. These letters produced some twenty positive replies and about six refusals, with the remainder not responding. (The refusals were exclusively from urban groups, while the nonresponses were almost all rural groups, implying paranoia in the cities and diffidence in the countryside). Of the thirteen groups eventually making up the 1970 sample, five had approved my visit in advance, and five others were known to me in advance but either had not been contacted for lack of a mailing address or had not answered my query. The remaining three were not known to me in advance and were instead discovered by chance, rumor, or personal referrals. For visits to all these groups I had either group permission or some form of personal sponsorship from one or more members, although in three cases (all open-land groups) neither permission nor sponsorship was necessary.

Altogether I visited about thirty communes over a four-month period beginning in Colorado in July 1970 and ending in Oregon in October, traveling in a 1954 Ford and camping out along the way. A number of these groups were urban. They were later dropped from the sample with my decision to focus exclusively on rural groups, which seemed to me far more serious and interesting experiments in social organization. No group that I visited ever turned me away outright, although two or three cut my stays shorter than I wished on the grounds that my presence would interfere with communal life. On two other occasions I left voluntarily before I had finished with my questions and observations, once because of fear (but not threats) and once because of the overbearing intensity of the place.

Another group, the Hog Farm in New Mexico, was reluctantly dropped from the sample because of insufficient information. The Hog Farmers spent most of their time scattered all over America in an assortment of old school buses on missions of mercy (crowd control at the famous Woodstock Festival in 1969) and madcap adventure (taking their mascot "Pigasus" to seek the Democratic nomination for president at the Chicago convention in 1968), coming home to New Mexico only sporadically to rest and recoup. I never learned enough about these communal gypsies to analyze them as an organization. Since then, however, the antics of this zaniest commune of them all have been set down for posterity in *The Hog Farm and Friends* (Links Books, 1974) by chief tripster and Hog-Farm guiding light Hugh ("Wavy Gravy") Romney.

As a representative sample of all the rural communes existing in America in 1970, the final collection of thirteen appearing in this study clearly has some limits. Numerically it is quite small, of necessity and circumstance. But I feel now as I did then that a smaller sample of case studies based on personal fieldwork was much preferable to a larger sample based on mailed questionnaires, which bring notoriously low response rates and unreliable answers (if any at all). Qualitatively, the sample overrepresents open-land groups like Morning Star East and Wheeler's Ranch, which were more a phenomenon of the West than of the East. Other than this, the differences between eastern and western rural communes were mainly cultural. In the East, the communards absorbed the traditional New England culture of crafts, gardening, cottage industries, and domestic self-sufficiency. In the West, communards were more interested in building, technological innovation, nomadics, and Indian lore. It was also my general impression that the communes of the West, in character with their locale and heritage, experienced many more episodes of internal and external violence.

Significantly, however, the settlement pattern of the new com-

munes was much the same in the East as in the West. Almost invariably they were located in broken, low-income mountainous and hilly
areas where land was cheap and unsuitable for commercial agriculture
and where social visibility was low. In the West, communal settlements were concentrated in the Rocky Mountains, the Sierras, and
the coastal ranges. In the East, they were concentrated in analogous
territories like rural New England, upstate New York, the Appalachi-
ans, the Smokies, and the Ozarks. It is worth noting that most communal settlements of the nineteenth century were located in the flat,
open farmlands of the Midwest and the Great Plains, reflecting more
interest in producing income that in retreating inconspicuously to isolated valleys and hillsides.

This sample may also underrepresent the more secretive and
unpublicized groups like Crook's Creek or LILA (where I was told
that if I published the photos I took my safety would be in danger).
Communes like these were little known in 1970 even on the rumor
circuit, and there were many hundreds like them which I never heard
from. On the other hand, there was little I found that distinguished
the character, organization, or internal life of these groups from
others which were better known, except for the fact that they were
less often subsidized. Other than these limitations, I consider the
thirteen groups taken together as a fairly accurate cross section of the
commune scene around 1970. By 1973 more account would have had
to be taken of religious and sectarian groups, but in 1970 they were
clearly no greater a proportion of the commune movement than the 15
percent (or 22 percent including the quasi-religious LILA) included
here. Another change since then has been the development of unusually large (over two hundred members), charismatically led groups
like Alan Noonan's Messiah's World Crusade (California), Steve Gaskin's The Farm (Tennessee), or Mel Lyman's Renaissance Church
(Massachusetts). But in 1970 such groups were either in precommunal
phases or in urban settings. I knew of none existing in rural areas
anywhere in the West that were not holdovers from an earlier age.

In the country of the young around 1970, sociologists were only
slightly more savory characters than narcotics agents and reporters.
With the growth of the antiwar movement in the late 1960s, the very
idea of research itself had come to mean collusion with the government and other agents of social control for perverted political ends. It
was a time when anyone coming along with questionnaires tended to
be considered just another kind of spy—perhaps a well-intentioned
one, but a spy nonetheless. It has probably always been the same for
anyone trying to study "deviant" groups. Being young and sympathetic to the commune movement myself, I had every good intention
with my work. In the usual way I hoped it would help. But I soon

learned that identifying myself as a sociologist "tagged me with a jacket," as convicts say, that tended to make my intentions beside the point. It called forth the notion that if I was not doing the devil's work itself, then at best I was on a fool's mission.

When I originally began planning this study in 1969, there were a number of different types of information about modern communes I hoped to acquire. In addition to a thirteen-page structured interview devised to find out about each group's social organization (the gist of which is reproduced in appendix B), I also planned to solicit responses to two different questionnaires from each member of each commune. One sought personal background information and personal feelings about life at that commune to pair with what I learned about organizational structure. The other, designed to measure moral development, asked for opinions on a wide variety of social and ethical issues. Although I did convince a couple of dozen people along the way to fill them out, I soon realized that this was going to be an erratic method with limited utility and that it was considered offensive or even threatening by many of my communal hosts. Simply having a questionnaire in hand often brought out great groans and not uncommonly a stream of sarcasm too. Since my main interests were organizational and not personal, I left my questionnaires in the trunk if I felt that bringing them out might be disruptive and jeopardize my chances of learning anything at all. I never entirely abandoned trying to get people to fill them out, but refusals were so frequent and cooperation so spotty that in the end I got little I could consider useful.

The same sort of difficulties applied to the structured interview I devised. My first experience in using it convinced me that it was irksome and awkward to go around asking questions with my clipboard, suspiciously jotting things down. I therefore memorized the protocol and asked my questions unobtrusively and informally, writing down the responses later, usually in private. Similarly, I was also rather secretive in keeping a private journal of the events I observed in everyday communal life and things I learned about each commune's history. This sometimes made me feel as if I were indeed a spy, but it was the only way I thought I could consistently get the information I wanted without being evicted as one. Of course I had my justifications for these elements of deception, but it was a lonely feeling to be suspended between responsibility and rationalization, accountable to no one but myself. I made many acquaintances in my travels, but few friends, though perhaps that was for the best.

On the average I stayed at each of the communes I visited less than a week, and sometimes for as short a period as two days, depending on my welcome and how the task of information gathering went. This length of stay was perfectly adequate for learning what I wanted to know about group structure and organization but left me open to the charge that I could never really understand communes without actually living in one. This criticism is as reasonable now as then, but I felt I could learn much more by observing a number of communes from a disciplined, comparative perspective rather than devoting my energies to living in one or two for extended periods. In retrospect it is clear that there have been many more good accounts of modern communal life produced from the latter point of view than from the former.

Another question of interest is the process of information gathering itself. My approach to this varied somewhat with the circumstances of my arrival at each of the communes I visited. In those cases where I had prior permission to visit, the postcard reply I had received was usually signed by an individual. I would seek to meet this person as soon as possible when I arrived. He or she usually acted as my primary informant (though not always). In cases where I did not have prior permission, the task of finding a primary source of information was more intuitive. Whenever possible I would try to learn from one commune the name of someone who lived at the next group I hoped to visit and then seek that person out as soon as I arrived. I explained that I was "gathering information for a book that I hoped would help other communes make better choices for themselves" and asked if I could visit for a few days.

In cases where I had no names and arrived cold, I usually behaved like just another visitor until I met someone who seemed interested in talking and/or who seemed to have at least some respect for what I was attempting to do. Ordinarily I would seek out the leader if there was one. If not, then I sought out other members who were older or who had lived with the group longest and knew the group's history. In a few communes I was subjected to scrutiny and questioning from an assembled group as a whole. In one instance a hitchhiker I brought along "blew my cover" publicly in the communal dining hall immediately upon our arrival ("Hugh here is taking a sociological survey"), and I had to talk fast to bail myself out of the jeers and hostility. In another I was invited to stay the evening but asked to leave the next day. Most often, however, I was not examined by groups as a whole and was either ignored by most members or sheltered behind the personal sponsorship of one or more of them.

The most common suspicions or reservations about me were that I was an informer for the law, that I might want to become a member when new members were not being sought, or that I might reveal specific names and locations through the media and bring a Haight-Ashbury–style invasion of visitors and crashers. In one case I was rejected by a leader I never met when she asked a lower-ranking member acting as an intermediary if I was "a beautiful person"; when told that I was not especially beautiful, she sent word that I should leave. By and large, however, my receptions were quite cordial and occasionally even enthusiastic. In light of all the revelations about government and police infiltration during that period, confirming practically every suspicion then held in the underground, it is amazing I wasn't scrutinized or evicted more often.

One thing that helped increase my welcome at most groups was contributing something by way of food, beer, tobacco, money, work, or transportation. In my more self-critical moments, it occurred to me that this was not unlike manipulating the savages with wampum, but it was also a principled action in the interests of leaving as much or more with each group as I accepted or took away. Several communes were so impoverished that it seemed as if I were walking among the survivors of a war (as indeed I was). In general I found that small gifts of cigarettes, fresh groceries, a case of beer, or a few dollars (my self-financed budget being $500 for the first trip and $300 for the second) were much appreciated. But what helped most, and was also most enjoyable for me, was pitching in on the daily chores and projects. Washing dishes, weeding the garden, chopping firewood, digging irrigation ditches, framing a house, planting trees, harvesting blackberries, cooking supper, feeding the chickens, milking the goats, scavenging materials, driving a dump truck, making adobe bricks, taking somebody to town—these were the real activities of the daily round and also the best occasions for asking questions.

In general, getting my questions answered usually involved locating the leader or an older or more experienced member as my primary source of information, following him/her around, helping with his/her work, and asking questions whenever the opportunity arose until the interview protocol was complete. As a check on the accuracy of what he/she told me, I relied on conversations with other members as secondary informants, on marginal members or ex-members having another point of view whenever I encountered them, on my own experiences and observations, on the accounts and observations of various journalists, and on various self-descriptive books and statements produced by the communards themselves. Scoring the interview protocol was usually straightforward and uncomplicated, but when sticky problems arose, I sometimes had only my own judgment to use in determining the accuracy of my perceptions, which is scarcely the best means to establish the reliability of information. For the errors which inevitably slipped by, I apologize to those affected.

Ethnographic Protocols

Community _____

Location _____ Founded _____

Visited _____ 1970 _____ 1973 (Disbanded: _____)

Population 1970:   Men ___   Women ___   Children ___

Average Adult Age 1970: 21/Under ___ 21–25 ___   25/Over ___

Average Adult Education: H.S./Less ___ 1–2 Yrs. College ___

                                                3/More College ___

Incorporated: Yes _____ No _____

Acreage: _____

1970 Turnover

Founders:	_____ Original (First 6 Months) Founders Remaining
	_____ % 1970 Population
Recent Membership:	_____ Members Also Here 6 Months Before
	_____ % 1970 Population
	_____ Members Also Here 12 Months Before
	_____ % 1970 Population
Transience:	_____ People Come and Gone Last 12 Months, Not Counting Visitors
	_____ % 1970 Population
Seasonal Flux:	_____ Smallest Population Last 12 Months
	_____ Largest Population Last 12 Months
Visitors:	_____ Average Number Visitors/Week, Winter
	_____ Average Number Visitors/Week, Summer
	_____ Average Visitors/Week, Overall

1970–1973 Turnover

_____ 1973 Adult Population
_____ 1970 Members Remaining 1973
_____ % 1970 Membership
_____ % 1973 Membership

Index of Prosperity, 1970–1973 (Score: _____)

Buildings Standing 1970:	Declined	−1	Same	0	Improved	±1
Buildings in Progress 1970:	Uncompleted	−1	None	0	Completed	±1
New Buildings Since 1970:	Fewer	−1	None	0	Completed/In Progress	±1
Utilities: ·	Declined	−1	Same	0	Improved	±1
Garden:	None/Worse	−1	Same	0	Bigger/Better	±1
Food Animals:	None/Fewer	−1	Same	0	More/Better	±1
Property Holdings:	Less	−1	Same	0	Increased	±1
Community Industry:	Declined	−1	Same	0	Grown	±1
Population:	Declined	−1	Same	0	Grown	±1

Sacrifice (Total: _____)

Abstinence (Subtotal: _____)

		Allowed	_Not Allowed_
Oral:	Alcohol	0	1
	Tobacco	0	1
	Coffee	0	1
	Meat	0	1
	Drugs	0	1
Sexual:	Continence	No	Yes
	Preferred	0	1

Austerity (Subtotal: _____)

Built Own Buildings:		None	0	Some	1	All	2	
Utilities:	Electricity	Hookup	0	Generator	1	None	2	
	Gas	Dwellings	0	Kitchen	1	None	2	
	Water 1	Some Pipes/Taps	0	All Hand Carried	1			
	Water 2	Storage/Year-round	0	No Storage/Seasonal	1			
	Sewage	Tank	0	Outhouse	1	Neither	2	
Winters:		Mild	0	2–4 Mos. Snow	1	5 Mos. Snow	2	
Use Food Stamps:		All Do	0	Some Do	1	None	2	

Investment (Total: _____)

	Don't Use	Use
Physical Participation:		
Must Build Own Shelter	0	1
Nonresident Members Prohibited	0	1
Financial Investment:		
Fee or Contribution for Admission	0	1
Property Signed Over at Admission	0	1
Sign Over Property Received While Member	0	—
Turn Over Some Income While Member	0	1
Irreversibility of Investment:		
No Records of Contributions	0	1
Defectors Not Reimbursed for Monetary Contributions	0	1
Defectors Not Reimbursed for Property Contributions	0	1

Renunciation (Total: _____)

Insulation (Subtotal: _____)

	Low	High
Ecological:Neighbor (± .5 mi.)	0	1
Inc. Town (± 5 mi.)	0	1
City of 50,000 (± 50 mi.)	0	1

	Present/Common	None/Uncommon
Media: Radio	0	1
Newspapers/Magazines	0	1
Movement Publications	0	1
Television	0	1
Telephone	0	1

Cross-Boundary Control (Subtotal: _____)

Average Member

Travels Outside: Daily ____ 0   Weekly ____ 1   Biweekly ____ 2

Monthly ____ 3   Less Often ____ 4

	Don't Use	Use
Visitation Rules:		
Fee Charged	0	1
Time Limits	0	1
Whom Visitors May Talk To	0	1
Limit to Number of Visitors	0	1
Areas Visitors Kept Away From	0	1
Certain Attitude or Purpose	0	1
Other_____	0	1

Screening New Members:	*Don't Use*	*Use*
Fee Required	0	1
Probation/Instruction Period	0	1
List of Required Reading	0	1
Formal Oath/Agreement	0	1
Unanimous Acceptance	0	1
Particular Skills	0	1
Particular Religious Beliefs	0	1
Particular Family Situation	0	1
Probationary Sponsor	0	1
Have Formally Blackballed Before	0	1
Have Ejected Member Before	0	1

Communion (Total: _____)

Homogeneity (Subtotal: _____)

Age: Many Over 5 Years Apart; Some Over 10   0
        Few Over 5 Years Apart; None Over 10   1

Prior Acquaintance 6 Months or Less   0   1 Year or Less   1
   Most Members: 1–2 Years   2   More Than 2 Years   3

Communistic Sharing (Subtotal: _____)

	No	*Yes*
Property Signed Over on Admission:	0	1
Income or Fee Turnover Required:	0	1
Community as a Whole Owns Land:	0	1
All Bldgs. Except Dwellings	0	1
All Bldgs. Including Dwellings	0	1
Some Tools, Furniture, Autos	0	1
All Tools, Furniture, Autos	0	1
Land Title in Community's Name, Not Individuals':	0	1
Single Community Garden:	0	1

Communistic Labor (Subtotal: _____)

Communal Dwellings: None 0   Some 1   All 2
Communal Dining: Weekly/Less 0 Daily/Once 1   Daily/More 2
Inviolable Private
   Places: Yes 0   No 1
% Day Spent with
   Others: 50%/Less 0   51–75% 1   76%/More 2
Fixed Daily Routine: No 0   Yes 1
Group Meetings: Monthly/less 0 Bimonthly 1 Weekly 2 Daily 3

Group Meetings: Spontaneous__0   Scheduled__1

Diameter Enclosing
  Dwellings: 100 Yards/More__0   100 Yards/Less__1

Ratio Acreage/
  Population_____: 1.0/More__0   .5 to .99__1   .49/Less__2

Ritual (Subtotal: _____)

Group Meditation/
  Ceremonies: None/Seldom__0   Weekly__1   Daily__2
Group Singing/Dancing: Monthly/Less__0   Several/Mo.__1   Daily__2
Mealtime Prayers: No__0   Yes__1

Persecution Experiences (Subtotal: _____)

Incidents of Legal Harassment
  (Last 12 Months):   None__0   Once__1   Twice/More__2
Vigilante Harassment
  (Last 12 Months):   None__0   Once__1   Twice/More__2
Harassment Previous
  History: None__0   Once/twice__1   Several__2
Perceived Negativity
  Locally: 25%/less__0   25–50%__1
                         50–75%__2   75%/more__3
Perceived Economic   Not Serious__0   Somewhat__1
  Discrimination Locally: Serious__2

Mortification (Total: _____)

Mutual Criticism (Subtotal: _____)

Meetings Devoted to
  Encounter, Mutual Criticism: No__0   Yes__1
As Part of Business Meetings: Yes__0   Sometimes Special__1
Informal Encounter: No/Seldom__0   Yes/Irregularly__1
                             Yes/Regularly/Daily__2

Spiritual Differentiation (Subtotal: _____)

Members Distinguished on
  Moral, Spiritual Grounds: No__0   Yes__1
Formally Structured Deference to
  Those of Higher Moral Status: No__0   Yes__1
Formal Probation Period,
  Limited Privileges for New Members: No__0   Yes__1
Formal Instruction in
  Community Doctrines: No__0   Yes__1

Transcendence (Total: _____)

Institutional Awe (Ideology) (Subtotal: _____)

Ideology Explained Essential Nature of Man:	No__0	Yes__1
Ideology Complete, Elaborate Philosophical System:	No__0	Yes__1
Magical Powers Imputed to Certain Members:	No__0	Yes__1
Magical Powers Imputed to Community as Whole:	No__0	Yes__1
Ideology Specifically Relates to Great Teachers, Figures of Historical Importance:	None Specifically__0 Several, None in Particular__1 One in Particular__2	

Institutional Awe (Power and Authority) (Subtotal: _____)

Single Person Embodies Community:	No __0	Yes/Secular__1	Yes/Sacred__2
Authority Hierarchy:	No __0	Yes/Secular__1	Yes/Sacred__2
Impeachment or Recall Privileges:	Yes__0	No__1	
Special Leadership Prerogatives:	No__0	Yes__1	
Special Residence for Leader(s):	No__0	Yes__1	
Top Leaders Founders or Their Named Successors:	No__0	Yes__1	

Programing (Subtotal: _____)

Fixed Daily Routine:	No__0	Yes__1
Detailed Specification of Routine:	No__0	Yes__1

Ideological Conversion (Subtotal: _____)

Commitment to Ideology Required:	No__0	Yes__1
Recruit Expected to Take Vows:	No__0	Yes__1
Procedure for Choosing New Members:	No__0	Yes__1

Tradition

Community Derived from Prior
  Organization or Organized Group: No__0__   Yes__1__

Index of Political Equality (Total: _____)

Decisions (Officially): Single Leader   __0__
                         Minority Rule   __1__
                         Majority Rule   __2__
                         Unanimity   __3__

Decisions (De Facto):   Single Leader/Lieutenants   __0__
                         Self-Selected/Nonlegit/Minority   __1__
                         Emergent/Legit/Minority   __2__
                         Voting/Committees/etc.   __3__

Community Decisions Outside Benefactor/Intervention   __0__
  Subject to   Outside Benefactor/No Intervention   __1__
  Benefactor   No Outside Benefactor   __2__
  Approval:

Participation Key   Distinct Minority   __0__
  Decisions: Less Than Full Membership   __1__
                     All Members/Exclude Aspirants   __2__
                     All Members, Aspirants/Exclude Transients   __3__
                     All Members, Aspirants, Transients   __4__

Tenure of Community Permanent   __0__
  Functionaries: Informal Delegation/Volunteer   __1__
                     Rotated/Terms   __2__

Participation of   Traditional Tasks Assigned/
  Women: Unequal Political Participation   __0__
                     Traditional Tasks Self-Selected/
                       Unequal Political Participation   __1__
                     Traditional Tasks Self-Selected/
                       Equal Political Participation   __2__
                     Traditional Tasks Rotated/
                       Equal Political Participation   __3__

Commitment Scores*

	Ananda	Crook's Creek	Drop City (X)	Guild of Colo.	Lama Foundation	Libre	LILA (X)	Maharaj Ashram (X)	Morning Star East (X)	Reality Const. Co. (X)	Saddle Ridge	Talsalsan (X)	Wheeler Ranch (X)	Mean (S.D.)
Sacrifice	9	8	5	7	11	8	9	15	12	11	5	4	9	8.69 (3.09)
Abstinence	3	0	0	0	3	0	2	5	0	0	0	0	0	
Austerity	6	8	5	7	8	8	7	10	12	11	5	4	9	
Investment	5	7	3	2	4	4	4	4	3	4	3	1	4	3.69 (1.44)
Participation	2	2	0	1	2	2	2	1	0	1	0	0	1	
Financial	2	2	0	1	1	0	0	1	0	0	0	1	0	
Irreversibility	1	3	3	0	1	2	2	2	3	3	3	0	3	
Renunciation	22	17	6	7	18	17	14	14	7	16	8	10	10	12.77 (5.10)
Ecolog. Isolation	3	3	0	1	2	3	1	0	1	1	2	2	1	
Media Isolation	5	4	5	1	4	4	4	4	5	4	4	1	5	
Visitor Control	5	3	0	0	3	3	4	3	0	4	1	1	1	
Screening Members	7	5	1	5	8	6	4	7	0	6	0	5	1	
Outside Trips	2	2	0	0	1	1	1	0	1	1	1	1	2	
Communion	16	25	19	33	32	16	24	22	24	19	21	20	19	22.31 (5.33)
Homogeneity	2	3	1	4	3	3	0	0	1	3	3	0	0	
Comm. Sharing	5	7	6	7	7	6	6	5	5	5	5	7	3	
Comm. Labor	3	5	2	4	7	2	5	4	3	5	5	6	2	
Regular Contact	4	6	8	11	9	0	9	8	7	4	7	4	4	
Ritual	2	1	1	0	5	1	4	5	2	0	0	0	2	
Persecution	0	3	1	7	1	4	0	0	6	2	1	3	8	
Mortification	4	3	1	2	6	2	2	5	1	1	3	3	1	2.62 (1.61)
Mutual Criticism	0	2	1	2	2	1	1	1	0	0	3	2	0	
Spiritual Diff.	4	1	0	0	4	1	1	4	1	1	0	0	1	
Transcendence	17	3	0	7	15	6	6	20	3	6	1	2	9	7.31 (6.33)
Ideology	6	0	0	0	5	2	0	6	1	0	0	0	2	
Power & Authority	8	2	0	4	5	1	1	8	1	3	0	0	6	
Programing	0	0	0	0	2	0	2	2	0	1	0	0	0	
Conversion	2	1	0	3	3	2	2	3	0	2	0	1	0	
Tradition	1	0	0	0	0	1	1	1	1	0	1	1	1	
Totals	73	63	34	58	86	53	59	80	50	57	41	40	51	57.39(15.39)

*Groups followed by an (X) did not survive the period 1970–1973.

Bibliography

Ald, Roy. *The Youth Communes.* New York: Tower, 1970.

Aldridge, John. *In the Country of the Young.* New York: Harper & Row, 1970.

Allen, James R., and Louis J. West. "Flight from Violence: Hippies and the Green Rebellion." *American Journal of Psychiatry,* 125 (September 1968), 364–370.

"Ananda Cooperative Village." *Communities,* no. 3, 1973.

Atcheson, Richard. *The Bearded Lady: Going on the Commune Trip and Beyond.* New York: John Day, 1971.

Beale, Calvin L., and Glenn V. Fuguitt. "The New Pattern of Nonmetropolitan Population Change." Paper read at the Conference on Social Demography, July 15–16, 1975, at the University of Wisconsin—Madison. Published by the Center for Demography and Ecology, University of Wisconsin (CDE Working Paper 75–22), August 1975.

Berger, Bennett, et al. "The Communal Family." *Family Coordinator,* 21 (October 1972), 419–427.

Berger, Bennett, and Bruce M. Hackett. "On the Decline of Age-Grading in Rural Hippie Communes." *Journal of Social Issues,* 30 (1974), 163–183.

Blowsnake, Jasper [pseud.]. "Reality Construction Co." *The Modern Utopian,* 4 (Summer-Fall 1970), 15.

Bookchin, Murray. *Post-Scarcity Anarchism.* Berkeley, Calif.: Ramparts Press, 1971.

Brand, Stewart, et al., eds. *The Whole Earth Catalog.* Menlo Park, Calif.: Portola Institute, Fall 1968–present. (Semiannual through Spring 1971, since revived as an occasional).

————. *Difficult But Possible Supplement to the Whole Earth Catalog.* Menlo Park, Calif.: Portola Institute, January 1969–March 1971 (quarterly).

Brown, Joe David, ed. *The Hippies.* New York: Time-Life Books, 1967.

Cohn, Norman. *The Pursuit of the Millennium.* 2nd ed. New York: Harper Torchbooks, 1961.

Community Publications Cooperative. *Communities.* December 1972–present (bimonthly).

Coser, Lewis, and Irving Howe. "Images of Socialism." In *The Radical Papers,* edited by Howe. Garden City, N.Y.: Doubleday, 1966.

Davidson, Sara. "Open Land: Getting Back to the Communal Garden." *Harper's*, 240 (June 1970), 91–100.

Diamond, Steven. *What the Trees Said: Life on a New Age Farm.* New York: Delta, 1971.

Ellen, Brian, Margot, Don, Marlene, Carol, eds. *Communitas: A New Community Journal,* 1 (July 1972). One issue only.

Fairfield, Richard. *Communes U.S.A.: A Personal Tour.* Baltimore: Penguin Books, 1972.

———. *Utopia, U.S.A.* San Francisco: Alternatives Foundation, 1972.

———, ed. *Alternatives! Directory of Social Change: Complete Updated List of Communes, Communal Matchmaking.* Published as vol. 3, no. 4 of *The Modern Utopian* (Fall 1969).

———, ed. *The Modern Utopian.* September 1966 through 1971 (quarterly).

Fogarty, R. S. "Communal History in America." *Choice,* 10 (June 1973), 578–590.

Gardner, Hugh. "Crises and Politics in Rural Communes." In *Communes: Creating and Managing the Collective Life,* edited by Rosabeth Moss Kanter. New York: Harper & Row, 1973.

———. "Your Global Alternative." *Esquire,* 74 (September 1970), 106–109.

Goodman, Mitchell, ed. *The Movement Toward a New America: The Beginnings of a Long Revolution.* Philadelphia: Pilgrim Press, 1970.

Goodman, Paul. *People or Personnel.* New York: Vintage, 1968.

Gottlieb, Louis, et al. "Open Land: A Manifesto." Bodega Bay, Calif.: Wheeler Ranch Defense Fund, 1970.

Gustaitus, Rasa. *Turning On.* New York: Macmillan, 1969.

Hedgepeth, William, and Dennis Stock. *The Alternative.* New York: Collier Books, 1970.

Hillery, George A., Jr. *Communal Organizations: A Study of Local Societies.* Chicago: University of Chicago Press, 1968.

Hinckle, Warren. "The Social History of the Hippies." *Ramparts,* 5 (March 1967), 5–26.

Hinds, William A. *American Communities.* New York: Corinth, 1961.

Hine, Robert V. *California's Utopian Colonies.* New Haven, Conn.: Yale University Press, 1953.

Holloway, Mark. *Heavens on Earth: Utopian Communities in America, 1680–1880.* New York: Dover, 1966.

Horwitz, Elinor Lander. *Communes in America: The Place Just Right.* Philadelphia: J. B. Lippincott, 1972.

Houriet, Robert. *Getting Back Together.* New York: Avon Books, 1972.

Howard, John R. *The Cutting Edge: Social Movements and Social Change in America.* Philadelphia: J. B. Lippincott, 1974.

Jenson, Krishna Kaur. "Shakti Yagna: The Celebration and Preservation of Women's Purity and Innocence." *Beads of Truth* #18 (June 1973).

———. "Drinking the Amrit (Nectar of God)." *Beads of Truth* #18 (June 1973).

Jerome, Judson. *Families of Eden: Communes and the New Anarchism.* New York: Seabury Press, 1974.

Kanter, Rosabeth Moss. *Commitment and Community: Communes and Utopias in Sociological Perspective.* Cambridge, Mass.: Harvard University Press, 1972.

———. "Commitment and Social Organization: A Study of Commitment Mechanisms in Utopian Communities." *American Sociological Review,* 33 (August 1968), 499–517.

———, ed. *Communes: Creating and Managing the Collective Life.* New York: Harper & Row, 1973.

Katz, Elia. *Armed Love.* New York: Holt, Rinehart and Winston, 1971.

Kaur, Shakti Parwha. "What's in a Name?" *Beads of Truth* #18 (June 1973).

Kinkade, Kathleen. *A Walden Two Experiment: The First Five Years of Twin Oaks Community.* New York: Morrow, 1973.

Kovach, Bill. "Communes Spread as the Young Reject Old Values." *New York Times,* December 17, 1970.

Krippner, Stanley, and Don Fersh. "The Mystical Experience and the Mystical Commune." *The Modern Utopian,* 4 (Spring 1970), 1–9.

Kriyananda, Swami. *Cooperative Communities: How to Start Them, and Why.* Nevada City, Calif.: Ananda Publications, 1971.

Lilly, John C., M.D. *Programming and Metaprogramming in the Human Biocomputer.* New York: Julian Press, 1972.

"A List of Intentional Communities That Are Open or Public." Freeland, Md.: Heathcote Center, 1970.

Lofland, John. *Doomsday Cult.* Englewood Cliffs, N.J.: Prentice-Hall, 1966.

Mandell, Arnold J. "Don Juan in the Mind." *Human Behavior,* 4 (January 1975), 64–69.

Mankoff, Milton. "The Political Socialization of Radicals and Militants in the Wisconsin Student Movement During the 1960's." Ph.D. dissertation, University of Wisconsin, 1969.

McLuhan, Marshall. *Understanding Media: The Extensions of Man.* New York: McGraw-Hill, 1964.

Melville, Keith. *Communes in the Counter-Culture: Origins, Theories, Styles of Life.* New York: Morrow, 1972.

Miller, David, et al., eds. *Communitarian.* 1 (March/April 1972). One issue only.

Mueller, John H., and Karl F. Schuessler. *Statistical Reasoning in Sociology.* Boston: Houghton Mifflin, 1961.

Mungo, Raymond. *Total Loss Farm: A Year in the Life.* New York: E. P. Dutton, 1971.

Nordhoff, Charles. *The Communistic Societies of the United States.* New York: Schocken, 1965.

Parsons, Talcott, and Edward Shils, eds. *Toward a General Theory of Action.* New York: Harper & Row, 1962.

Perlman, Eric, and Havertat [pseud.], eds. *Spiritual Community Guide for North America (1975–1976).* San Rafael, Calif.: Spiritual Community Publications, 1974.

Pitts, Jesse R. "On Communes." *Contemporary Sociology: A Journal of Reviews,* 2 (July 1973), 351–359.

Potter, Paul. *A Name for Ourselves.* Boston: Little, Brown, 1971.

Rabbit, Peter [pseud.]. *Drop City.* New York: Olympia Press, 1971.

Ram Das, Baba, et al. *Be Here Now.* San Cristobal, N.Mex.: The Lama Foundation, 1971.

Reed, Roy. "Rural Population Gains Now Outstrip Urban Areas." *New York Times,* May 18, 1975, p. 1.

Richard, Jerry, ed. *The Good Life: Utopian Communities and Communes in America.* New York: Mentor, 1973.

Roberts, Ron E. *The New Communes: Coming Together in America.* Englewood Cliffs, N.J.: Prentice-Hall, 1971.

Romney, Hugh [Wavy Gravy]. *The Hog Farm and Friends.* New York: Links Books, 1974.

Roszak, Theodore. *The Making of a Counter Culture: Reflections on the Technocratic Society and Its Youthful Opposition.* Garden City, N.Y.: Anchor Books, 1969.

Rothchild, John. "American Communes: Voluntary Maoism." *Washington Monthly,* June 1975, 16–23.

Runyon, Richard P., and Audrey Haber. *Fundamentals of Behavioral Statistics.* 2nd ed. Reading, Mass.: Addison-Wesley, 1972.

Sale, Kirkpatrick. *SDS.* New York: Random House, 1973.

Shuttleworth, John, ed. *The Mother Earth News.* January 1970–present (monthly).

Singh, Khushwant. *The History of the Sikhs.* 2 vols. Princeton, N.J.: Princeton University Press, 1963 and 1966.

Skinner, B. F. *Walden Two.* New York: Macmillan, 1962.

Slater, Philip. *The Pursuit of Loneliness.* Boston: Beacon Press, 1970.

Smelser, Neil J. *Theory of Collective Behavior.* New York: Free Press, 1963.

Sosenski, Jim. "Wheeler Ranch." *The Modern Utopian,* 4 (Spring 1970), 17.

Stewart, Jon. "Splitting Apart and Holding Together in New Mexico." *Scanlan's Monthly,* 1 (September 1970), 23–33.

Stickney, John. *Streets, Actions, Alternatives, Raps.* New York: Putnam, 1971.

————, and John Olson. "The Commune Comes to America." *Life,* July 18, 1969, pp. 16B–23.

Sundancer, Elaine [pseud.]. *Celery Wine: Story of a Country Commune.* Yellow Springs, Ohio: Community Publications Cooperative, 1973.

Swann, Robert S., et al. *The Community Land Trust: A Guide to a New Model for Land Tenure in America.* Cambridge, Mass.: Center for Community Economic Development, 1972.

Taylor, Gordon Rattray. *Rethink: A Paraprimitive Solution.* New York: E. P. Dutton, 1973.

Thibaut, John W., and Harold H. Kelley. *The Social Psychology of Groups.* New York: Wiley, 1959.

Thompson, Hunter S. *Fear and Loathing in Las Vegas.* New York: Popular Library, 1971.

Turner, Victor W. *The Ritual Process: Structure and Anti-structure.* Chicago: Aldine, 1969.

Veysey, Lawrence. "Individualism Busts the Commune Boom." *Psychology Today*, 8 (December 1974), 73–79.

———. *The Communal Experience: Anarchist and Mystical Counter-Cultures in America*. New York: Harper & Row, 1973.

War Resisters League et al. "Alternatives." *WIN*, 4 (January 1, 1969).

Whittaker, David, and William A. Watts. "Personality Characteristics of a Nonconformist Youth Subculture: A Study of the Berkeley Nonstudent." *Journal of Social Issues*, 25 (April 1969), 65–89.

Wolfe, Burton H. *The Hippies*. New York: Signet, 1968.

Yablonsky, Lewis. *The Hippie Trip*. New York: Pegasus, 1968.

Zablocki, Benjamin. *The Joyful Community*. Baltimore: Penguin Books, 1971.

INDEX

Abstinence, 25, 79–80, 96, 108–109,
141, 160, 222
See also Celibacy; Sexual
continence
Abundance, 3, 11–15, 243, 245
Activism, 35, 36, 51–52
See also Political protest
movement
Ahimsa Church, 146, 147
Alianza Federal de Mercedes, 108
Allen, John, 235–236
Alpert, Richard, 75–78
See also Ram Dass
Altamont, California, Rolling
Stones concert at, 9
Alternate Society (periodical), 19
"Alternatives Foundation, The," 47*n*
Ananda Cooperative Village, 58,
79–80, 82, 87, 88, 150–169,
220, 228, 232–234
commitment mechanisms at,
160–166
communion at, 162–164, 166
investment in, 160–161
mortification at, 164, 165
1967–1970, 150, 153–160
1970–1973, 166–168
renunciation at, 161–162, 165
sacrifice at, 160
transcendence at, 164–165
Anarchistic communes, 141, 223,
233, 234, 243–249
*See also specific anarchistic
communes*
Anonymous Artists of America,
59*n*
Architecture, 35, 50–51, 73, 142
Austerity, 25, 41, 54, 80, 109–110,
141, 160, 175, 185, 204, 223–
224

Authoritarian communes. *See*
Religious communes
Authority, 28, 43, 45, 56, 66, 88, 89,
98, 99, 115, 128, 144–145, 165,
178, 190, 211, 232–234, 240
See also Leaders
Awe, institutionalized, 28, 232
See also Authority; Ideology;
Power

Baer, Steve, 51, 73, 75
Baker, Dick, 152
Beale, Calvin, 249
Be Here Now (Baba Ram Dass),
77–78, 90, 91
Benefactors. *See* Subsidies
Bhagavan Das, 77
Bhajan, Siri Singh Sahib Yogi, 120–
132, 248
Blowsnake, Jasper, 117, 118, 119*n*
Bountiful Lord's Delivery Service,
90
Break-up rate, 32*n*
Building
at the Lama Foundation, 75, 81
at Libre, 50–52, 54
Buildings, 73–75, 89–90, 95, 198,
212
See also Geodesic domes;
Housing
Bureaucratization, 12, 14

Caen, Herb, 5
Capitalism, Ananda Cooperative
Village and, 168
Cathectic-cohesion commitment,
22–26
Catholic Workers, 3
Celibacy, 167, 222
See also Sexual continence
Charisma, 27–28